"Complexity, wicked problems, big–data, and a growing of what chief executives must understand in today's conte successful. Mental Models can aid in the decomposition of these complexities. Dr. Mitchell's book is the first to amalgamate the concept of Mental Models and police decision-making by providing a critical thinking framework for police leaders to follow in a pragmatic, easy to follow format. Dr. Mitchell's teachings will challenge the readers' assumptions on how they make decisions. As police leaders, it is time we move the needle forward and examine how we make policy decisions in society's name. This book is a bold step forward."

Commander Chris G. Vallejo, *Austin (TX) Police Department*

"Dr. Renée Mitchell does an outstanding job of discussing her unique approach to utilizing mental modeling to incorporate the use of data and research in the most important areas of the policing realm – making it easily digestible for every reader. As police administrators, we must ensure we are well-educated in the use of data in day-to-day decision-making. Renee outlines this process – utilizing her twenty-one mental models to help strengthen police leadership – in a simple yet progressive way. This is a must-read for every police leader!"

Chief Ken Clary, *Bellevue Nebraska Police Department*

"If there is one book on policing you should read it is this. It's a well-worn phrase but seriously, all police leaders and commissioners SHOULD read this. Renée has taken the content of hundreds of insightful papers and books and distilled it into a relevant and page turning guide to policing. She highlights pitfalls and opportunities, all with the intention of improving the service we deliver. The problem with the Atlantic difference between the US and Europe means the continued reference to math instead of maths which will drive the European reader mad, but forgive the bad English and instead learn the lessons, some of which you already know and some you won't. There are three things that stand out to me; its relevance, its objectivity and finally its writing style – the perfect fusion of an author that has her feet in the world of policing and academia. I know Renée, and I have to say she is slightly crazy – but nothing great ever comes from mediocrity and it takes someone like Renée to put together something as good as this. The timing is perfect; the erosion of trust meets the opportunity of empirical analysis. Renée quotes Ben Goldacre and I would do the same in motivating people to read this: 'anyone who is going to trade in numbers, and use them, and think with them, and persuade with them, let alone lock people up with them, also has a responsibility to understand them'. This book enables us to start doing just that."

Alex Murray, *Commander Metropolitan Police Service*
Founder of the Society of Evidence-based Policing

"Dr. Renée Mitchell expertly blends her academic insights with her wisdom gained through her career as a police officer to create this much-needed, easily accessible book. At a time when there is a historic focus on the role and actions of police in America, Dr. Mitchell distills how best to advance the profession in a simple, compelling framework: if you want to improve the way police act, you first must improve the way they think."

Maureen McGough, *Chief of Staff NYU School*
of Law Policing Project

Twenty-one Mental Models That Can Change Policing

This book goes beyond other police leadership books to teach practitioners how to think about policing in a structured way that synthesizes criminological theory, statistics, research design, applied research, and what works and what doesn't in policing into Mental Models. A Mental Model is a representation of how something works. Using a Mental Model framework to simplify complex concepts, readers will take away an in-depth understanding of how cognitive biases affect our ability to understand and interpret data, what empirical research says about effective police interventions, how statistical data should be structured for management meetings, and how to evaluate interventions for efficiency and effectiveness.

While evidence-based practice is critical to advancing the police profession, it is limited in scope, and is only part of what is necessary to support sustainable change in policing. Policing requires a scientifically based framework to understand and interpret data in a way that minimizes cognitive bias to allow for better responses to complex problems. Data and research have advanced so rapidly in the last several decades that it is difficult for even the most ambitious of police leaders to keep pace. The Twenty-one Mental Models were synthesized to create a framework for any police, public, or community leader to better understand how cognitive bias contributes to misunderstanding data and gives the reader the tools to overcome those biases to better serve their communities.

The book is intended for a wide range of audiences, including law enforcement and community leaders; scholars and policy experts who specialize in policing; students of criminal justice, organizations, and management; reporters and journalists; individuals who aspire to police careers; and citizen consumers of policing data. Anyone who is going to make decisions about their communities based on data has a responsibility to be numerate and this book, *Twenty-one Mental Models That Can Change Policing: A Framework For Using Data and Research For Overcoming Cognitive Bias*, will help you become just that.

Renée J. Mitchell served in the Sacramento Police Department for twenty-two years and is currently a Senior Police Researcher with RTI International. She holds a B.S. in Psychology, an M.A. in Counseling Psychology, and an M.B.A., a J.D., and a Ph.D. in Criminology from the University of Cambridge. She has taught and lectured internationally on evidence-based policing and is best known for being the first policing pracademic to run a randomized controlled trial. She was a Fulbright Police Research Fellow and is the co-founder and executive committee member of the American Society of Evidence-Based Policing. She has two TEDx talks, "Research Not Protests" and "Policing Needs to Change: Trust me I'm a Cop," where she advocates for evidence-based policing. She has published her research in the *Journal of Experimental Criminology, Justice Quarterly*, and the *Cambridge Journal of Evidence-Based Policing*. Her books include *Evidence Based Policing: An Introduction* and *Implementing Evidence-Based Research: A How-to Guide for Police Organizations*.

Routledge Series on Practical and Evidence-Based Policing

Books in the Routledge Series on Practical and Evidence-Based Policing disseminate knowledge and provide practical tools for law enforcement leaders and personnel to protect and serve the public and reduce crime. With an aim to bridge the "translation gap" between frontline policing and academic research, books in this series apply sound scientific methods as well as practical experience to make everyday police work safer and smarter. These books are an invaluable resource for police practitioners, academic researchers, public policymakers, and students in law enforcement and criminology programs to guide best practices in all aspects of policing.

Police Misconduct Complaint Investigations Manual, 2nd Edition
Barbara Attard and Kathryn Olson

Guidelines for Investigating Officer-Involved Shootings,
Arrest-Related Deaths, and Deaths in Custody
Darrell L. Ross and Gary M. Vilke

Twenty-one Mental Models That Can Change Policing
A Framework for Using Data and Research for Overcoming Cognitive Bias
Renée J. Mitchell

Twenty-one Mental Models That Can Change Policing

A Framework for Using Data and Research for Overcoming Cognitive Bias

Renée J. Mitchell

Routledge
Taylor & Francis Group

NEW YORK AND LONDON

First published 2022
by Routledge
605 Third Avenue, New York, NY 10158

and by Routledge
2 Park Square, Milton Park, Abingdon, Oxon, OX14 4RN

Routledge is an imprint of the Taylor & Francis Group, an informa business

Library of Congress Cataloging-in-Publication Data
Names: Mitchell, Renée J., author.
Title: Twenty-one mental models that can change policing: a framework for using data and research for overcoming cognitive bias / Renée J. Mitchell.
Description: 1 Edition. | New York: Routledge, 2021. | Series: Practical and evidence-based policing | Includes bibliographical references and index.
Identifiers: LCCN 2021009173 (print) | LCCN 2021009174 (ebook) | ISBN 9780367481476 (hardback) | ISBN 9780367480080 (paperback) | ISBN 9780367481520 (ebook)
Subjects: LCSH: Community policing. | Criminal justice, Administration of.
Classification: LCC HV7936.C83 M65 2021 (print) | LCC HV7936.C83 (ebook) | DDC 363.2/3—dc23
LC record available at https://lccn.loc.gov/2021009173
LC ebook record available at https://lccn.loc.gov/2021009174

ISBN: 9780367481476 (hbk)
ISBN: 9780367480080 (pbk)
ISBN: 9780367481520 (ebk)

DOI: 10.4324/9780367481520

Typeset in Bembo
by KnowledgeWorks Global Ltd.

Access the Support Material: www.Routledge.com/9780367480080

To Mark, thank you for suffering through all my crazy pursuits and still loving me despite them.

Anything, anytime, anywhere.

To Cole and Kyle, I love you fiercely. And no matter where you go and what you do in life, please base your beliefs on empirical research.

Contents

PART VIII
How to Apply It All

Figures

Tables

Acknowledgments

Many people aided in the completion of this book and for their help I am beyond grateful. First and foremost, I must thank the one person I would have never been able to finish this book without and that is my husband Mark Greenlee. If it were not for him cooking every night, helping with the kids, and editing most of the book I would not have gotten past the first chapter. My life is complete because of you and nothing else. Cole and Kyle, thank you for existing. Your mere presence in the world makes my heart happy and you need to do nothing more. Then to my friends, who read chapters for me and gave me critical feedback that helped shape this book in so many ways, thank you. Especially those of you that took to time to add in all the commas everywhere I forgot them. I have a special thank you to Captain Jason Potts who introduced me to Shane Parrish and Mental Models, without you telling me about his book I would have never stumbled on this framework. Also, thank you to Rachel Tolber for not only editing, but just being my friend, our phone calls help me be a better mom, wife, writer, researcher, and person. I am lucky to have such a large group of brilliant people who are willing to read my work, give me feedback, and edit for me. I really do appreciate every single person in my life. And in no particular order, Jim Bueermann, Maureen McGough, Jason Bruder, Michael Reese, Luke Bonkiewicz, Nick Petitti, Eric Dlugolenski, Eric Jones, Wendy Stiver, Cody Stephens, Corey Falls, Stephen Bishopp, Ashley Heiberger, Justin Risley, Cory Haberman, Chase Wetherington, Ryan Keck, Greg Stewart, Paige Vaughn, Jonas Baughman, Brandon del Pozo, Rich Johnston, Alex Murray, Jeff Egge, Jeremiah Johnson, Natalie Hiltz, Ken Clary, Matthew Barter, Joshua Young, Stuart Greer (Handsome Stu), Simon Williams, Bruce O'Brien, Brian Acken, Chris Vallejo, Dave Norris, James Nolette, Obed Magny, Daniel Ortega, Heather Prince, Dan Jones, Jason Rohde, Troy Gay, Kathryn Greenbeck, Ross Hendy, Matthew Ashby, Tim Mashford, and Sara Davis – Thank you!

Prologue

The Shoulders of Giants

It is not enough to be busy; so are the ants. The question is: What are we busy about?

Henry David Thoreau

This book is the result of people who are smarter and wiser than me taking their time to teach and mentor me about applied criminology, research, and data management. Since one serendipitous moment in 2010, I have had the opportunity to learn from the greatest minds in criminology and policing. I have been lucky enough to have been guided and mentored by Chief (Ret.) Jim Bueermann, Chief (Ret.) Ed Flynn, Chief (Ret.) Sheriff Mike Reese, Chief Eric Jones, Chief Sylvia Moir, Captain Mark Greenlee, Dr. Cynthia Lum, Dr. David Weisburd, Dr. Chris Koper, Dr. Larry Sherman, Dr. Barak Ariel, Dr. Cody Telep, Dr. Jerry Ratcliffe, Dr. David Klinger, and Dr. Geoff Alpert. I come nowhere near their understanding of and experience in the field and am grateful that they all took the time to teach me about policing and the field of police research. This book is my effort to condense their wisdom into a digestible form that can be applied in the field. I wanted to write this book for a couple of reasons.

The main reason for writing this book is policing has evolved as a profession that now relies on data to drive its decision-making and resource allocation, yet throughout a policing career police officers are never taught to be numerate. This is not another indictment of policing's lack of training. Medical doctors and other practitioners who make vital decisions for our communities are not taught how to interpret data either. Practitioners, no matter the field, are taught how to "do" the practice, not evaluate the practice. Police are taught how to interpret and apply laws, to drive at high speeds safely, to take someone into custody, and to shoot accurately, just as medical doctors are taught to "do"—diagnose, prescribe, and possibly operate. Most professions that teach a practice (the art of doing) are not required to learn how to understand, interpret, and apply data to their practice. For policing, being numerate has now become an important skill, as the introduction of CompStat (Computer Comparative Statistics) by NYPD in the 1990s forced police executives into interpreting data and making decisions based on those interpretations. And unlike medicine where patients voluntarily consent to treatment, in policing the community is often an unwilling or unknowing recipient of those decisions. The public can decide if they want to see a physician when they become sick and often they can see a different doctor if they do not like the opinion of the first. Even though the cornerstone of some police agencies is policing by consent, the public is not actively involved in daily police decisions in the same way they are in their medical decisions. The public relies on the police to make the best decisions for their communities and recently it is apparent that many communities, especially communities of color, do not like the decisions the police are making for them.

Once CompStat became the de rigueur, agencies rushed to follow NYPD's example and CompStat meetings flourished across U.S. police departments. Police were thrown into a management meeting that required them to interpret data with no training on how to understand, interpret, and apply data correctly. If policing strategies are based on data and the police have no training on how to interpret data, then therein lies the gap in knowledge that remains to be filled. I have watched many police executives struggle to articulate how they use data and statistics. The most common use of data in policing is to react to increases in crime data by sending officers to the area to do "something." Then, when examining that "something" in the aggregate, the data often looks as though certain communities are being subjected to disparate policing. Cognitive biases inherent in humans are not reflected in individual data points but are reflected in the aggregate. Without understanding how to interpret data, police managers are at a disadvantage. Humans are born with an innate ability to understand language, but not an innate understanding of numbers. We are not naturally numerate. Before numbers, cavemen generally knew what 1 was, and that $1 + 1 = 2$, but anything after that was just "many". Being numerate is hard. It does not come naturally to any human being. This book is not intended to criticize policing. I wanted to write this book because most police agencies use data to make resource allocations and as Dr. Ben Goldacre states in his book *Bad Science*, "Anyone who is going to trade in numbers, and use them, and think with them, and persuade with them, let alone lock people up with them, also has a responsibility to understand them."

This book develops a framework using Mental Models to understand data and research in a way that can be easily understood, interpreted, and applied. A Mental Model is a framework that takes a complex idea and boils it down to simplistic components. It is the mind's way of making sense of something. We create frameworks in our minds to understand the world every day. There are Mental Models we construct in our minds based on our experience of the world and then there are 'known' Mental Models that have been verified by empirical data. From the time you were born, your mind was creating a framework around how social interaction works. You do not think deeply about standing in line and who goes next when waiting to purchase movie tickets, but you know when someone violates a social custom based in your culture and tradition—that is a Mental Model. One Mental Model that is a well-known shibboleth is "Correlation is not causation." It is one of those common phrases that people say but they do not apply it in real life. This hackneyed phrase reminds me of the scene from *The Princess Bride*, when Inigo Montoya says to Vizzini, "You keep using that word. I do not think it means what you think it means," after Vizzini uses the word "inconceivable" incorrectly. Correlation is Not Causation is Mental Model #13 and I review it because although you have heard it before—I do not think it means what *you* think it means.

This book structures twenty-one "known" Mental Models in a precise order to help you think about data. I know there are not many people in the world who are going to be excited by that statement, but if your responsibility is to use data to make decisions related to resource allocation in policing, then I would argue that you have an ethical responsibility to educate yourself about how to make those decisions. I chose these Twenty-one Mental Models because I thought these were the most important concepts for policing. There are more "known" Mental Models than the twenty-one I describe here, but these twenty-one are the concepts that repeatedly came up the most often over the years when I was teaching police executives how to apply criminology to data management. As I said at the beginning of this prologue, I am not nearly as wise and experienced as the people who have mentored me along my evidence-based path, but my hope with this book is that I have condensed their teachings to the Twenty-one Mental Models that will give you just enough knowledge to assist with your thinking and not so many that you are overwhelmed. *Twenty-one Mental Models That Can Change Policing: A Framework For Using Data and Research For Overcoming Cognitive Bias* is a labor of love meant to fill a knowledge gap in policing that is difficult to acquire on one's own.

Introduction

What is a Mental Model and How Does It Help Policing

> We should be humble about what we think we know and even humble about what we can know. And I think that if we just were more comfortable with not knowing the answers to things, we would be less confident about the answers that we come up with and we would be less inclined to make confident predictions based on really shaky assumptions, right? And I believe that would help us to avoid some particularly damaging overreaches associated with hubris.
>
> Dr. Duncan Watts

The idea of Mental Models arose from Charlie Munger's famous talk at USC Business School in 1994 entitled "A Lesson on Elementary Worldly Wisdom." Munger described Mental Models as theories in our brains about how the world works in easily accessible, usable forms, that is, models. He explained to the USC business students that to be successful stockbrokers they had to have multiple models in their heads across several different disciplines, otherwise "To the man with the hammer, every problem looks like a nail." The concept of Mental Models has been expanded since Munger first described them in his 1994 speech with researchers and authors taking known concepts and describing them as Mental Models. In the book *Complexity*, M. Mitchell Waldrop links the idea of prediction to Mental Models and gives one of the best explanations to date:

> But the concept of prediction also turns out to be at least as subtle as the concept of building blocks, says Holland. Ordinarily, for example, we think of prediction as being something that humans do consciously, based on some explicit model of the world. And there are certainly plenty of those explicit models around. A supercomputer's simulation of climate change is one example. A start-up company's business plan is another, as is an economic projection made by the Federal Reserve Board. Even Stonehenge is a model: its circular arrangement of stones provided the Druid priests with a rough but effective computer for predicting the arrival of the equinoxes. Very often, moreover, the models are literally inside our head, as when a shopper tries to imagine how a new couch might look in the living room, or when a timid employee tries to imagine the consequences of telling off his boss. We use these "mental models" so often, in fact, that many psychologists are convinced that they are the basis of all conscious thought. But to Holland, the concept of prediction and models actually ran far deeper than conscious thought – or for that matter, far deeper than the existence of a brain. "All complex, adaptive systems – economies, minds, organisms – build models that allow them to anticipate the world" he declares.

DOI: 10.4324/9780367481520-1

Although there are more than just twenty-one Mental Models known to man, *Twenty-one Mental Models That Can Change Policing: A Framework for Using Data and Research for Overcoming Cognitive Bias* reviews the Twenty-one Mental Models that can specifically assist police executives with how to understand, interpret, and apply data to reduce our natural cognitive biases and better allocate police resources in the field.

The book is broken up into eight parts, grouping three mental modes together at a time to build a broader concept. This book only reviews empirical Mental Models based on rigorous research and not Mental Models based on experience. Some Mental Model chapters are longer than others either because the concept takes more time to explain or in some cases, I had better stories to tell. At the end of each of the seven sections there is a section describing how to apply the models in practice, Mental Models in Practice. These smaller applied sections are the building blocks for the final section, The Mental Model Method: How It All Fits Together, that demonstrates how to apply all Twenty-one Mental Models in the field. Each of these applied sections synthesizes the Mental Models in a way that, by the time you finish the book, you should be able to apply the Mental Model Method with little assistance.

Twenty-one Mental Models That Can Change Policing: A Framework for Using Data and Research for Overcoming Cognitive Bias begins with **Part I—How We Think** which explains the Mental Models that are important for understanding How We Think. The first Mental Model reviews how our brains digest data, **Mental Model #1—System 1 and System 2** thinking discusses Dr. Daniel Kahneman's work on how humans think about statistics, risk, and the world. His work lays out a Mental Model for explaining how humans think and why we make errors in judgment and reasoning. It explains why understanding these systems are important to police decision-making. System 1 is our "blink" reaction to the world. It engages our limbic system and our reactions based on gut, intuition, and feel rather than logical thought. System 2 engages our frontal cortex and is used for complex math and problem solving. The challenge for policing is that we are often using System 1 to make decisions although we believe we are using System 2 (a typical human error). Explaining the way our cognitive abilities are limited is an important concept for policing to understand as it contributes to our implicit biases. **Mental Model #2—Cognitive Biases** reviews the many cognitive biases that we have and why they have come to be. This section examines the assumptions police make about crime using these cognitive biases. It explains how relying on intuition, gut instinct, and anecdotes weakens the effectiveness of policing strategies and potentially damages the public perception of the police. **Mental Model #3—First Principles Thinking** examines the common assumptions in policing that have driven police practice for decades. Mental Model #3 defines First Principle Thinking and ascribes it to the research in policing. What assumptions have been made in policing that we have been building on for decades that are not supported by science? What fundamental ideas are hidden in the research that can transform how we approach policing? Examining our beliefs about policing and crime is the first step in removing the barriers that inhibit us from interpreting data correctly.

The next section, **Part II—How We Think About Math**, begins our journey into the math. Do not be alarmed. I too became a cop to avoid ever doing math again, yet here I am writing a book about policing that is founded in mathematical and statistical concepts. To understand and interpret data there are some foundational mathematical concepts that we all need to understand, otherwise our interpretations of the data will be wrong. **Mental Model #4—False Linear Thinking** explains how we often extrapolate numbers as though it increases infinitely but certain things cannot increase forever, for example height and crime. We cannot grow to 200 feet and crime will never reach an infinite daily amount, there is variance—highs and lows of both height and crime that is bounded. **Mental Model #5—Binary Percent Changes** examines how percent increases and percent decreases are not equivalent due to differing base rates. For example, if a number decreases by 50 percent, then increases by 50 percent, it does not return to the original number (try it with the number 100). **Mental Model #6—Second Order Thinking** is not a mathematical concept but should be introduced early in the book to begin thinking about how your decisions affect downstream outcomes. What you do today can have everlasting effects. Thinking through those effects before you make any decision should be a part of a management meeting process.

As we move into **Part III—How Things Concentrate**, we begin to think about how the world works and how some patterns we observe in the world are also relevant to policing. One of these patterns we commonly see is concentration. We review the Pareto Principle in **Mental Model #7—The Pareto Principle** is the idea that 80 percent of the results come from 20 percent of the effort, 80 percent of a business's income comes from 20 percent of their customers, and 80 percent of system crashes are caused by 20 percent of bugs. This phenomenon is also observed in policing, where **Mental Model #8—The Law of Crime Concentration** demonstrates that police agencies consistently find 5 percent of their city street segments generate 50 percent of their crime and **Mental Model #9—The Felonious Few** that 10 percent of the most criminally active people are responsible for 66 percent of the crime.

Part IV—How Things Vary outlines the statistical Mental Models that set the groundwork for applying natural laws to policing. This section uses layman's terms, graphs, charts, and policing examples to explain each of the phenomenon occurring, how these phenomena pertain to policing, and why understanding causality is important to police performance. Starting with **Mental Model #10—Distributions** we see how most phenomenon in the world follow the natural law of the normal distribution. Most natural phenomenon do not increase in perpetuity. There is a bounded limit such as with weight, there are people on the left side of the distribution who are extremely thin and people who are on the right side of the distribution who are extremely heavy, but no adult can weigh 5 or 3,000 pounds. **Mental Model #11—Law of Large Numbers** explains a normal distribution and helps the reader understand that looking at weekly CompStat data, divided into specific crime categories, creates too few observations to develop a true understanding of crime. The Law of large numbers states that as data accumulates, the mean number becomes closer and closer to depicting the actual population. CompStat weekly data is typically so small that it cannot be accurately generalized to the population, yet police executives make strategic decisions based on these numbers. The Law of Large Numbers (MM#11) is then connected with **Mental Model #12—Regression to the Mean** to underscore the idea that decision-making based on small data is a misguided effort. Regression to the Mean (MM#12) is a statistical phenomenon that occurs when a variable (like crime) is affected by both stable and chance factors that causes data to vacillate around a mean without any outside influence. Regression to the Mean (MM#12), unless understood, can lead to the misinterpretation of data as in the case of making strategic decisions based on a week's worth of crime data. In most policing organizations, departments tend to react to crime spikes by throwing police patrols (standard model of policing) at the issue without considering that crime most often will naturally regress to the mean. This traditional way of examining crime (percent changes, binary comparisons, managing by crisis) is flawed as it leads to resource allocation and policy decisions that result in treading water. Administrations will be served better if a "normal" level of crime or average is established across crime categories and geographic sections of a city. This will allow for building control limits and an index that measures deviation from the norm. Fluctuation around the mean causes police managers to react to small increases in crime, thereby wasting valuable resources. Mental Models #10, #11, and #12 will help with understanding the *why* underlying the fluctuations.

Next, we delve into **Part V—How to Determine Causality** which continues by reviewing statistical Mental Models that people think they understand, but often do not, like the age-old adage of **Mental Model #13—Correlation Is Not Causation**. Correlation is explained in a way that sheds light on the incorrect causal assumptions often made in policing. This can be observed when police executives, city leaders, and the media attribute citywide crime drops to their most recent programs, policies, or resource allocations. We often mistakenly use correlation to attribute causality; thus, Mental Model #13 reviews the fundamentals of correlation so you can avoid doing this in managerial meetings and help your city leaders and local media do the same. **Mental Model #14—Causal Inference** explains how to determine causation, the importance of a comparison group and why understanding causation is mission critical knowledge for policing. Moving policing from correlational thinking to causal and probabilistic thinking is an important paradigm shift if we want to advance our professional knowledge. **Mental Model #15—Bayesian (Probabilistic) Reasoning**, also called probabilistic reasoning, is an approach to update our thinking with new relevant information for uncertain outcomes. We need a system to understand what information is relevant and what is not.

Here we shift into **Part VI—How to Think Scientifically** which explains the importance of knowing the difference between rigorous research and poorly designed research. The chapter begins by asking readers to check their assumptions **Mental Model #16—Peer Review Your Perspectives** by asking yourself, "How do I know that?" "How did I develop that assumption?" Peer review means to check your opinion by examining your sources to determine if they are credible sources, such as information from empirical studies, academic journal articles, or books written by academic experts. Google, social media, and best practice are often poor sources of information, but people let those sources guide their thinking. Police often use what they consider to be "best practice" to support their position, which is really just common practice as many police "best practices" have never been empirically tested. This moves us into examining how to test police practice with the scientific method—**Mental Model #17—The Scientific Method**. This chapter explains the scientific method (MM#17) as a Mental Model and demonstrates how crime theories have been developed over the last half century and supported through the scientific method. Routine activities theory, rational choice theory, deterrence theory, and focused deterrence theory are important theories for understanding why some interventions work and others do not. Mental Model #17 also explains how to use the Maryland Scientific Methods Scale as part of the scientific method for rating scientific rigor. Then we get to **Mental Model #18—Evidence-based Practice** which reviews how the Evidence-based Medicine paradigm shift occurred and how Dr. Larry Sherman built the evidence-based policing model from the medical model. It reviews the seminal evidence-based policing article "Preventing Crime: What Works, What Doesn't, What's Promising" to demonstrate how each of the principles apply to policing. This Mental Model #18 is built on the mathematical and cognitive foundation of the previous Mental Models which demonstrates why understanding statistical models is important for policing.

The last Mental Model section **Part VII—How to Make Decisions** explains strategies for evaluating police interventions, harm indexes, and a decision-making method to assist police departments with being more systematic in their approach to crime reduction and more thoughtful about how their interventions affect the community. This section explains how to structure, organize, and think about data to inform police executives in a way that can be easily understood, interpreted, and turned into actionable plans beginning with **Mental Model #19—Targeting, Testing, and Tracking**, an approach created by Dr. Larry Sherman. Sherman suggests a model of targeting problems by evaluating data, testing interventions to determine effectiveness and efficiency, and tracking data to ensure the program continues as implemented. **Mental Model #20—Harm Indexes** introduces the idea of a harm index, an index that creates an equal base rate across crimes for focusing police resources rather than using traditional crime counts. A harm index accounts for low volume/high harm crimes like homicide and high volume/low harm crimes like shoplifting by using sentencing days to determine the level of harm to a community. Advocates argue that harm indexes are a better way to measure crime than crime counts. Dr. Jerry Ratcliffe's harm index is reviewed here as an alternative harm model. He includes police activity as a measure in the index to balance the positive and negative outcomes that police activity can create in communities. The last model, **Mental Model #21—Decision-making Models** reviews the rational decision-making approach. It describes and explains steps for decision-making to determine whether programs, projects, or interventions are achieving their desired outcomes. Program evaluation does not have to focus on crime reduction alone. Public relations programs, such as Cops and Coffee, where the intent is to develop relationships can be evaluated too. Here Mental Model #21 creates a framework for understanding what an agency is trying to accomplish and if the goals of the program match the measures identified as priorities. If agencies uncover programs that are not achieving the intended outcomes, it will be suggested that they discontinue the program no matter how beloved it is; to in essence "kill their darlings."

Understanding how to apply Mental Models in the field is important for crime reduction, improving community perception, reducing cognitive biases, and improving the health and wellness of police officers and the community. The data will drive where and what an organization should focus on. **Part VIII—How to Apply It All** finishes the book with the **Conclusion: How the Twenty-one Mental Models Can Improve Policing and Reduce Cognitive Bias** is an epilogue of the book and the **Mental Model Method: How It All Fits Together Mental Model 1–21** is an overview of how to apply all Twenty-one Mental Models. Each Part I–VII concludes with an "applied" section— **Mental Models in Practice**—which explains how to apply the preceding three Mental Models. This final segment of the book combines all seven parts into an overall guide in the hopes that following the Twenty-one Mental Models will assist you with monitoring your thinking for cognitive biases, mining and interpreting your data in a way that will help with understanding what is occurring in your city, and give you a strategy that will help your agency become more effective and efficient while generating the least possible harm to your community.

Twenty-one Mental Models That Can Change Policing: A Framework for Using Data and Research for Overcoming Cognitive Bias is an attempt to synthesize statistical, psychological, sociological, and criminological theoretical models into a concise framework for police, policy makers, and community advocates. The Mental Models are arranged as building blocks to create a critical thinking structure around policing issues. Using these Mental Models to examine data will assist police with examining societal issues in a way that can reduce crime and calls for service efficiently and effectively without creating harm to the community. By using the Mental Models to think about police issues, we will be better equipped to reason, explain, predict, design, communicate, act, and explore a variety of issues in policing. It will encourage police to build their own latticework of theories for which to place their facts upon. Many policing books teach specific strategies for officers in their agencies. It removes the requirement of deep understanding of crime and is a disservice to policing. It assumes police are not capable of understanding sociological theories and statistics. Understanding the why behind crime and removing cognitive biases is integral for moving policing to a new era of thinking, which in this moment of time is critical.

Part I

How We Think

System 1 and System 2

> The instinctual shortcut that we take when we have "too much information" is to engage with it selectively, picking out the parts we like and ignoring the remainder, making allies with those who have made the same choices and enemies of the rest.
>
> Nate Silver

I was sitting in my office when one of my co-workers, George (names have been changed to protect the innocent), stopped by to say hi after he had finished testifying at court. Collapsing into one of my chairs, he said, "I just had the weirdest experience." I was immediately intrigued, because this officer, a normally steely-eyed, sarcastic, unflappable veteran officer looked astonished, so I immediately asked, "What happened?" Looking a little bewildered he started to explain:

> I just got done testifying in court on a gun case. When I was on the stand the district attorney asked me what happened on the traffic stop, so I explained the series of events step by step. I pulled the suspect over, he stepped out of the vehicle and as he stepped from the vehicle, a gun dropped to the ground. When I saw the gun hit the ground, I immediately ran towards the suspect and before he could reach the gun, I engaged him, and the fight was on.

I nodded, thinking to myself that sounds like a pretty typical flow of events. He continued explaining: "There was a passenger in the car. When the fight started, they got out and walked towards the front of the vehicle, but then turned and left the scene. I called for cover and we eventually got the suspect into custody." I responded: "Well that seems pretty normal," to which George shook his head in disbelief and replied, "No that's not the weird part. It was the defense attorney's follow-up questions."

George went on:

> The defense started asking me about the movements of the passenger. She asked if there was a passenger in the vehicle which I told her "Yes, there was a passenger." And then she asked, "What did the passenger do while I was fighting with the driver?" I explained to the jury, that the passenger got out of the car walked to the front passenger side of the vehicle and then walked away. The defense attorney asked whether the passenger come back after they left. I said "No." Then she asked, whether the passenger ever walked around to the driver side of the vehicle where the gun was, and I said "No."

DOI: 10.4324/9780367481520-2

Listening to George tell his story, I could already figure out where the defense was headed; they were trying to create reasonable doubt that the gun was not the suspect's but the passenger's. George explained, "I told the court, 'no—the passenger never went to the front of the vehicle' and the defense again asked, 'Are you sure?' I again said no the passenger was never near the front driver side of the vehicle. At this point the defense attorney then asks the court if they can show my body-worn camera video and the judge agreed."

George looks at me and says,

> I was fine showing the jury my body-worn video because at this point I was like "Go ahead and show it because it will substantiate what I am saying." The defense attorney starts the video so the court and I could watch it. And this is what I saw—while the fight was occurring, the passenger gets out of the vehicle, walks to the front passenger side of the car, watches the fight for a second, and walks away just like I said he did. And in my head, I am thinking, see he walks away. And then this is when it got weird, he comes back. The passenger comes back and walks over to the front of the driver side of the car near the gun and the fight. Stands there watching for a bit and then walks away again.

Looking dumbfounded, George says,

> Here is the thing though, I can't see it in my mind. It's not there. I can see everything in my memory. I can see when he first got out. I can see when he was near the front of the passenger side of the car, but after that he is nowhere in my memory. I can visualize the whole area where the fight was occurring, so it is not that there was something blocking him from my view. I can see exactly where he is standing in the video. It is just that *he's* not standing there in my memory. He is not there. I watched the whole video. The guy is there. I close my eyes and he is not. In the video he is pretty close to me and where the gun was lying during the fight, but I can't *see* him in my mind. He is not in my memory, and no matter how much I try to remember, he is just not there.

He sat back, "This is the most bizarre thing that has ever happened to me. It's so effin' weird." So, like most conversations I have in my life, I steered it towards research and asked George if he had to watch the "Invisible gorilla experiment" video in the academy.

The Invisible Gorilla experiment was an experiment run by Simons and Chabris published in 1999, examining the effects of inattentional blindness. Inattentional blindness is failing to notice something that is a fully visible but unexpected object because your brain is otherwise occupied with another task. The study became famous for the novelty of the research and its unexpected outcome. The experimenter devised a simple test. They video-taped two teams of three people passing a basketball back and forth to each other. One team wore black shirts, and one team wore white shirts. The players were in a wide-open space in front of a bank of three elevator doors and moved about randomly while they passed the basketball. The teams would pass the ball in a specific order: player 1 to player 2 to player 3 then back to player 1. They would use bounce passes and aerial passes and moved in rhythm with the passing of the basketball. Individuals then watched the videos and were assigned to count passes; they were either assigned to count the white team passes or the black team passes and to count all the passes (easy) or only count the aerial or bounce passes (hard). The four conditions were thus:

1 white/hard,
2 white/easy,
3 black/hard,
4 black/easy.

And while the observers were watching the teams pass the basketball either a person in a gorilla suit or a woman with an umbrella would walk through the scene. This created sixteen conditions and each observer only participated in one condition. When the participants were finished with the experiment, they were asked four questions with increasing specificity, beginning with asking them if they saw anything unusual and ending with did you see a gorilla or a woman with an umbrella.

The Invisible Gorilla experiment was designed to determine if someone's attention was focused elsewhere, would they essentially become "blind" to another stimulus. What Simons and Charis found was that 46 percent of the people participating in the study across all conditions failed to notice the gorilla or the umbrella woman. And when comparing the easy to hard condition, they found that almost 20 percent more people failed to see the gorilla or the umbrella woman, 64 percent compared to 45 percent relatively. This study found that when people were engaged in a heavy cognitive load, they had a hard time paying attention to the things around them.

Police are trained to work through high stress events by using "combat breathing" to avoid tunnel vision caused by a rush of adrenaline. The difference between tunnel vision and inattentional blindness is that adrenaline narrows the field of perception in your vision, whereas with inattentional blindness you see the entire perceptual field, but you do not "see" something within that field. This is what happened to George during his fight, it was not tunnel vision, it was inattentional blindness. His attention was on the suspect he was fighting and even though he could "see" the passenger in the beginning of the fight, after the passenger left and returned, George's brain no longer could "see" the passenger.

Human brains are tricky. What psychologists and neuroscientists have been learning through research is that our brains do not process information the way we think we do, especially when faced with uncertainty. Humans view their life experiences as facts and their memories as correct, even though experiences like George's and experiments like the gorilla experiment demonstrate that our brains our fallible. We think we make rational choices in life, but often our choices are influenced by our beliefs rather than logic. Our brains do not function in a rational matter. Instead of thinking we understand the world and everything that occurs within it, we must learn about how we think before making assumptions about the world we live in. Thinking about our thinking was what one psychologist named Daniel Kahneman spent his life studying.

In 1967, Dr. Daniel Kahneman was working on experiments examining the relationship between pupil dilation, cognitive workload, and perceptions well before Simons and Chabris added a gorilla to the mix. Kahneman wondered if there was an objective measure that represented the cognitive workload of the brain. He wondered if pupil dilation reflected how hard a human brain worked. Kahneman, along with Jackson Beaty, tested the idea that as a brain works harder, the pupils dilate in sync with how hard the cognitive load is. Their theory was if they had an objective measure of cognitive load then this would assist them in learning how the brain works. They found that the pupils dilate as large as possible during maximum workload and immediately constrict once the brain is finished thinking. When they confirmed that pupil dilation was an indicator of cognitive workload, they moved on to examining what the brain attends to when taking on a workload. They designed 'add-1' experiments. Participants were asked to listen to a string of four numbers and then add 1 to each number and verbally respond with the new number. For example, a participant would hear 4872 ($4 + 1 = 5$, $8 + 1 = 9$, $7 + 1 = 8$, $2 + 1 = 3$) and they would respond 5983. Pupil size was documented by taking a photo of the pupil at a rate of one per second. Participants were then shown the letter K on a display that was only 40 cm from their eye. At the end of the test, they were asked if the letter K had appeared during any time in the trial. What they found was over the course of the 10 seconds of the test, participants almost never missed a *K* at the beginning or at the end of a test, but during the period where the cognitive load was the greatest, they missed the *K* half of the time.

Kahneman was in search of learning how we processed the world. And what he found after decades of research is that our brain generally works in two separate ways. He defined these processes in his book, *Thinking, Fast and Slow*, as System 1 and System 2—Mental Model #1. Kahneman describes them,

> System 1 thinking "operates automatically and quickly, with little or no effort and no sense of voluntary control." System 2 "allocates attention to the effortful mental activities that demand it, including complex computations. The operations of System 2 are often associated with the subjective experience of agency, choice, and concentration."

In policing, System 1 thinking is the mental effort that is typically being activated in patrol and System 2 thinking is the prolonged mental effort that tends to occur in investigations. System 1 is our quick response system, the one that notices a speeding car and immediately goes after it or when a suspect runs and you immediately start chasing. System 2 is the system we use when we are solving a problem that requires a greater mental effort. Interviewing a suspect requires thought and planning about what questions you are going to ask, what order are you going to ask them, and determining what outcomes you are looking for from the interview.

System 1 and System 2 are relatively easy frameworks for understanding how our brain processes information. It defines how the brain processes information and informs us as to how a human will react. If you see a lion in the jungle, System 1 engages, and you run. When helping your kid with common core math, System 2 will kick in as you engage your long-term memory and recall the rules of math learned in your childhood. Your brain will restructure that knowledge into a common core framework, and then conceptualize how to explain it in a way that your child understands. This requires a big cognitive effort. I am sure that if you paused for a moment, you would be able to think of all kinds of activities that would fall under either System 1 or System 2. Here are some of Kahneman's examples of both systems shown in Table 1.1.

Table 1.1 Kahneman's Examples of System 1 and System 2 Thinking

System 1	System 2
Drive a car on an empty road	Park in a narrow space
Orient to the source of a sudden sound	Search memory to identify a surprising sound
Answer to $2 + 2 =$	Fill out a tax form
Detect hostility in a voice	Check the validity of a complex logical argument

Here are some policing examples of System 1 and System 2 thinking shown in Table 1.2.

Table 1.2 Policing Examples of System 1 and System 2 Thinking

System 1	System 2
Unholstering a gun when feeling threatened	Examining crime data in CompStat
Driving a squad car	Driving and giving updates during a pursuit
Chasing a fleeing suspect	Interviewing the suspect once they are caught
Read someone their Miranda rights	Trying to solve a crime from physical evidence

The tricky part about System 1 and System 2 is that people often think they are engaging System 2, being logical, rationale, and using their intellect when deciding. But System 1 has a sneaky way of influencing System 2 without System 2 even knowing it. It is tricky because of the way we view ourselves. We view ourselves as rational, logical people who think through our decisions in a precise, logical manner, based on facts. In actuality, our System 1 processing works so quickly that often if something makes sense to us, we adapt it into our beliefs. If an idea is salient to System 2, we do not "fact check" the information. Think about it this way: System 2 stays in sleep mode while System 1 runs our brains. System 2 "wakes up" when complex thinking is required, but most often System 1 is just running along making sense of the world through impressions, intuitions, intentions, and feelings while checking in with System 2 to turn it into a belief.

Annie Duke summarizes how we view our own thought processes in her book, *Thinking in Bets*. She summarizes how we *think* we form beliefs and how we *actually* form beliefs.

This is how *we think* we form abstract beliefs: 1. We hear something; 2. We think about it and vet it, determining whether it is true or false, only after that 3. We form our belief. It turns out, though, that we actually form abstract beliefs this way: 1. We hear something; 2. We believe it to be true; 3. Only sometimes, later, if we have the time or inclination, we think about it and vet it, determining whether it is, in fact, true or false.

This is due to cognitive load. As Kahneman and others have shown, when we are over-loaded cognitively, we shut down and stop processing information. George's story at the beginning of the book was an example of this in practice. As we process more information, our pupils dilate, our heart rate increases, and it requires more effort to critically think through something. As a species, we do not have time for the inefficiencies of System 2. We have System 1 to help us navigate the world. You cannot sit at a stop sign processing every bit of information in the world. If you did, it would take you ten minutes to put your foot down on the gas pedal. It is simpler to rely on our intrinsic responses. System 1 jumps in with a model of how we should perceive the world and, voila, beliefs are transferred from hearing something to believing something. And once System 1 decides something is true, all the information in the world that System 2 receives will now be viewed through the lens of System 1 and its biases. System 1 is an efficient system but depending on the situation it may not be an effective one.

During the COVID-19 pandemic, all kinds of information was being put out on Facebook and Twitter about what was true and what was not. One video that went viral was of a Dr. Frank Hahnel, who was advising people to take quinine and if they could not find it, then he advised people to drink three to four ounces of tonic water a day to get quinine and zinc into their system as a way to prevent COVID-19. He claimed a "friend" of his who was a doctor was successfully treating COVID-19 patients with hydroxychloroquine and zinc. He used this information as evidence of how to prevent COVID-19. He made the claim that quinine "acts similar to hydroxychloroquine as a transport chain to let nutrients into the cells" and that everyone needed to listen to him and immediately start taking zinc and drinking Schweppes tonic water to prevent COVID-19. He covered his liability by saying that he was not giving medical advice. It was posted on a Facebook feed of a friend of mine. To peer review (MM#16) the information, I googled "Who is Dr. Frank Hahnel?" Based on the absurdity of his claims, I was not surprised to find that Dr. Hahnel was a chiropractor who runs a "wellness" center. I *was* surprised that his name was not Dr. Frank Hahnel, it was actually Dr. Eric Nepute. Based on his website claims, Dr. Nepute's chiropractic education has made him an expert in a variety of medical fields—he offers a concoction of vitamins administered intravenously that he claims will cure migraines, asthma, seasonal allergies, and chronic fatigue. He works with mothers who want children, he calls this preconception care: "This is when parents come to us at least 2 years before conceiving a child to first correct unidentified health issues with them in order to prevent those genes from being passed down." I found it interesting that a chiropractor, a person trained to relieve musculoskeletal pain through manipulation, feels comfortable giving medical advice to the masses on a health pandemic and future mothers on genetics. I also wondered how he was going to "prevent" genes from being passed down.

After I read his biography, examined his website, looked up the school where he received his education, I decided that this was not a person that ANYONE should be listening to for medical advice concerning COVID-19. I went back to my friend's Facebook post and attached a link to the good Doctor's website stating that this person was not Dr. Frank Hahnel, his name was Dr. Eric Gapute, and he was a chiropractor from St. Louis. My friend's response on Facebook was, "I agree he may not be legit, who knows who is nowadays and the source, I didn't investigate him, but I like some of his common sense approach to the whole thing which is getting out of control." My friend, in order to hold on to her belief that something can prevent COVID-19, disregarded all the relevant information about this person's education by focusing on the "common sense" part of what she believed he was saying. Her System 1 had created a model of the world she accepted, therefore System 2 was not allowed to follow a logical, rational, or methodical evaluation of the evidence presented. If it had, she may have looked up the fact that the FDA banned the sales of all drugs that contained quinine in 2006. They found, through empirical research—not anecdotes—the only thing quinine was useful for was the treatment of malaria and the side effects of taking quinine could be serious illness or death. The FDA, although they do make mistakes, rely on, and learn from science, thus their view versus a chiropractor who makes a lot of dodgy medical claims should be more valued.

Our brains have evolved into efficient systems that "minimizes effort and optimizes performance." System 2 engages when System 1 cannot make sense of something in the world. For parents raised in the 1980s and 1990s, Common Core will always be a function of System 2. Yet, if System 2 were engaged all day, taking in information, analyzing it, walking through a set of organizational decision-making processes, we would get nothing done. Therefore, many activities that engage System 2 in the beginning can get moved to System 1 through building expertise. Officers learning to shoot for the first time may have to walk through the five-step process for pulling a gun out of a holster, but by the time they hit the streets will pull their weapon automatically without thought. Our brains are remarkably effective at creating shortcuts to move an activity or thought process from System 2 to System 1. We want to be efficient at moving about the world. But because System 1 creates models for how the world works *and* operates automatically *and* cannot be turned off, "errors of intuitive thought are difficult to prevent." Which means our brains are susceptible to Mental Model #2—Cognitive Biases.

Cognitive Biases

Sometimes bad things happen even when good people are doing their best. This is very hard to accept psychologically. Bad outcomes cast a halo around everything that came before them and its next to impossible to see through the halo to reality .... This halo effect really is very deep and profound and hard to shake, right? We think we are evaluating a process that led to some outcome but really we're just reflecting the outcome itself and this really gets in the way of evaluating the process.

Dr. Duncan Watts

System 1 works efficiently to create shortcuts in our thinking, making us able to respond quickly to the world. This means that since the day we were born we are taking in information about the world, attempting to understand it, and then creating action to effectively get through life. Therefore by the time you are a functioning adult, your brain has created thousands of short cuts in System 1. And these short cuts represent *your* beliefs about the world, but it does not necessarily make them true (all the time, for every person). These beliefs come from your experience of the world. Our lives become complicated when System 1 has created a belief, and if it is inaccurate, System 2 rarely stands a chance of overcoming it. As Kahneman explains, System 1 works pretty well to get us through life. Its predictions are typically accurate, its reactions are swift and usually appropriate, and its model of familiar situations is usually right on. The problem that occurs in human processing is that System 1 creates models for quick access and these models create bias through which all System 2 information is now filtered.

It is important to understand System 1 and System 2 and the resulting cognitive biases that are produced because policing has evolved over the last three decades and now uses data to drive decision-making. System 1 is good at detecting simple relationships, such as crime increased by 5 percent this month and attributing it to a generalized cause, that is, burglary series, summertime, holiday, and so on. As indicated before, although you may be able to simplify a phenomenon with System 1 thinking, it does not mean it is correct. When interpreting data, especially something as complicated as crime data, System 1 fails. I repeat System 1 *fails*. As Kahneman says, "System 1 ... excels at integrating information about one thing, but it does not deal with multiple distinct topics at once, nor is it adept at using purely statistical information." Data interpretation as the basis for strategic decision-making has become the backbone of police decision-making in most police departments. Thus, if agencies are using data to allocate resources, which thereby directly effects their communities, they should make every effort to do this in a manner that eliminates cognitive bias. This

DOI: 10.4324/9780367481520-3

begins with understanding System 1 and System 2 thinking and the multitude of cognitive biases that accompany them.

One important point to understand at this juncture is that everything discussed in Kahneman's book is not about intelligence. Kahneman references Keith Stanovich's work in *Thinking, Fast and Slow* where he states that rationality is distinct from intelligence. Intelligence is the ability to acquire knowledge and rationality is to apply knowledge in a systematic way. Stanovich implies that being susceptible to cognitive errors is "lazy" thinking. Relying on System 1 because it is easy, rather than doing the analysis required of System 2, is my definition of lazy thinking. This book advocates for System 2 thinking when we are doing long-term problem solving, when we can take the time to use System 2 thinking, and only falling back on System 1 thinking when in the field and reaction time requires it.

Cognitive biases are rational deviations from logic that effect our judgments and decisions that arise from heuristics created by System 1. Heuristics are useful as when a ballplayer catches a flyball using a gaze heuristic rather than estimating the ball's velocity, angle, and distance, if they stopped to do the math, they would miss the ball. Heuristics can be useful and can be harmful. Think of heuristics as short cuts our brains use to evaluate the environment around us. Heuristics are our brains narrowing in on small bites of information in the environment that allow us to act fast. In Tversky and Kahneman's 1974 paper, "Judgment under Uncertainty: Heuristics and Biases," they discuss how cognitive biases are the outcome of heuristics or rules of thumb that people apply to the world. These "rules of thumb" are where our stereotypes come from. System 1 is efficient at simplifying the world, but this simplification tends to lead to errors in rational thought. Some of the most common cognitive biases we see in policing are:

- Availability heuristic—Overestimating the likelihood of events by using what is "available" in your memory, which tends to be events that occurred recently, were unusual or were emotionally charged.
- Base rate fallacy—Focusing on an individual or event, rather than examining the probability of the phenomenon occurring in the population (or as I call it, the "I know a guy" effect).
- Confirmation bias—Only finding or seeing data that confirms one's preconceived notions.
- Clustering illusions—Seeing patterns, clusters, or streaks in large samples of random data.
- Insensitivity to sample size—Underestimating the variation in a small sample or, as Tversky and Kahneman called it "The belief in the law of small numbers."
- Hindsight bias—The belief that past events are predictable at the time the event occurred.
- Outcome bias—The tendency to judge a decision based on the outcome rather than on the quality of the decision.
- Gambler's Fallacy—The belief that past events will predict future outcomes.
- Semmelweis effect—The tendency to reject evidence if it contradicts with a current paradigm.
- Bandwagon effect—The tendency to do or think things based on other people doing or thinking the same.

The first three biases (availability heuristic, base rate fallacy, and confirmation bias) are common in policing, especially when it comes to the types of people we come across in the field. In a procedural justice training course developed by the Chicago Police Department, under the guidance of Yale Law Professor Dr. Tom Tyler, students are shown a slide depicting the percentage of the population that police officers encounter. This slide is shown to demonstrate that due to the nature of police work, the majority of people that the police deal with are a small representation of the total population. The point of the slide is to demonstrate that policing beliefs about certain populations are most likely not attributable to the whole population. This slide demonstrates the "I know a guy effect." Instead of examining the likelihood of an occurrence based on the whole population, people will search their minds for a close representation of that person and apply it to the whole population. Tversky and Kahneman demonstrated this phenomenon by giving written descriptions of a person to study participants and asking them to choose what type of job that person would have. Subjects were given the following description. "Steve is very shy and withdrawn, invariably helpful, but with little interest in people or in the world of reality. A meek and tidy soul, he has a need for order and structure, and a passion for detail." They were then asked if he was more likely to be a farmer or a librarian. Instead of using logic, as to how many farmers there are versus librarians to determine a base rate of probability, most people will use the description to determine what "type" of person Steve represents, a librarian. If humans were logical, then we would examine the "likelihood" of someone having a certain occupation based on what is statistically represented in our society, and disregard information about what we think their personability reflects. Tversky and Kahneman showed that resemblance as a heuristic was more powerful than statistical base rates. We observe this in policing when recruiters meet applicants and based on an initial intuition, decide whether someone "resembles" a police officer.

When officers apply to police departments, they usually have to pass a succession of tests before getting to their background check. Once in their background check, they meet with a background investigator who will assess whether they believe the applicant will make a good police officer. This process reminds me of the story told in the book *MoneyBall* where scouts believed they were better at choosing baseball players based on how the player looked on the field (comfortable, confident, and relaxed), the scouts' opinions about their abilities, and whether the players fit with their model of what a good ball player should look like. When Billy Beane came up with a statistical model of assessing players' abilities, he demonstrated that evaluating ability based on data rather than gut feelings produced better outcomes. The scouts did not believe this was a better approach. They had their "I know a guy" stories and how they have seen hundreds of ball players over the course of their careers, in consequence they felt their experience should trump data. The issue with experience is that if you do not have a constant feedback loop that tracks your successes and failures you will not learn from your choices (this will be reviewed more thoroughly in Mental Model #15—Bayesian (Probabilistic) Reasoning). Like most humans, when the scouts thought about their experience, they most likely activated System 1 and remembered the most recent player they scouted (availability heuristic) and used it as an example of their success. Because of Billy Beane and his success with using statistics to build a baseball team, in the end choosing players became a blend of art and science. He used statistics as a feedback loop to improve his scout's ability to choose better players. Human judgment is flawed due to how System 1 and 2 work. Imagine what a recruiting unit would look like if police agencies analyzed the data to determine what qualities determine an applicant's success and used this to create a statistical method to evaluate candidates, rather than using a backgrounder's intuition or "gut feelings" as a predictor of success. Availability heuristics, confirmation bias, and base rate fallacy all contribute to police confidence about their ability to pick out a good police recruit, nick a bad guy on the street, or decide who is qualified to be promoted. Understanding the limitations of our mind could help us to better serve our communities by helping us make better rational decisions based on data rather than beliefs.

However, even when using data to drive decision-making, interpreting data can still be subject to cognitive biases. Tversky and Kahneman demonstrated two heuristics common when evaluating data: clustering illusions and insensitivity to sample size. It is not too hard to understand why, as human beings, we often fall back on heuristics. Our brains need to make sense of the world and we have a powerful drive to see cause and effect. If we could not figure out the cause of something, then we would come to view the world as random and scary. Look at how far science has come over the last few centuries. Human desire to understand and control our environment has driven progress. Imagine how scary a place the world would be if we still believed that hurricanes were angry gods and earthquakes were demons from beneath trying to escape the netherworld. Being able to predict what is going to happen in the world allows us to feel safe. This need to feel safe and connect cause and effect makes our brains susceptible to finding reasons even when none are there. Tversky and Kahneman have shown that when you show people random data, they will see patterns in the data where none exist. Kahneman and others, when explaining this bias, commonly refer to the story of the World War II German bombings and William Feller. Feller was a leading mathematician in the study of statistics and probability who decided to examine the bombings that occurred in South London. During the War, the English developed a belief that the Germans had spies in London based on where bombings clustered on a map. The English saw large gaps in bombing patterns and decided German spies must be hidden somewhere in the area where no bombs landed. Using a Poisson Distribution, a distribution of the number of events occurring during a time interval over quarter kilometer areas, Feller determined that the bombs were dropped at random and there was no pattern in the bombings. He stated, "To the untrained eye, randomness appears as regularity or tendency to cluster." Picture what a policing crime map looks like. If presented with dots on a map, our brains will make connections that do not exist. Without understanding our tendency to see patterns, police can make the mistake of seeing patterns in crime maps where there are none and mistakenly redistribute resources. Tversky and Kahneman showed this same bias with something inherently random, coin flips. Even though one coin flip has no effect on the next coin flip (you have a 50:50 chance of getting a head or tail) people still perceived that HTHHTT was a random process versus HHHHHH, even though both patterns were as equally likely. Humans will see patterns where there are none.

The focus of crime analysis is to determine crime patterns and trends and report on crime data. Understanding cognitive bias is important because crime analysis is not only affected by a clustering illusion bias, but also by an insensitivity to small number bias. When I left the crime analysis unit, my replacement was under immense pressure to apply some type of "predictive policing" component to his weekly management briefings. The department had vetted a couple of different software programs that advertised a predictive component. Although none were purchased, the expectation remained. Thus, the crime analysis supervisor just took to circling an area where the most crime occurred that previous week and saying this was their "predicted" focus area for the following week. He did not do any type of analysis. No statistical computations. He did nothing more than circle the area where most of the dots clustered and presented it as predictive policing. Everyone was happy and there was no more discussion of purchasing predictive policing software. Using dots that cluster together made everyone feel as though they were focusing their resources in the right areas. And I know there are some who will say, "What is wrong with that strategy? Go where the crime occurs." Well, if you want to proactively prevent crime, then you need to be where crime is going to happen and not where it has already happened. Conceivably, the Law of large numbers would hypothesize that by examining a week's worth of data, police are responding to the noise or variation in the data rather than what the data would really show if the data set were larger. Altering resources to respond to a cluster of crimes based on a week's worth of data is falling victim to the belief in small numbers or insensitivity to small numbers bias.

The belief in small numbers is our tendency to take a small amount of data and generalize it to a population. Sometimes we use a number as small as a sample size of one (n-of-1) seeing as we often use "I know a guy" as an example of how things work in the world. Insensitivity to small numbers bias or small sample bias is slightly different than base rate fallacy. Base rate fallacy says that we will predict the likelihood of something occurring based on the representation of a person rather than the whole population. We do not consider the proportion of occurrence in the population to make a prediction. Whereas the belief in small numbers originates with a lack of understanding of the variance that occurs with a small sample size. It is taking the occurrence of a phenomenon in a small population and applying it to the whole. I have taught classes where I explain the research evidence demonstrating that, overall, Drug Abuse Resistance Education (DARE) is not an effective intervention for reducing the use of drugs and alcohol except for one study that shows positive results for 14-15-year-old girls of Hispanic descent who live in Southeast Arizona. This program has extremely limited effectiveness and in some cases has been shown to have a backfire effect where it has increased the use of drugs and alcohol in some groups. Inevitably, I will have someone in my class raise their hand and say something to the effect of "That may be true, but I had this kid who …" It is the "I know a guy" defense. What is interesting about cognitive bias is that often having an emotional story to go along with a sample of one creates a belief more powerful than data from hundreds of kids can overcome. If we are applying programs nationally or to a large group of kids, then the program should demonstrate efficacy over a whole population, not just one person. Police must be good stewards of taxpayers' monies and spending resources on an ineffective program wastes tax dollars.

The belief in small numbers means that when police see a week's worth of data in a crime management meeting, they will believe that these numbers are representative of the crime in their city rather than random fluctuations that could have occurred by chance. Crime data and crime itself is greatly influenced by chance. First, there is the chance that a citizen may or may not report a crime. The victim influences the likelihood of reporting. The suspect is influenced by chance as they may change their mind about committing a burglary when a homeowner comes home from work in the middle of the day because they forgot their lunch. When chance influences data, then small amounts of data will have large variance. One week of crime data, broken down by crime type, can have large changes week to week. Therefore, CompStat data often reflects 30 or 50 percent increases because there were only two robberies the previous week and this week there were three. When the numbers are small, there is too much potential for variance in the data. Extreme examples within small data sets can skew the average of an overall data set. Statisticians call this variance—noise—as it drowns out the signal the data is trying to convey.

Belief in small numbers also goes hand in hand with the Gambler's Fallacy heuristic in that people have misconceptions about the fairness of the laws of chance. People will place bets on red during roulette if the last six spins landed the ball on black. They believe that chance has an element of fairness, that because it was black so many times before that, eventually chance will switch directions and cancel out the previous six spins. The laws of chance do not work that way. Statistically speaking, the ball has the same probability of landing on green, black, or red every time the wheel is spun no matter the color it landed on previously. Yet people will believe that the laws of chance dictate the next spin to be different. They believe that the spins will cancel each other out. "The laws of chance … do not work that way: deviations are not canceled as sampling proceeds, they are merely diluted."

"Merely diluted" is the best way to understand what is occurring as data accumulates and why large data sets reveal the signal within the noise. When determining whether HHHHHH is more random that HTHHTH, you may understand that there is a 50:50 chance of a coin landing on heads or tails but the way humans perceive it is that HHHHHH cannot be random because *the set* does not reflect the possibility of a 50 percent probability. They feel *the set* should reflect this probability. It is not that either set is not random. It is that as you add datum, both data sets will be diluted by new datum. As you continue to flip the coin over time, the variance will get closer and closer to 50 percent heads and 50 percent tails. As the datum increases, the variability of the data set is diluted, and the true average comes to light. Flipping coins is how statisticians came to understand the population and sample distributions (MM#10). Therefore, looking at a weekly increase or decrease of crime data is an ineffective way to interpret data. Because the sample is small, the data reflects the variance that occurred within that week rather than the average of what is occurring over a period of six months or a year. It is better to gather enough data to dilute the variance so you can see the true signal in your data and determine where resources should be allocated.

Even if the law of small numbers makes sense to you, transitioning a police agency from weekly data to a moving six-month or year average will be difficult because of the last two cognitive biases on the list, the Groupthink bias and the Semmelweis effect. Most people have heard of the groupthink effect where people believe something because most people in the room or population believe it. They have even conducted studies where a study participant is unaware that everyone else in the room is actually a part of the study. The group is asked a question and one of the dummy participants gives a wrong answer. The rest of the group then agrees with the wrong answer. Even though the study participant knows the answer is wrong they will often agree with the rest of the group. The power to act in concert with others is strong in human beings; going along to get along is deeply embedded in our DNA. In addition, when presented with findings that are contrary to our understanding of the world, we will reject them no matter how much data and evidence there is that demonstrates our way of thinking is wrong. This bias is called the Semmelweis effect.

The Semmelweis effect is named after Dr. Ignac Semmelweis, a Hungarian medical doctor who worked at the Allgemeine Krankenhaus in Vienna in the 1800s. He is famous for discovering the cause of puerperal fever (childbirth fever) that killed thousands of women annually (and attempting to unsuccessfully change medical practice that would have saved these women from an untimely death). When Semmelweis began working at the Allgemeine Krankenhaus, he knew there was a problem in the hospital with women dying after labor from puerperal fever. And it was not just that the women were dying at the hospital, it was that the women who were cared for by the doctors and medical students during labor on the one side of the hospital died at a greater rate than the women who were cared for by midwives on the other side. The death rate on the doctor's side was six times higher than the midwife side. The rate of disparity was so high even the patients knew it existed. If Viennese women went into labor on a day they would be assigned to the doctor's side of the hospital, they would wait and, if necessary, have their babies on the street instead.

When Semmelweis started working at the hospital and noticed the disparity, it became his passion to figure out why there was such a disturbing difference between the outcomes of what appeared, on the surface, to be the same treatment. He applied the scientific method to his field work to determine what variable was different between the doctors and the midwives' method. He went so far as to make the doctors and the midwives stood in the same spots when assisting with labor, made sure they had the same religion, had them both use the same tools, and so on. He performed autopsies on the women when they died after childbirth to see if that would give him any clues about what was causing the different rates in death. When he performed the necropsies on the cadavers, the smell was horrific as their insides would be covered in pus and abnormalities. He could not make sense of it though, because the pus often covered different parts of the intestines or organs. Semmelweis could not discern why some organs were affected and not others or why organs unrelated to childbirth were affected at all. Semmelweis kept a running list of details, meticulously writing down every objective data point he observed to construct a theory as to what was causing puerperal fever. Even with all the data points he collected, it was not until his close friend died of the same symptoms that he gained insight into the cause. His friend Dr. Jakob Kolletschka died after nicking himself with a knife while conducting an autopsy. Before he died, Kolletschka developed a fever similar to mothers who died of puerperal fever. When the autopsy was performed, his organs looked indistinguishable from the deceased mothers. From this event, Semmelweis finally developed a theory as to the cause of death.

As was common for the time, the medical students all performed autopsies on cadavers before they went into the delivery room. When doctors were teaching medical students how to deliver babies, the doctors would put their hands inside the women demonstrating how to check on the baby's health. Once they showed the technique to the students, they would have the students repeat the technique to demonstrate they understood what they were being taught. Often the women would have multiple different doctors inserting their hands inside them to check on the condition of the baby. Between his friend's death and the medical practice of the doctors, Semmelweis finally made the connection. He hypothesized that the doctors were transmitting tiny dead particles from the cadavers to the women and this was what was causing them to die. He knew the hospital used a chloride of lime solution to help eliminate the smell that emitted from the dead bodies during autopsies. Connecting the two events, Semmelweis wondered if chloride of lime, besides eliminating the smell, could also eliminate the dead body particles clinging to the doctors' hands. He immediately instituted the practice of doctors dipping their hands in a chloride lime solution before treating women during childbirth and the death rate dropped immediately. After implementing the chloride washing, the rate of death from childbirth when the midwives or the doctors assisted were finally equal. Semmelweis solved the issue of childbirth puerperal fever, but his battle had only just begun.

When Semmelweis discovered that merely dipping one's hand into a solution of lime chloride diminished the rate of death from puerperal fever, he knew he had to get this information out into the medical field so women around the world would stop dying after childbirth. Like anyone who makes a medical discovery that could save thousands of lives, he immediately started telling doctors in other countries about the necessity for chloride cleansing of their hands before assisting with labor. The medical field did not listen. When encountering a new paradigm for which we already have an ingrained belief, no matter the substance of evidence, we rarely shift our beliefs. He even transferred to another hospital and achieved the same reduction in maternal deaths through the implementation of chloride cleansing, and still the medical establishment did not change their views on hand washing. This is why this heuristic—the inability to shift our beliefs in the face of new evidence—is called the Semmelweis effect.

When Semmelweis addressed physicians and nurses in his hospitals he told them *what* to do, but he did not do a particularly good job explaining the theory behind his *why*. Simon Sinek, in his book *Start with Why*, talks about the golden circle where the "what" of an organization is in the outer ring, the "how" is the center ring, and the "why" is the innermost ring of the bullseye. He states that most organizations know *what* they do and *how* they do it, but they often do not know *why* they do what they do. To inspire people, Sinek states, they need to know the *why*. They need to understand the purpose, cause, or belief. Many historians have written stories about Semmelweis and have given many different reasons why the medical establishment ignored his advice. Some said Semmelweis was too rigid and stern, closely watching the physicians and nurses to make sure they were clean and washing their hands. Being too militant, if a mother came down with puerperal fever, he tracked down his staff until he identified the person who failed to wash their hands. Sinek is incorrect about how human nature works when it comes to shifting beliefs. Even though Semmelweis told his staff the "what"—delivering healthy babies and caring for mothers, the "how"—by staying clean and washing hands with lime chloride, *and* the "why"—to save mother's lives, it did not work to change their behavior. It did not work because their behavior was attached to their belief system that had already created a strongly embedded System 1 belief—the Semmelweiss heuristic. The difference between what Sinek advocates for in his book - inspiring workers to work harder in something they already believe is different than inspiring someone to change their fundamental beliefs about the world. Inspiring someone to change their beliefs is nearly impossible.

Thomas Kuhn coined the phrase paradigm shift about the painful process in science when a new way of thinking overcomes an old way of thinking. This process is not an easy one, and usually occurs once there are more people in the field who adhere to the new way of thinking versus the old. As Max Planck once said, "A new scientific truth does not triumph by convincing its opponents and making them see the light, but rather because its opponents eventually die, and a new generation grows up that is familiar with it." This is the *why* behind why we see the Semmelweis effects continue generation after generation, yet it still will not inspire anyone to change.

Over the last several decades data has taken center stage when police agencies and city governments make decisions about police resources and programs. Yet, the profession has not kept pace with these changes by educating itself about data, cognitive bias, and research. When I began this book, COVID-19 and the "defund the police" movement did not exist and yet police still should have understood cognitive bias. Now that we have been through this turmoil it seems now more than ever police executives should have an in-depth understanding of our cognitive biases, especially how they affect us when interpreting data. Without understanding how the human mind makes sense of information and data, the police and the public will continue to inaccurately interpret data. At least one side of that equation has a responsibility—the police to educate themselves as they have a duty to keep their communities safe. These cognitive biases manifest themselves through resource allocation which can mean the over-policing and underserving of some populations. It can mean defunding the police because System 1 thinking is overriding System 2 thinking. Without understanding how System 1 creates shortcuts that lead to bias, we will assume our interpretations of data are correct and continue business as usual. Understanding System 1 and System 2 thinking and our cognitive biases can help police executives and city leaders identify when their cognitive biases are getting in the way of their rational thinking. The first step in making this change is by defining the commonly held assumptions in policing by community members, city leaders, and the police themselves, then determining which are based on accurate data and information and which ones are not.

First Principles Thinking

"He believed in getting to the heart of the problem," says Arthur. "Instead of solving incredibly complicated equations, he taught me to keep simplifying the problem until you found something you can deal with. Look for what made a problem tick. Look for the key factor, the key ingredient, the key solution."

~ Brian Arthur speaking about Professor Stuart Dreyfuss

Our assumptions about the world are generated by our System 1 thinking, many of them are accurate. We learn as small children that if we touch the hot stove our hands will get burned. This gets rapidly assimilated into our understanding of the world and we no longer touch the stove. Many of our assumptions about the world are also incorrect. We tend to incorporate things we hear or read into our understanding of the world without vetting the information first. Annie Duke discussed how our beliefs about the world are created in her book *Thinking in Bets*. Rather than hearing or reading about something and vetting it for validity, we hear or read something and if it makes sense, we believe it and reshare it on social media.

A favorite classroom activity of mine is to display a list of generic beliefs on a slide and ask the room by a show of hands what assumptions are true and which are false. I compiled my list from Duke's book and googled some topics to find research that refuted some of our common beliefs. My list includes the following:

- Sugar makes kids hyperactive
- Milk increases mucus
- We only use 10 percent of our brain
- We lose the most body heat through our heads
- We have dominant learning styles from which we learn best—auditory, visual, and tactile
- Rust causes tetanus
- Hair and nails continue to grow after death
- Spicy foods cause ulcers
- Sir Robert Peel created Peel's Principles

After I go through all the bullet points, I reveal to the class that all the statements are false. I ask for someone who said true to any of the statements to be a volunteer. Once they divulge which statement or statements they thought were true, I ask them, "How do you know

DOI: 10.4324/9780367481520-4

that?" And most people cannot tell you how they know what they know. Some might say "my mom told me that," but the most common response is "I don't know." Duke points out the reason people do not know how they know what they know is because of how we ingest information. We hear something. We believe something. There is no vetting of the information, so a lot of our assumptions are based on things we have heard that sound reasonable. It is System 1 at its finest.

First principles thinking is a method that, if employed properly, can help you overcome your System 1 assumptions. First principles thinking assists with this by breaking down complex problems into basic facts that are supported by data and evidence, before moving to solution-seeking actions. This approach to knowledge requires you to walk back your thinking by examining every assumption you make about a topic to determine if your assumptions are correct. First principles thinking was popularized by Elon Musk and his drive to privatize space travel. When examining the feasibility of space travel, Elon ran into the same issue that had thwarted those before him, the astronomical cost (pun intended) of rockets. Rather than adopting conventional wisdom of that time—ordering rockets from another company—he decided to figure out what was needed to build a rocket. Rather than adopting the market practice of purchasing expensive rockets, he priced out the components needed to build a rocket and figured out he could build his own rockets for substantially less. By rethinking the conventional approach and breaking down the problem into the smallest parts, he was able to approach the problem in a different manner. System 1 assumptions are often barriers to progress.

First principles thinking, as described by Shane Parrish in his book, *The Great Mental Models Volume 1*, "is about systematically delving further into a statement or concept so that you can separate reliable knowledge from assumption." It requires stripping a problem down to its basic components until you are only left with the truths that define the problem. When examining the assumptions surrounding a problem ask yourself a simple question: "How do I know that?" If the answer is not from an empirical study or data, then you might want to start looking for data and evidence that supports your assumptions. Otherwise, how do you know whether you are trying to solve a problem based on a set of false assumptions?

A false set of assumptions can keep a discipline from advancing their knowledge for decades. This occurred in the medical field in the 1980s when doctors believed that the stomach was a sterile environment. Due to this assumption they dismissed clinical evidence as to the cause of ulcers, bacteria, for almost nine decades. Bacteria in the stomach was found by scientists as early as 1886 and confirmed by 1906. But because the scientist who discovered them, W. Jaworski, wrote his treatise in Polish, much of this information did not inform the international medical establishment. In 1910, Dr. Karl Schwarz published a case study on 14 patients in which he excised ulcers in the abdomen, throat, and duodenum, from which he deduced that the ulcers only occurred where acid was present, thus the saying, "no acid, no ulcer" became conventional wisdom of the time. After this case study, doctors began prescribing antacids for ulcers which gave patients some relief. Then in 1954, Dr. Eddie Palmer examined the cells of 1,180 ulcer patients and found no bacteria, and even though this was counter to three other scientists' findings, Doenges, Freedburg, and Barron, he surmised that bacteria were not the cause of ulcers. Despite three other studies showing otherwise, Palmer's study firmly entrenched the dogma that bacteria could not survive in the stomach. From then on doctor's believed the stomach was a sterile environment.

If you would have seen a doctor for a stomach ulcer in the 1960s or 1970s, the recommendation would have been to reduce your stress level, as stress increases stomach acid and acid causes ulcers. This was a System 1 error in logic, just because two things occur simultaneously—acid and ulcers—does not mean one causes the other, as you will see in Mental

Model #13—Correlation is Not Causation. After advising you to reduce your stress the doctor would have followed up with a prescription for an antacid and sent you on your way. The problem was that antacids helped with the symptoms but did not stop the ulcer from bleeding because the cause of ulcers was not acid. Even though some patients had to have their stomachs removed and others bled to death, the medical field stayed firmly ensconced in the belief that stomach acid caused ulcers and although antacids did not cure the problem, at least it gave patients some relief.

It was not until the 1980s that Drs. Robin Warren and Barry Marshall published a paper that revealed the presence of the bacteria Helicobacter pylori (H. pylori) in patients with ulcers, yet once again a stubborn System 1 would not believe the findings until 1995 when the medical establishment finally began using antibiotics to treat it. Warren had been collecting peptic ulcer samples for years well before the 1980s. When he observed the samples under a microscope, he could see the H. pylori bacteria, but culturing the bacteria was a difficult task as it did not grow at the expected rate in a petri dish compared to other bacteria. And if he was to prove the bacteria existed in the ulcer, he needed to classify the bacteria, and in order to classify the bacteria he needed to culture it. He made attempts to explain to practitioners in the field that he could see bacteria in the samples but was getting nowhere without cultures to show the bacteria growth. As he explained during a 2005 interview, "Every time I spoke to a clinician they would say, 'Robin, if these bacteria are causing it as you say, why hasn't it been described before?'" The dogma was so entrenched in the medical establishment, no one believed him. Then in 1981 a young new doctor, Barry Marshall, approached Warren and asked if he could work on his research project with him. From the moment Warren showed Marshall his slides, Marshall believed that Warren was on to something.

Part of the reluctance of the medical establishment to believe Warren was the 1954 study conducted by Palmer. His sample size was larger than the other three studies that contradicted his findings and because Palmer had the largest sample of all the studies performed it was assumed that his findings were correct. When they began working together Warren explained to Marshall the reason his findings were different to Palmers was that he used a silver stain that allowed him to see the bacteria under a microscope, while Dr. Palmer did not. Thus, having 1,180 samples was meaningless if you were not using the correct method in the first place. The problem was that no one knew the method was wrong, which meant Warren and Marshall had to set about getting enough samples to demonstrate to the medical field that the bacteria were present, so Marshall's first task as Warren's partner was to go out and find 100 samples.

The bacteria observed under the microscope by Warren was the same bacteria as seen by Doenges, Freedburg, and Barron (the three scientists discounted by Palmer) but because the assumption of a sterile stomach was already established by Palmer, the information was discounted. When confronted with information that conflicts with previous beliefs, humans will reconstruct the information rather than reconstruct their belief system; this is another attribute of System 1 that Kahneman has discovered. And this psychological response is a strong one. Marshall presented a paper at a small local conference presenting the 100 ulcer samples that were riddled with bacteria and was met with patronizing scorn. Then, when Warren and Marshall finally wrote their paper, it was met with skepticism and was initially rejected because *The Lancet* could not find reviewers who thought it was an important enough study for the medical field. The two had to write a letter to *The Lancet* describing their study to get the esteemed journal to publish it. It was only due to the support of a microbiologist from the U.K., Dr. Martin Skirrow, that the article was finally published. Warren had convinced the microbiologists that the bacteria existed, but they had no skin in the game because they were not the ones working with the patients. The gastroenterologists were the doctors prescribing treatment to patients and they were confident in their belief, despite conflicting research, that the stomach did not contain bacteria. They were also involved in a 3-billion-dollar (U.S.$) industry performing endoscopies on ulcer patients and since there were no cures, ulcer patients were perpetual money makers for the doctors. In a 2010 interview with Dr. Marshall he described gastroenterologists' position on ulcers: "They made the connection between ulcers, stress, and acid without any proper double-blind studies, but it fit in with what everybody thought." Fewer people were dying from their ulcers in the 1980s, but they had to live on $100-a-month medication and the antacid industry was making billions of dollars. There was no reason for anyone to pay attention to Warren and Marshall, as demonstrating that ulcers could be cured with antibiotics rather than maintained with antacids would undermine a whole industry.

In addition to the cultural challenges, one of the scientific challenges Warren and Marshall faced was human testing. They first had trouble cultivating the bacteria in a petri dish. At the time it was believed that anything that did not grow in two days did not exist. Just by happenstance a lab tech forgot to clear out some of Marshall's petri dishes and he found the H. pylori bacteria growing. It was a slow-growing bacterium; unlike anything they had ever seen before. They also ran into trouble trying to cultivate the bacteria in an animal; it could not be cultivated in lab mice. Next, they attempted to cultivate the bacteria in piglets and failed there too. Without being able get the bacteria to replicate in an animal, they were prohibited from experimenting on humans. Finally, in 1984, desperate to produce evidence, Dr. Marshall took a culture from one of his ulcer patients, mixed it into a broth and drank it. Within five days he developed stomach pains, began vomiting, and after ten days he finally had an endoscopy and it showed his stomach was covered in H. pylori, the bacteria that caused ulcers. He then showed that antibiotics could clear up the bacteria and cure his ulcers. He thought, just like Semmelweis did, that he had enough scientific evidence to prove to the medical field once and for all that ulcers were not caused by acid. He had physical evidence from a human that H. pylori caused the ulcers, he had pictures published in The Lancet showing the H. pylori bacteria in ulcers and yet gastroenterologists did not budge. Using antacids as the primary treatment for ulcers lasted over another decade before the Food and Drug Administration (FDA) and the National Institute of Health (NIH) finally stepped in and started pushing information out to the American medical establishment. Finally, between 1993 and 1995, doctors began prescribing antibiotics for ulcers. Once doctors began prescribing antibiotics, ulcers *and* stomach cancer were all but eradicated, as we now know stomach cancer is the result of a long-term H. pylori infection. Thankfully, Warren and Marshall persisted in spite of the professional ridicule and difficulties they faced, and in 2005 they were awarded a Nobel Prize for their discovery.

History is laden with stories of conventional wisdom being wrong. The story of Drs. Warren and Marshall could also have fit into Mental Model #2—Cognitive Bias as an example of the Semmelweis effect, but it fits here better because it shows how once an industry decides that a belief or assumption is true, it can take decades to undo. Dr. Palmer's inadequate research dominated the field for almost 40 years. If scientists would have used first principles thinking they could have broken down the problem of ulcers into the smallest components and examined what was true and what was not. There was evidence of H. pylori in the human gut beginning in 1886 yet scientists chose to ignore the evidence, by relying on the assumption that having many cases—1,180—in one study (Palmer's) was stronger evidence than the evidence from multiple scientists (Doenges, Freedburg, Barren, Warren, & Marshall) over many decades.

When examining our assumptions in policing we must begin examining where our ideas came from. Did they come from our academy or from our colleagues? If we learned them in a class, who taught the class and where did they get their information from? One of the classes my former agency was required to take was a class on procedural justice. I took one of the train-the-trainer courses to be an instructor. We adopted our class from a class taught by Chicago PD developed with the oversight of Dr. Tom Tyler, a well-known procedural justice researcher. The class was certified by California Police Officer Standards and Training (POST). Every time we got to the slide on Peel's Principle my co-instructor would look at me, laugh, step back, and say "Go ahead." He knew that I could not cover the slide without giving the class my disclaimer. First, I would ask the class if they had been taught Peel's Principles in the academy to which they would all respond "yes." And then I would explain that there is no evidence of a primary source connecting Sir Robert Peel to those statements. It was purely an invention of textbook writers from the 1970s and 1980s. I would explain that they were taught that Peel said these things, when nowhere in our history books can anyone find a direct reference to Peel saying these tenets. The only place you will find them is in criminal justice textbooks starting in the 1960s and most of them do not cite their source. If you read the newer criminal justice textbooks when they mention Peel's Principles, they cite the textbooks from the 1960s and 1970s. You know the saying about a lie being true if you say it often enough? Well, thanks to criminal justice textbooks we now have the well-entrenched story of Peel's Principles, and no one is going to uproot that story from policing folklore, in the words of Dr. Warrren, "it fit(s) in with what everybody thought."

First principles thinking requires us to dissect policing problems down to the basic components, as Musk did with his rocket problem. Once a problem is stripped to its basic components then you must examine the assumptions behind every fact you believe is true. Many times, when we try to address a problem in policing much of the thinking rests on preexisting assumptions. For example, CompStat and crime analysis rests on preexisting assumptions that crime data should be separated into crime type and examined weekly. CompStat was created in the 1990s by the New York Police Department (NYPD). CompStat is a performance management tool to reduce crime and to hold area commanders responsible. This is accomplished through tracking crime data by crime type on a weekly basis. CompStat has four principles: 1). Timely and accurate information or intelligence; 2). Rapid deployment of resources; 3). Effective tactics; 4). Relentless follow-up. CompStat was developed to generate strategic problem-solving, yet what it evolved into was a "de facto substitute for any broader problem-solving approach, thereby restricting or narrowing both the types of problems police can address and the range of solutions they are able to consider." This narrowing may have occurred over time due to the way crime data was displayed and continues to be displayed.

CompStat meetings tend to display data in binary terms, meaning this set of data compared to this other set of data created this percent change. Agencies will compare the current week to the previous week or the current week to the same week the previous year. Crime data is generally displayed similarly to the example from Austin Police Department (see Figure 3.1):

Data requires interpretation. Displaying crime data as a binary percent change, determining whether it goes up or down compared to another arbitrary data set leads people to examine data as though it is a linear function. They do this by assuming the data will follow a linear trajectory and this is not always the case. A binary comparison does not reflect the variance that occurs naturally in data and because police executives typically are not trained on how to interpret data, they will make decisions based on inaccurate assumptions. Mental Model #4—False Linear Thinking will explain why linear assumptions will lead to false conclusions which in turn will lead to inaccurate resource allocations. If something as

Offense Category	MTD	MTD LM	MTD LY	MTD % Var	YTD	YTD LY	YTD % Var	CR YTD	CR YTD %
HOMICIDE	5	3	2	150%	19	17	12%	17	89%
RAPE	40	50	60	−33%	294	409	−28%	99	34%
BANK ROBBERY	2	3	1	100%	11	19	−42%	10	91%
BUSINESS ROBBERY	14	19	12	17%	131	142	−8%	74	56%
INDIVIDUAL ROBBERY	81	63	40	103%	428	404	6%	118	28%
AGG ASSAULT No FV	100	100	95	5%	654	603	8%	205	31%
AGG ASSAULT FV	112	82	115	−3%	619	707	−12%	382	62%
Total	354	320	325	9%	2,156	2,301	−6%	905	42%

Figure 3.1 Example of Austin Police Department's CompStat Violent Crime Report

simple as how we display data can lead to worse outcomes, then it might be time to employ first principles thinking about why we display data in a binary manner.

CompStat tracks crime by type. Police agencies examine all the burglaries that occur across the city and group them into one category then use percent increase or decrease as an indicator of whether they should intervene or not. Research has shown that burglaries can have patterns or trends due to being linked to a particular burglar or particular area, but a burglary that occurred in the north area of the city could have absolutely nothing to do with a burglary that occurred on the south side of the city, yet they will be grouped together and treated as such during CompStat. Studies have shown that there is an increased likelihood of burglary on the same street as the initial burglary and increased likelihood of repeat victimization in the next month. Yet, police agencies examine burglary numbers in totality across the city or area, rather than looking at it by neighborhood or street segment. It has also been shown that crime concentrates in micro places such as a specific building, apartment, or street and that concentration rarely varies over long periods of time.

Police agencies could use first principles thinking for deconstructing their CompStat or crime management meetings. In doing so, they might find that the way they digest and interpret their data comes from how other agencies think about crime, rather than from research or data. The medical establishment based years of treatment on something they thought was a first principle—"acid creates ulcers"—but the first principle they built their treatment model on was wrong. This was not uncovered until one person began to examine every fact that supported the acid assumption, until he found instances where the facts did not hold up. Policing has not examined their assumptions about crime, disorder, and calls for service for several decades … if ever. Displaying crime as binary can lead to, as Inspector Guilfoyle says, "a catalyst for groundless assumptions about (potentially non-existent) trajectories within data." Shane Parrish in his book, *The Great Mental Models Volume 1*, suggests the following steps for engage first principles thinking:

1   Clarifying your thinking and explaining the origins of your ideas. (Why do I think this? What exactly do I think?)
2   Challenging assumptions. (How do I know this is true? What if I thought the opposite?)

3 Looking for evidence. (How can I back this up? What are the sources?)
4 Considering alternative perspectives. (What might others think? How do I know I am correct?).
5 Examining consequences and implications. (What if I am wrong? What are the consequences if I am?)
6 Questioning the original questions. (Why did I think that? Was I correct? What conclusions can I draw from the reasoning process).

This is where policing should begin. Why do we categorize data by type rather than by community? What evidence is there that demonstrates what is more closely related to each other, crime types or crimes within communities? How do I know crimes are related? Is all crime of the same type related to each other? What are my root assumptions about crime and how do they influence my decision-making? Why do we make binary comparisons evaluating one week of data compared to another week? What are assumptions about the changes in crime data week to week? What is our understanding of data interpretation? Where does our knowledge about data interpretation come from? CompStat has been replicated across the country by thousands of police departments: the question should now be with what we know today, is CompStat still the best model on which to interpret data, drive decision-making and allocate resources from? Can CompStat still be used as a meeting to drive decision-making while changing how we think about data? CompStat as a performance management meeting may be a useful framework, but the data that is used to populate that framework and the questions being asked might need updating.

The Mental Models in Practice I—Mental Models 1–3

System 1 and System 2, Cognitive Biases, and First Principles Thinking

Applying the first three Mental Models is about examining your own thinking and the assumptions your organization bases its strategies on. Police officers make many assumptions about how to best prevent crime, punish offenders, and engage the community. Many of these assumptions are based on what we have experienced in the field, learned from our field training officers, or just picked up over the years from other police officers. Below I list some ideas about how to examine your agency's current thinking to determine if the underlying assumptions are correct. Begin with Mental Model #3—First Principles Thinking to break down your assumptions into smaller and smaller ideas and then ask yourself: "How do I know that?" to determine what you are basing your assumptions on.

1 Examine your agencies core beliefs about crime, calls for service, social disorder, community engagement, and employee issues by having your executive management write down their beliefs about each topic that impacts the police and have them indicate where their information comes from (*how do you know that?*). Collect the information anonymously and have an assistant combine the answers into a report.

2 Begin the exercise by asking clarifying questions about their thinking on topics such as:

    a   Calls for service:

        i What percent of these calls do you think involve mental health issues?

            1 Of these calls, how many do not need a police response?
            2 Do you know if these calls occur in one part of the city over another?

        ii What percent of these calls do you think involve homelessness related issues?

            1 How should the department address homelessness issues?

        iii What percent involve civil disputes?

            1 How should civil disputes be handled?

    b   Crime

        i What police interventions reduce crime?

            1 Do different police interventions reduce different types of crime?
            2 What are the underlying causes of crime?

    c   Community engagement:

        i What types of community engagement programs reduce crime?

    d   Diversion:

        i What kind of diversion programs reduce crime?

    e   Social disorder:

        i What types of social disorder do we face in our city—loud music calls, illegal dumping and camping?
       ii What drives these behaviors?

    f   Employee issues:

        i What improves the morale of an organization?
       ii What is the best way to change behavior in an organization?
      iii What is the best way to prevent illegal or immoral behavior?

    g   Data:

        i How do we display our data in management meetings?
       ii Why do we compare week to week data sets?
      iii Is there a better way to understand our data?
      iv How do we decide when to intervene based on data?

The questions above are a sample of possible questions to elicit the beliefs and values of your executive managers and to determine what assumptions their beliefs are based on. Every single one of these questions should be followed by "How do you know that?" Like Elon Musk demonstrated, by breaking things down into the smallest components possible, an organization can discover where their thinking is faulty, and that shift in perception can lead to innovative new ideas.

Additionally, this exercise is not structured to gain consensus. The intent of the exercise is to get at how you think as an organization—defining the organizational beliefs and values and most importantly understanding where your organizational information comes from, especially around data management. The current approach to displaying and interpreting data in management meetings is flawed and can potentially lead to biased-based policing. The ideas that are based on the best possible source (unbiased research) are the ideas that should be moved forward. Rank does not rule in this exercise (and really never should when it comes to research), the reliability and validity of the evidence does.

Part II

How We Think About Math

False Linear Thinking

The belief that the change between two static points in time is sufficient to identify trending has left a majority of departments in a cycle of chasing variability. The unconscious false association of linearity that inevitably follows results in the perception that the problem will continue unless a response is initiated. The primary disconnect is that the decision-makers' belief that they are being proactive is based solely on limited data that describes only what has already happened. The problem that they are trying to address, the continuance of a perceived trend, is actually an artifact of their cognitive bias.

Nick Petitti

How data is displayed and interpreted in policing is extremely important because an executive manager's interpretation of data affects their decisions about resource allocation. Currently, most police departments display data on a weekly basis, showing raw numbers and percent changes from last week to this week, last month to this month, or the current month to the same month last year—binary percent changes—comparing one number to another to determine a percent change. Mental Model #4—the idea of false linearity—highlights the danger of thinking about data as though it follows along a straight line rather than a curved one. For when it comes to crime, the data lines both curve and snake, moving up and down, and back and forth, wrapping their serpent line around some imaginary center. To demonstrate how we typically display data in policing, I recreated a portion of a table from the Nashville Metropolitan Police Department's CompStat Report. The report was published on 01/18/2020, two days before the U.S. saw its first case of COVID-19. The data was taken from http://compstat.nashville.gov/2020/20200118_CompStat_Report.pdf which is publicly available. Table 4.1 shows the results comparing the most current 8 weeks of data to the previous 8 weeks of data.

Table 4.1 Nashville Metropolitan Police Department's CompStat Data from 01/18/2020

West Precinct	Rolling Sixteen Weeks Last 8 Weeks to Prior 8 Weeks		
	Violent Offense	Property Offenses	Part I Offenses
Prior	65	538	65
Last	49	501	49
% Change	−24.6%	−6.9%	−8.8%

DOI: 10.4324/9780367481520-5

As you can see from the table, the Commander of the West Precinct could ostensibly sit back and pat himself on the back. Whatever he has been doing in the previous eight weeks to combat crime has apparently had a massive effect, especially on violent crime. An almost 25 percent drop in violent crime in a two-month period is an accomplishment, right? You can almost picture the commander at the podium, pointing at the negative percent points, and without saying a word, dropping the mic and walking back to his seat. If you go back and read the quote that begins this Mental Model, Nassim Taleb sums it up nicely when he says that our emotional apparatus is designed for linear causality. We assume if crime is dropping, it will continue to drop, and if it is dropping, it must be causally linked to some variable. We cannot fathom the notion that crime data may experience random, indeed, even dramatic fluctuations across time.

In his book *Intelligent Policing: How Systems Thinking Methods Eclipse Conventional Management Practices*, Simon Guilfoyle devotes a whole chapter to binary comparisons titled "Binary Comparisons: Compared to What?" What he means is: what do binary comparisons really tell you when you compare one meaningless data set to another meaningless data set? What does the difference between one week of crime data and the next tell you about that crime type, and with so many variables affecting crime, how are you creating meaning from those variables? Watching a number or line on a graph shift up or down is meaningless.

Examining data in a traditional CompStat model—a binary fashion—leads to thoughtless linear extrapolation which is based on Mental Model #4—False Linear Thinking. When I say thoughtless, I do not mean to imply that police are being inconsiderate, rude, or selfish, I *literally* mean the root basis of the word: without thought. When we see data exhibited in a binary form, week two compared to week one, System 1 will kick in and examine the data as though crime is a linear function, and if there are changes, our brain assumes the changes are significant. "Crime as a linear function" means our brains perceive that crime will continue to increase in perpetuity unless someone does "something," similar to our belief that object in motion will remain in motion unless acted on by an unbalanced force. Yet physical science is starkly different to social science, and the "laws of motion" do not apply to crime and policing data. One of my executive police students explained the thinking like this: "If crime is going up and I don't do anything in my area command, crime will continue to go up." In reality, however, that statement invites a nuanced critique. Yes, it may go up, but it does not go up forever. Crime fluctuates. It goes up and it goes down due to police interventions, social interventions, economic factors, and as we have seen in 2020, public health factors as well. Crime is not a linear phenomenon, yet when we examine binary data and start to think about solutions to our problems, System 1 will attribute a false linearity to the data. System 1 wants you to do "something."

If you recall your eighth-grade pre-algebra class, a linear function is $y = f(x) = a + bx$, where the independent variable is x and the dependent variable is y. When graphed on an x/y-axis a linear relationship looks like Figure 4.1—this graph depicts a fake relationship between the height of a weed and days of growth. There is no variation in the growth each day and it continues increasing indefinitely.

If my student's hypothesis about the relationship between crime and policing interventions were true, then crime would continue rising day after day without stopping. But because crime is influenced by many other variables naturally, crime will *not* continue increasing in a linear fashion. Take, for example, one of the most common assumptions in policing: crime increases with hotter temperatures. Any street cop knows this to be true (How do you know that?), because they have been subjected to the increase in calls for service every summer. Here, our cognitive biases kick in because we have seen anecdotal evidence every summer for however many summers we have spent on patrol, but do we know whether crime and temperature increase linearly?

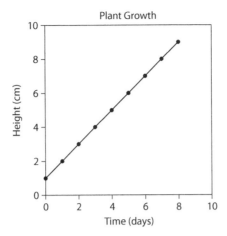

Figure 4.1 Linear Plant Growth Height in Centimeters Over Time in Days

Two emergency room doctors who saw violent crime victims in their emergency rooms decided to test the hypothesis that crime goes up during the summer by analyzing homicides, rape, and assaults that occurred in Dallas, TX, from 1993-1999. Using a multivariate analysis (simultaneously comparing the effects of different variables on one outcome (homicides, rape, and assaults)), they found that although violent crime does increase when temperatures increase, as temperatures near 90 degrees Fahrenheit, violent crime plateaus, and then begins to drop back down to pre-90-degree levels. The graph in Figure 4.2 depicts the relationship between temperature and aggravated assaults.

Unlike the weed growth graph, the relationship between temperature and aggravated assaults is not linear, it is curvilinear, meaning rather than increasing in a straight line, the line curves in one direction or the other as one variable increases. Viewing crime as

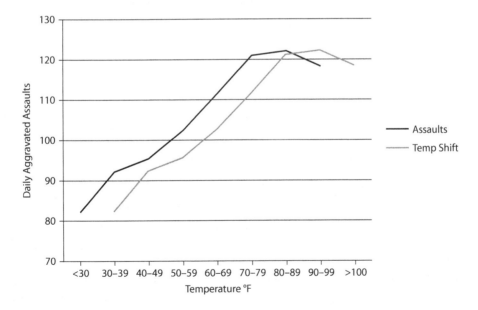

Figure 4.2 Relationship Between Daily Aggravated Assaults and Temperature in Dallas, TX

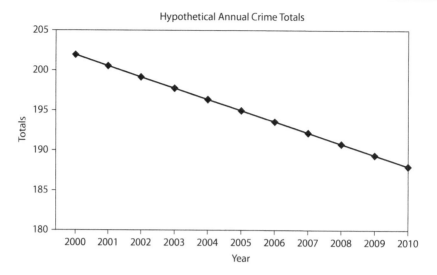

Figure 4.3 Hypothetical Linearly Decreasing Crime Totals

a linear phenomenon can cause police to make decisions based on inaccurate assumptions (MM #1, 2, and 3). Crime does not continue to increase or decrease in a straight line like the weed growth chart. The data does not look like Figure 4.3. It increases and decreases more like the graph in Figure 4.4.

The graph in Figure 4.4 was created by Nick Petitti, the Director of Business Intelligence of the Rochester Police Department in New York, for a blog series he wrote for his management team to assist them with understanding crime data. As you can see in the title,

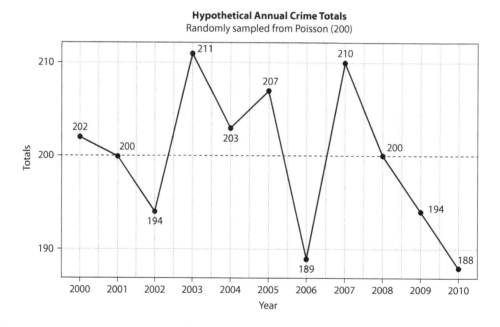

Figure 4.4 Hypothetical Annual Crime Totals Randomly Sampled from Poisson (200)

he utilizes a Poisson distribution employing 200 as the average. What this means is he instructed software to create a random distribution of numbers over an 11-year period based on a base parameter of 200. The different numbers generated are depicted on the graph—202, 200, 194, 211, 203, 207, 189, 210, 200, 194, 188 which, when you add them up and divide by 11, equals 199.81, almost the 200 average inputted. This graph represents what the data would look like if crime data were completely random. We know in policing that crime is not exactly random. There are *stable* variables that influence crime and *chance* variables that influence crime. Because there are both stable and random variables that influence crime, crime will never increase linearly, and conversely it will also never look like Figure 4.4 and be all over the graph. Crime data fluctuates over time incrementally which is why using large data sets to see what the natural variation looks like, and to determine the average amount of crime over a long period of time is a better way of examining data and comparing data points. This phenomenon is not just something that occurs in policing, it is a natural phenomenon that occurs regularly and because of our System 1 thinking we are lured into examining data with false linearity. If you would like to see this explained using stick figures, please check out Inspector Simon Guilfoyle's blog "Straight Lines" at https://inspguilfoyle.wordpress.com/2014/02/19/straight-lines/.

This idea of false linearity is not just something that affects police decision-making, it is something that effects everyone. Jordan Ellenberg, in his book, *How Not to be Wrong*, explains how linear thinking occurs even in baseball. Ellenberg discusses the April 2012 ESPN blog written by Eric Karabell in which he states: "Matt Kemp is off to a blazing start hitting .460 and on pace for 86 homeruns, 210 RBIs and 172 runs scored." Ellenberg mentions that most people in baseball use the term "on pace" as a tongue-in-cheek term as they do know that even if someone kicks off their season with amazing stats, maintaining those stats are impossible over a long period of time. Yet even though it is said in a sarcastic manner, people still report on those statistics, leading some to believe staying "on pace" might be achievable. But staying "on pace" means that batting average would be a linear equation—the rate of hitting homeruns would remain the same. A baseball player would have to continue his rate of hitting in perpetuity. As Ellenberg explains, the math works like this:

Kemp hit 9 homeruns in 17 games, so his homerun rate is 9/17
Multiplying his rate by the number of games will give Kemp's average homerun rate
Homeruns = Games × Rate
There are 162 games per season thus
HR = 162 × 9/17 = 85.76 or rounding up 86 Homeruns.

The problem is that this assumes that the two variables, homeruns and times at bat, are linearly related. It assumes that every time Kemp is at bat, he will hit a homerun at the same rate—nine times out of 17 times at bat. The problem with this approach is batting average is affected by multiple variables other than a baseball player's ability. The weather can affect both the pitcher's ability and the batters. One pitcher can be better than another or be having an extremely good or extremely bad day. Kemp himself could have a poor night's sleep the night before or have personal stressors that affect his ability. Finally, there is just random chance. Random chance is what killed Kemp's "on pace" batting average that year. Just one month after the ESPN blog published, Kemp tore a hamstring which caused him to end the season with only 23 homeruns.

False linearity in policing can cause police to do "something" when they should not. By using binary data to compare week-to-week fluctuations in data, police can mistakenly

Table 4.2 Nashville Metropolitan Police Department's CompStat Data from 01/18/2020

	Rolling Two Week	Rolling Eight Week	Rolling Sixteen Week	Year to Date	Rolling Twenty-Four Month
	Last week to prior week	*Last 4 Weeks to Prior 4 Weeks*	*Last 8 Weeks to Prior 8 Weeks*	*Current YTD to Prior YTD*	*Last 52 Weeks to Prior 52 Weeks*
West Precinct Violent Offenses					
Prior	10	21	65	18	450
Last	7	28	49	22	410
Percent Change	−30%	**33.3%**	−24.6%	**22.2%**	−8.9%

see trends where there are none. Without understanding how to interpret data, they will ascribe meaning to weekly changes in police data. They interpret week-to-week increases as a signal to "do something." As Guilfoyle discusses in his book: "It (binary comparisons) disregards variation and is incapable of communicating accurate information about trends, trajectories, or outliers, while appearing to do precisely that." If you reread his quote and think about what he is saying, he means that comparing week-to-week data is not useful, despite the powerful temptation or executive pressure to do so.

This is what happened to the Nashville West Precinct Commander as he was walking away from the podium after his mic drop. Just as he was sitting down, the full slide showed up on screen and a new data set for his violent crime was revealed in Table 4.2.

Guilfoyle argues that comparing data set to data set is meaningless and this exercise can reveal why. Comparing the last eight weeks to the previous eight weeks looks fantastic as violent offenses are dropping, but when you look at the last four weeks compared to the previous four weeks the violent offense rate looks horrible. Looking at data when it is constructed like this can make a police executive feel unsure about how to proceed. The problem is not about your interventions being useless. It's about examining the data in a way that informs you as a police professional and remaining cognizant of the pitfalls of false linear thinking. When our solutions are built on faulty logic, they aren't really solutions, only well-intentioned shots in the dark.

Crime is a complex problem that requires using analytical techniques that uncover the signal in the data rather than the noise. Binary data comparisons force our brains into thinking about crime data as though it is a linear phenomenon. If crime starts to rise, we think if we do nothing, it will continue to rise in perpetuity like Kemp's astronomical "on pace" batting average. This thinking leads police to reacting to natural variation in the data. As an area commander, if you do "something" just because you observe crime going up, the subsequent variance you witness may be just a random fluctuation in the data. Reacting is predicated on two faulty, common assumptions. First, assigning police resources to an area where crime is increasing "causes" the crime to go down, and second, assigning police resources to an area only has a positive effect.

Binary Percent Changes

> The only possible interpretation of binary comparisons are either 'we are doing fine', inviting complacency when the unseen long term picture may actually indicate that urgent action is required on the system, or 'things are getting worse' (even when it isn't); both risk unnecessary organizational responses to fix the 'problem'. Binary comparisons can never tell the full story, and when percentages are introduced into the equation inappropriately, it gets really messy.
>
> Dr. Simon Guilfoyle

Viewing police data as a binary percent change forces management into comparing raw number changes against an arbitrary baseline. Binary percent change is just a fancy, concise way of saying what the percent change is between two numbers. For example, the binary percent change between 100 and 200 is 100 percent. That is the percent change between the two numbers (binary). The formula for percent change is

$$C = x_2 - x_1 / x_1,$$

where C equals the relative change and x_1 is the initial value and x_2 is the final value. I briefly touched on the concept of binary percent changes in Mental Model #4—False Linear Thinking as these two Mental Models intertwine. Binary comparisons contribute to false linear thinking and false linear thinking is why the brain has an affinity for binary comparisons. One of the main goals of this book is to understand how brain functioning contributes to lazy thinking and why it feels good, so that when we fall into System 1 thinking we recognize it, correct for it, and engage in better thought processes.

Comparing this month's data to last month's data to determine a percent change adds a level of misinterpretation to the data. All data has variation (noise), or more specifically, all statistical estimates have variance. Variance measures how far a set of numbers is spread out from their average value: for example, if an area experiences the number of crimes in Table 5.1:

Table 5.1 Hypothetical Monthly Crime Data

Jan	Feb	Mar	April	May	June	July	Aug	Sept	Oct	Nov	Dec
12	7	9	14	11	18	17	17	11	9	7	12

DOI: 10.4324/9780367481520-6

Adding the crime counts from January to December and dividing by 12, the mean number of crimes per month equals 12. The variance equals (monthly crime count − mean)^2/mean.

$$\left(12-12\right)^2+\left(7-12\right)^2+\left(9-12\right)^2+\left(14-12\right)^2+\left(11-12\right)^2+\left(18-12\right)^2+\left(17-12\right)^2+\left(17-12\right)^2$$

$$+\left(11-12\right)^2+\left(9-12\right)^2+\left(7-12\right)^2+\left(12-12\right)^2$$

$$=\left(0\right)^2+\left(-5\right)^2+\left(-3\right)^2+\left(2\right)^2+\left(-1\right)^2+\left(6\right)^2+\left(5\right)^2+\left(5\right)^2+\left(-1\right)^2+\left(-3\right)^2+\left(-5\right)^2+\left(0\right)^2$$

$$=0+25+9+4+1+36+25+25+1+9+25+0=160/12=13.333$$

The variance of this data set equals 13.333. The standard deviation is the square root of the variance, and the square root of 13.333 is ±3.65. This means if the crime count stays between 15.65 and 8.348 this is only one standard deviation from the mean and relatively close to the "norm." If a police department was simply looking at monthly crime count percent changes, the percent change between May (11) and June (18) is 63.6 percent.

Simple percent change calculations are unable to account for variation in the data. The percent change between May and June looks frighteningly large but taking the variation into account and viewing the crime counts through the lens of the standard deviation, the increase no longer seems so alarming. Ignoring the variation in crime occurrences across time eliminates the ability to identify true change. Examining percent changes gives the appearance of being data driven, but if the statistical estimate does not account for variation, then what are you being driven by other than randomness? Comparing and displaying data in this manner does not consider the random variation in a data set and will lead to incorrect interpretations of the data. Comparing 2020 to 2019 will produce a different percent change than comparing 2020 to 2018 or comparing 2020 to the average of 2017–2019. This is why Nassim Taleb dedicated a whole book to the topic, titled *Fooled by Randomness*. Humans are fooled by randomness in data because we do not innately understand data and statistics very well.

The typical CompStat model as depicted in the Nashville example in Mental Model #4—False Linearity displays weekly data comparisons. Nashville was thorough and used a wide range of weekly data sets, 1-week, 2-week, 4-week, 8-week, 52-week and year-to-date. Some agencies also use month-to-date data comparing a year's worth of data to the current year, meaning January-April 2020 compared to January–April 2019, then the next month it would be January–May 2020 compared to January–May 2020. Crime data for a CompStat meeting is traditionally displayed like Table 5.2.

The other issue, besides losing the variance, with comparing crime data in a binary matter is the underlying assumption it creates for police executives, which is: if there is a percent

Table 5.2 Hypothetical Crime Data Displayed in a Traditional CompStat Format

	Month to date	Month to date last month	Percent change	Year to date	Year to date last year	Year to date percent change
Homicide	5	3	66.6%	19	17	11.8%
Aggravated Assault	82	112	(−26.8%)	654	603	8.5%
Simple Assault	112	82	36.6%	619	707	(−12.5%)
Robbery	14	19	−26.3%	131	142	(−7.8%)

change increase then it is indicative of trending and the bigger the number, the larger the problem. Compare the monthly aggravated assault to simple assault data in Table 5.2, where both had the same raw score change (51). Simple assault counts went up the same amount as aggravated assault counts went down, yet the percent change is different, 36.6 percent compared to (−26.8) percent. Percent changes are influenced by the denominator, as seen by the equation at the beginning of the chapter. If the denominator is lower, then the percent change will be higher. If the denominator is higher, then the percent change will be lower. Using the simple versus aggravated assault example, the denominator is 82 for simple and 112 for aggravated assault, which is why the percent change is higher for simple assault—the denominator is smaller than the denominator for aggravated assault. This way of depicting data can be beneficial for policing when it results in cities panicking and shoveling more money into police resources. However, this way of depicting data can also lend itself to exhausting officers as police executives shift resources, create a new program of the day, or over police in a socioeconomically disadvantaged area thus weakening the police-community relationship. Be aware when making decisions about resource allocation that percent decreases in crime will always be smaller than percent increases in crime. Here is an easy way to understand it.

Using a fictitious burglary example below: Box 1 displays the percent change formula another way—(Value 2 minus Value 1) divided by Value 1 multiplied by 100 equals the percent change between the two values. Box 2 depicts burglaries increasing from 50 (V1) in January to 100 (V2) in February. Box 3 now depicts the burglaries in February, decreasing from 100 (V1) to 50 (V2) in March. Both are changing by the same raw numerical count (50) yet observe the massive difference in percent change, a 100 percent increase from January to February versus a 50 percent decrease from February to March.

$$(V2-V1)/V1\times100=X\%$$ $$(100-50)/50\times100=100\%$$ $$(50-100)/100\times100=-50\%$$

OR you can think about it in a different way—an old value versus new value.

Percent Change

$$\text{Percent Change} = \frac{\text{New Value} - \text{Old Value}}{\text{Old Value}} \times 100\%$$

If the result is positive, it is an increase.
If the result is negative, it is a decrease.

The old value or V2 is going to be the previous year, month, or week. If crime is increasing, the percent change will always be greater for the raw count compared to the same raw count decrease. Percent change is a poor metric for evaluating change in crime. If police examine their data in this manner, their System 1 will interpret the increases as more meaningful than the decreases and be tempted to intervene to stop the increase.

Relying on binary percent changes to drive decision-making influences police to act. System 1 takes over and decides that if the change is large enough, an intervention is required. The process of interpreting police data is appropriately summarized by Annie Duke's explanation of the way we think in Mental Model #1—System 1 and System 2—(1) we *read* the data; (2) we believe it to be important because it's *increasing*; (3) only sometimes, later, if we have the time or inclination, we think about it and vet it, determining whether it is, in fact, data we should be interpreting a signal from. This is the important part of the book to assimilate. System 1 thinking will assign meaning to data. System 1 thinking sees patterns in data where there is none. If there are no figurative caution cones put out to alert people to this fact, then the human brain will attribute meaning to binary comparisons. CompStat still maintains its binary comparison model. It was an innovative management tool in the 1990s and led to improvements in police management. Without CompStat, policing would not have started collecting and analyzing data, but now that we know how the brain works, policing should begin to think about better ways to depict and interpret crime and calls for service data.

Traditionally, police decided to act based on binary percent changes without discussing the variables that may be contributing to those changes and understanding if those changes are meaningful or just random fluctuations in the data. What police should be addressing is not the change in the direction of the numbers, but the cause of the change. Any data-driven analysis (no matter the type) should act as a flag to indicate a problem may exist and *not as an explanation of the problem*. This appears on the surface as a small nuance, but it creates a significant difference in *how* police data should be displayed, discussed, and considered. Reacting to a change in numbers alone may address the driver, but policing will never know if it was the intervention or the randomness that caused the change, because the problem was never properly identified in the first place.

To better understand if police imbue meaning to simple percent changes in numbers, Inspector Guilfoyle surveyed the entire U.K. police force to test this theory. He displayed binary crime comparisons in a traditional CompStat model and asked for their interpretation of the chart (comparable to Table 5.3). Additionally, Guilfoyle asked about their level of concern about the interpretation of the data, their likely tactical response to the data, and 4,917 police officers responded to the survey.

What Guilfoyle found was 86.6 percent of the respondents ascribed meaning to the binary percent comparison even though there was insufficient information to make that determination. This affirmed his hypothesis that police practitioners interpret data using false linearity and believe that the two date-in-time comparisons imply an increasing trajectory (crime will stay in upward motion unless acted on by a police force). Rather than viewing the data as "crime increased" they interpret it as crime *is increasing*, a subtle but significant difference in meaning. When interpreting data in this manner, he hypothesized police decision-makers will be more likely to have an emotional response and engage in some type of intervention. Guilfoyle called it a Disproportionate/Unwarranted Behavioural Response (DUBR). Kahneman would call it System 1 thinking. Allowing System 1 to drive thinking during a crime management meeting can lead to wasted resources. This happens because the decisions are made in response to the noise (the variance) in the data rather than the signal. Guilfoyle suggested a better way to depict data is through the Statistical Process Control method.

Statistical Process Control (SPC) was a method created by Walter A. Shewhart using graphs to depict large data sets over several years to identify patterns. Columns and rows of

Table 5.3 Depiction of Similar CompStat Data Given to Study Participants

CompStat Data			
Last Month	This Month	Change	Percent Change
1,942	2,089	147	7.6%

data are hard to interpret but graphs showing changes over time are easier for brains to process. By using large temporal data sets, the variance can be pulled out and depicted visually. Shewhart's graphs provided visual context to the variance that existed in the data through control limits. He showed the average of the data and then an upper and lower limit of the variance of the data.

Think about weight: an average woman might weigh 130 pounds, but her weight will vary between 127–132 pounds based on levels of dehydration, salt intake, alcohol intake, time of day, and so on. Overall, her weight is 130, but it fluctuates around the average. Variance is a naturally occurring process which is why your trainer will tell you not to step on a scale every day. As much as scientists want to understand every component of all the natural phenomenon in the world, there is always a small percent of each phenomenon that we just do not understand or cannot control, that can contribute to variance. What Shewhart and others have shown is that variance that is caused by the system is "common," and variance caused by an independent variable is "special." Think of it this way, the common variance is random variation in robberies in a bar district and special variation is rapid increase after a new bar opens.

To use a method analogous to Shewhart, police would need to extend the duration normally tracked in their data sets. Using small periods of time will limit an agency's ability to develop a good understanding of the variability contained within their data sets. Rochester PD is one police department that is dedicated to understanding and interpreting their data in a more accurate way than binary comparisons. They are shifting away from the use of year-to-year comparison statistics toward the process control method proposed by Shewhart. By plotting data over longer durations, Rochester PD can analyze their data to determine upper and lower control limits. Figure 5.1 is an example of the type of chart Petitti uses for Rochester PD's management meetings.

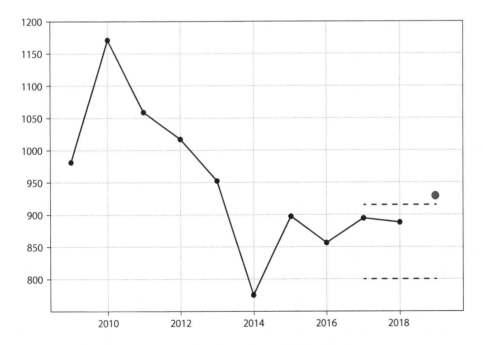

Figure 5.1 Petitti's SPC Chart Depicting Hypothetical Annual Crime Totals

In this chart the dashed lines represent the upper and lower control limits set as targets for the current three-year period (2017–2019) based on the previous five-year period. The large dot represents the current year-to-date projection for 2019—November at the time. It also provides ten years' worth of data to provide context around possible trending. In this example you can see that the long-term trend downwards since 2010 has plateaued in recent years but that would be completely lost if only two points in time were presented. Petitti advises his executive managers not to change their strategic approach unless the data approaches the upper control limits. Petitti sets his control limits algorithmically, based on the parameters chosen by his analyst early in the process, such as how many years of data to use and type of measure of center to use (mean, median, or weighted-average). As this chart depicts, this presentation of data included multiple years of data to provide context—a user is unlikely to wrongly interpret normal variance as a linear trend.

Petitti's chart will make it easier to determine common variation and special variation. Determining what caused the special variation and an appropriate response requires looking into the data more closely to determine what contributed to the special conditions. Guilfoyle favors depicting data this way stating,

> "The beauty of presenting the data using this method is that not only are extreme values immediately visible to the naked eye, but the calculations responsible for determining the lower and upper control limits effectively filter out the 'noise' of the common cause variation amongst the data, clearly exposing these two 'signals'. This provides reassurance that there is no need to react to the other peaks and troughs present between the control limits."

While there is a bit of upfront analysis work to get to this point, the beauty in SPC charting is that it allows for much more context to be conveyed about a problem (think crime type) and provides actionable trigger points for decision-makers. Control limits essentially act as flags to signal the need to conduct more in-depth analysis while not getting decision-makers distracted with random variation (noise) in the data. Control limits flag for potential 'special causes' driving the change in the data. If the data moves beyond the control limits, then executives should begin looking for the drivers of the change, until then they should remain tactically stable. By giving police executives permission to ignore the common variance in week-to-week or month-to-month data, they will be able to focus their efforts on proactive long-term improvements in the organization rather than chasing the tail of short-term variations in data. Petitti explained it this way:

> We like to think of our modified SPC as a combination of two products 1. Annual control limits/projections aimed at continual improvement (i.e. driving the limits down in subsequent 3-year periods) and 2. Weekly control views (based on the annual control) for more traditional (i.e. CompStat) looks at the data to determine if immediate action is necessary. In both cases the variance in the data is accounted for.

This was the original intent of Shewhart's SPC graphs—to show where the natural variation was occurring so organizations could focus on the areas where they could make organizational gains rather than constantly reacting to the noise in the data.

These small sets of data (the monthly or weekly data police agencies currently use) contain a lot of variance, a lot of "noise." What will commanders decide to do if the one-week percent change is up, the two-week is down, the four-week is flat, and the year-to-date is up? What statistic gets cherry-picked? Binary percent changes are arbitrary because the denominator influences the amount of the percent change and does not account for variance. If we want our police departments to work in an effective and efficient manner, while creating the least possible harm to the community, then crime data should never be displayed in a binary manner. It tricks our brains into interpreting the binary percent changes as meaningful and the biproduct of creating meaning is the redistribution of finite resources. CompStat can send mixed messages; SPC is more internally consistent. When resources are redistributed, there can be unintended secondary and tertiary consequences that reach beyond (community harm) the intended outcome (crime reduction). Even when an SPC chart indicates that there is a special cause (robbery series) moving the trajectory beyond a control limit, policing still needs to think through the potential downstream outcomes that could occur from reallocating resources. These secondary and tertiary outcomes are the focus of the next Mental Model #6—Second Order Thinking.

Second Order Thinking

> Just as great poker players and chess players (and experts in any field) excel by planning further into the future than others, our decision-making improves when we can more vividly imagine the future, free of the distortions of the present. By working backward from the goal, we plan our decision tree in more depth, because we start at the end.
>
> Annie Duke

Second order thinking is thinking about all the downstream effects of your decisions. When thinking about solutions for a problem, people often focus on the problem at hand rather than what can occur in the future and end up pairing a simple solution to a complex problem (System 1). For example, in the 1930s Australian sugar cane fields were being devoured by beetles. Sugar cane farmers were desperate for a solution but only wanted to use pesticides as a last resort. The farmers heard the Cane toad, a particularly large amphibian who could grow up to 4.5 pounds, could eat massive quantities of the beetles that were destroying the sugar cane fields. The farmers had been told the Cane toads were used successfully in Puerto Rico against the same beetle infestation. It was a simple solution to a complex ecological problem. Predator and prey do not have a simple relationship. The predator/prey relationship is often more complicated than it appears on the surface. Without thinking about the secondary and tertiary consequences beyond beetle eating, the Australians ended up importing one of their greatest menaces.

The farmers flew in 102 Cane toads in the 1930s to deal with one pest and instead the toads became the bigger pest. The farmers did not realize the Cane toads were lazy hunters; rather than hunting beetles the toads would lay under streetlights and wait until bugs would hit the lights and drop to the ground. Additionally, the toads create a toxin behind their eyeballs which, if you are inclined to lick a toad, will induce LSD-type hallucinations in humans, but in other animals it will kill them. Without any natural predators there was no way to keep the toad population in check. To make things worse, the toads are prolific breeders with ridiculous sex drives, so much so that they have been seen mating with rocks, tree stumps, and human feet. The female Cane toad will lay up to 30,000 eggs at one time. The farmers' experiment was a complete and total failure, and the toads, with no natural predators, a strong sex drive, and the ability to lay so many eggs at one time, rapidly took over Australia. Today there are over 1.5 billion Cane toads in Australia. The country has spent over 20 million Australian dollars on Cane toad eradication without making any substantial gains. The toads are still spreading, getting bigger, evolving to store water longer, and now have longer legs to move even faster. Simple solutions for complex problems often

DOI: 10.4324/9780367481520-7

have downstream consequences: we should expend efforts thinking about and anticipating what those consequences are.

Outcomes are not just attached to the decisions you make in the moment. There are often subsequent outcomes that arise not only from the initial decision, but can also evolve from the primary outcome. For example, during the COVID-19 crisis of 2020 the stay-at-home orders and closing of non-essential businesses led to a drastic drop in public crime because people were not out and about—a positive primary outcome. Consequently, because of the lack of cars on the streets, police reported an uptick in high-speed crashes and an increase of 100+ mile-per-hour citations, because with less vehicles on the street, street racers had unlimited roadway on which to drive uninhibited. The tertiary outcome (speeding vehicles) evolved from the secondary outcome (fewer cars on the road) which evolved from the decision to enforce stay-at-home orders (primary outcome). The stay-at-home order was not a decision made by the police, but were the governmental entity that had to deal with the secondary and tertiary consequences of that decision. Often, secondary and tertiary effects can come from decisions made outside an organization's control, but these decisions must still be examined and dealt with in an effective manner.

Policing suffered from secondary and tertiary effects throughout 2020. Cities, states, and the federal governments passed laws without input from police management, yet the police departments are the ones who have to deal with the unintended consequences. Recently cities and states have been passing laws banning the use of projectiles and gas at protests, yet without the use of less lethal munitions, police on the riot line are left using their batons to deal with crowds which can lead to unintended injuries. The City of Seattle is a prime example of how seeking a simple solution to a complex problem led to secondary and tertiary consequences. In reaction to citizens being injured during riots, the city council passed an ordinance that banned the Seattle Police Department from using tear gas, pepper spray, and projectile rubber bullets during protests. Responding to the ordinance, Chief Carmen Best sent a letter to the city's business owners stating that her department would not be able to protect their property. She explained that by limiting her officers' ability to safely deploy during violent riots, she could not in good conscience deploy them to prevent the destruction of property (secondary consequence). The ordinances crippled Seattle PD's ability to control protesters to the point that they were able to take over a small section of Seattle that the protesters named the CHAZ—Capitol Hill Autonomous Zone (tertiary consequence). The protesters controlled the area for approximately six weeks, had armed men patrol the entrances, and would not allow the police into the area. The area was recovered after two juveniles were gunned down by CHAZ security patrols for joyriding through the area in a stolen vehicle. When all was said and done, the business owners who were affected financially and emotionally by the violence and intimidation they suffered at the hands of the CHAZ occupants sued the City of Seattle for failing to protect them as taxpayers (quaternary consequences). The Seattle council persons were trying to protect the protesters in Seattle and to reduce their exposure for lawsuits and, in the end, they increased their exposure to lawsuits, increased the amount of property damage the city suffered, increased the number of homicides, and still ended up getting sued. When making decisions, second order thinking must be employed to avoid negative downstream consequences.

Laws and ordinances not only have effects on businesses, but decisions made by companies, public agencies, or cities can often have unintended effects on other businesses. For example, the development of the LED light reduced energy consumption by 80 percent compared to incandescent and florescent lights. If you only examine the primary consequence this is a positive outcome. Only 5 percent of the energy used by LEDs is turned into heat, the rest is turned into light which makes the LED light an amazing innovation. How they got this amazing bulb to work is interesting. LEDs are more efficient than a regular light bulb because they are not always "on." They stay illuminated using pulse-width modulation which means the lights are flashing 15 times per second, but to the naked eye they appear as though they are constantly on. The control circuits that keep the light flashing rely on frequencies between 30 and 300 MHZ and this frequency just happened to overlap with garage door opening frequencies which work between 280 and 360 MHZ. When people began replacing their garage door openers with LED light bulbs, Lift Master was inundated with complaints about failing garage door openers. Sometimes the garage door opener would work and sometimes it would not. It took Lift Master months of investigation before they realized that the two frequencies were interfering with each other causing the garage door remote controls to fail to connect with the opener. Now when you buy a Lift Master garage door opener the instructions and the website have a list of LED bulbs that can be installed that will not cause interference. An innovation's face value can be positive, but still have secondary or tertiary effects. Whether we are thinking about policies, practices, or innovations, we should also be engaging in secondary thinking—trying to think about all the long-term downstream effects not only for your agency but for other industries, or communities, or businesses and whether those effects are beneficial or detrimental and, most of all, if they are acceptable.

One way of doing this is conducting a premortem. A premortem is a managerial tool used to plan around potential downstream problems. The medical field uses a postmortem to review a case to determine how a patient's death occurred and what if anything could have been done to prevent the patient's demise. A premortem starts at the beginning, before the death of a plan, a project, or a program. A premortem assumes the project has already died spectacularly and failed. Then managers work backward to talk through the reasons why the project most likely failed. The idea of premortems were constructed from the work of Dr Deborah J. Mitchell of The Wharton School and colleagues who found when test subjects were presented with a future certain event, they produced 30 percent more explanations for the occurrence than when presented with past events or uncertain future events. Imagining the event occurring produced more responses rather than imagining a potential event (our usual approach to problem solving) or reviewing a past event (hindsight bias influences this process MM#2), thus the business world adopted the premortem.

Although a premortem is structured to help a management team think about all the potential problems they can avoid before starting a project, this process can be used to develop second order thinking processes. Second order thinking ultimately prioritizes long-term goals over immediate gains and in policing, many of our decisions have consequences that last generations. Conducting a premortem before you implement a new program or process can help flesh out all potential issues that can arise in the future. When conducting a premortem the project leader tells the group that the project failed and then has the group write down all the reasons why they think the project failed. Then as each person reads their reasons out loud, the project leader writes the reasons down on a white board. Because the program has not actually failed yet, there should be no political backlash or finger pointing, because no one has done anything yet. This is the beauty of a premortem. It allows for the exploration of the potential for problems which relieves some of the stress of the interaction. Once all the reasons are up on the board, then the team members can begin to explore solutions to the problems. Thinking through potential problems beforehand is important, because often, as we have seen in policing once a program becomes entrenched in the culture, it is difficult to dig it out.

Policing is not the only profession to have indoctrinated practices that once learned are difficult to unlearn. X-rays, a powerful innovation, were discovered in 1895 when Wilhelm Conrad Röntgen was using cathode tubes for his research at the University of Würzburg in Germany. He was wrapping the cathodes in black paper when he discovered that the rays emitted by the cathode tube would leave a green glow on a florescent board he had situated about one meter away. He kept experimenting with the rays, discovering that they went through most substances like paper and human flesh but could not pass through dense material. Realizing that he could use the X-ray to create images of human bones, he took an X-ray of his wife's hand that showed her bones and the wedding ring she wore. By the 1930s, X-ray machines were being used in hospitals to help physicians set bones and find bullets. X-rays were assisting doctors in the field, making their jobs easier. And even though there was emerging evidence that demonstrated X-rays were causing radiation poisoning, those secondary and tertiary effects were not a concern for doctors, because the primary benefit was too powerful a draw. Even in 1956 when Dr. Alice Stewart wrote a report that linked the X-rays of pregnant women to childhood leukemia, doctors still believed the immediate benefits of the X-ray machine (viewing the position of the baby) overrode the negative secondary effects (childhood leukemia). Dr. Stewart fought the medical establishment for over 25 years to stop the practice of X-raying pregnant women. Pregnant women were still X-rayed even though they knew their babies were more likely to end up with childhood leukemia. If doctors would have thought about and addressed the secondary effects of the X-ray machines in the beginning before the practice became entrenched, Dr. Stewart may not have had to spend 25 years fighting a bad practice. Once a practice becomes entrenched it becomes difficult to undo. Secondary thinking can help organizations work through thinking about the possible negative consequences before practices become best practices.

CompStat has been called "perhaps the single most important organizational innovation in policing during the latter half of the 20th Century." Yet, it also brought scandal to the NYPD when they were accused of doctoring data to make their outcomes look better than they were. Because CompStat created a simple approach, a binary percent change table, to address complex problems—organizational management, crime, community health, and statistical knowledge—it made it easier for police managers to manipulate the data than to address the multitude of issues. Additionally, by using binary percent changes, police managers were reacting to variations in the data rather than "special causes" in the data making CompStat ripe for secondary and tertiary consequences. Guilfoyle argued in 2013 that creating a performance management system based on statistics that are influenced by outside factors other than a commander's performance can lead to "the presence of perverse incentives, behaviours, and gaming within targets-based public sector performance management." The manipulation of the NYPD data was a secondary effect of creating a management system. Whenever "systems" are introduced into an organization there will be multiple effects and all of the potential outcomes should be thought through.

In the case of NYPD and CompStat, they could have implemented an oversight process to prevent statistical manipulations if they would have thought about the downstream process. Creating checks and balances for any organization should always be part of thinking about the downstream process and whether if what is being measured is an actual indicator of success and how a person's career can be affected by that process. Innovation, in the present moment, can appear as the quintessential answer to a problem, but just like the Seattle city council's decisions, without examining other potential outcomes, your dream project can turn into your nightmare.

To avoid a future nightmare, when thinking about implementing a new scheme, think about the secondary and tertiary effects that might arise from your decision. Using secondary thinking is useful at work and in your personal life. Thinking about the secondary and tertiary effects of sending your child to an out-of-state university versus an in-state university or of taking a credit line on your house will be beneficial to the "future you" who will be facing "present you's" consequences. This was another area of Kahneman's research—he examined the differences between the "present you" and the "future you" and he arugued the "present you" is always promising the "future you's" time. Think of the times you promised a friend to help them move and when that time comes around, the "present you" does not usually feel the same.

One method of developing secondary thinking is using the 10/10/10 method. Think about the issue and how you will feel about it ten minutes from now, ten months from now, or ten years from now, or in the case of helping your friend move—2/2/2 two minutes from now, two days from now, and two weeks from now when you are missing out on a rafting trip because you are helping your friend move. Using secondary thinking will help save the "future you" from your "present you's" decision. Another way to develop secondary thinking is using an Ishikawa diagram or as it is more commonly known as the fishbone diagram, which can help with thinking through problems proactively by defining these potential secondary and tertiary effects.

The fishbone diagram was created by Kaoru Ishikawa to show the cause and effects of a specific event. Ishiwaka was an organizational theorist who was well known for his quality management innovations. He thought about how to improve the quality of management to avoid process problems. He created the fishbone diagram to visually lay out all the reasons something *went wrong* if reviewing a past project or *could go wrong* if it were a future project. He created this process so management teams could be prepared to handle any potential problems. The idea behind his process was not to punish or single out individuals, but to examine how things functioned in the organizational environment and address potential issues before they became too large. Being a professor at the University of Tokyo allowed Ishiwaka to take this nonpunitive approach as an outsider and help organizations institute practices that would improve their outcomes. Figure 6.1 displays a typical fishbone diagram.

The head of the fishbone starts with the problem statement. If this tool is being used in a management meeting, then the group is responsible for defining the problem. To avoid the cognitive bias of groupthink (going along with the majority to keep the peace), ask the managers to write their answers on a piece of paper and turn them into a facilitator who will write them on a board. Do this for defining the problems and when asking the group

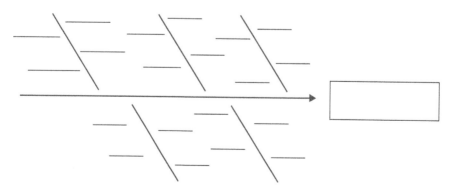

Figure 6.1 Typical Structure of a Fishbone Diagram

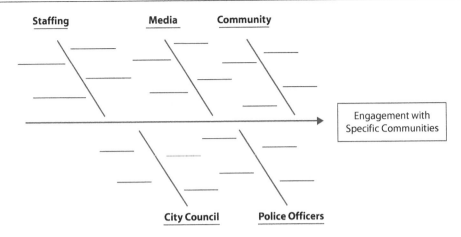

Figure 6.2 Problem Statement at the Head of the Diagram and Subgroup Headers

about cause and effect. This will keep one person from taking control of the group. There are studies that show the first idea to be presented, whether it is correct or not, is usually the one that dominates. Additionally, there is research that shows if there is only one woman in a group of men, she will have difficulty having her ideas heard. By having your executive management team turn in ideas by writing them down, this will help support the diversity of thought in the room. This fishbone diagram can be used for some of the difficulties police were facing in 2020. For example, if you use the fishbone diagram to think through the community relationship issues your agency is facing, you might be able to think of solutions to implement *and* think about the secondary and tertiary consequences of implementation. The head of the fishbone would be titled Engagement with Specific Communities. Figure 6.2 depicts what the beginning of the fishbone would look like.

The hard part of this process would be to define what parts of the community have poor relationships with the police department. Even though the Black community has been portrayed in the media as supporting the abolition of policing and defunding the police, we also know there are Black communities that want the police in their neighborhoods and Black citizens who support the local police. Community relationships are difficult because there is not a one-size-fits-all solution and often a solution that benefits one segment of a community could negatively impact another segment, which is why second order thinking was an appropriate approach to problem solving in 2020.

Once engagement with specific communities is placed at the head of the fishbone, police executives would go through the same process to decide the main categories that contribute to the problem. Police executives would write down the major categories they viewed as significant contributors to the problem and then write those categories as branches on the main arrow. There could be staffing, media, community, city council, and police officers. Then follow the written process again to brainstorm all the possible causes of the problem. Under the staffing section some of the issues could be that there are not enough officers to do the proper amount of community outreach or the right type of officer is not assigned to do the outreach. The next step is to ask the group "why would this cause occur" to determine if there are subgroups under the main categories. For staffing, this problem could arise from a supervision issue, a recruiting process, a training issue, or an interviewing process. Continue to ask "Why" to generate deeper levels of causes and continue organizing them under related categories. This process will help identify and then address root causes to

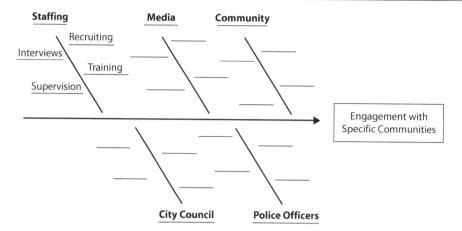

Figure 6.3 Fishbone Depicting the Possible Problems Contributing to Subgroup Issues

prevent negative secondary and tertiary outcomes. This process will not necessarily prevent them all, but at least it will help you think through some of them. Figure 6.3 demonstrates where to add the subgroups to the fishbone model.

Ishiwaka spent his life trying to help organizations perform efficiently and effectively, by examining how systems work to determine where an organization should focus their efforts. Today fishbone diagrams are used in a variety of ways—to determine cause and effect, find bottlenecks in a process, and for root cause analysis. Ishiwaka is credited with creating the Total Quality Management system: a program dedicated to improving system processes to avoid secondary and tertiary consequences of system processes. Second order thinking is a method used to avoid unintended downstream consequences and the fishbone method can help with this process. Our next Mental Model also involves Ishiwaka, who was the first to publish an example of a Pareto chart, also known as the 80/20 rule.

The Mental Models in Practice II—Mental Models 4–6

False Linear Thinking, Binary Percent Changes, and Second Order Thinking

This section of the Mental Models book grouped together somewhat divergent ideas. Just like Mental Model 4—False Linear Thinking, Mental Models just like crime and calls for service do not line up in a perfect order. While all the Mental Models give you a frame of mind with which to view the world and all of them are about how we think, some of them have to do with statistics and some of them have to do with decision making and some have to do with both. Here in Applying Mental Model 4-6 the first two Mental Models: False Linear Thinking and Binary Percent Changes are statistical Mental Models and Second Order Thinking is a problem-solving Mental Model. Here is how to apply them:

1 Start backward with this group of Mental Models with Second Order Thinking and 10/10/10.

  a What do you want to get out of your management meetings ten months from now and ten years from now?

  b Write management meeting on the head of the fishbone.

  c Write out all the categories that prevent you from changing your management meeting into the type of meeting that achieves your goals.

  d Underneath the categories, write out all the issues that prevent the meeting from making meaningful contributions to your department's mission and vision.

  e Make a commitment and assign a person directly responsible for making those changes and supervising the changes.

  f Conduct a premortem on changing your management meeting and the use of your data:

    i What would happen if you examined your data differently?

    ii What could go wrong if you changed the way you depict your data?

    iii If you changed the way your agency responded to the data, what is the worst thing that could happen?

    iv Problem solve the issues people see occurring.

2 Stop using binary percent change data.

3 Stop using small data sets.

4 Create Statistical Process Control Charts—figure out the average of crime using a minimum three years of data.

  a Create an upper and lower control limit using the standard deviation of the mean of the crime data. Nick Petitti in his Rochester PD blog uses two standard deviations which means that you will only be responding to crime that gets beyond a normal average. I would suggest looking at crime when it gets beyond one standard deviation. One standard deviation will keep you from reacting when crime is 18.26 percent above or below the average. I think it if is moving toward the high teens it is time to start thinking about making a move.

5   Sign up for Andrew P. Wheeler's email blasts and read his blogs on data www.andrewp-wheeler.com. His blogs can assist with developing SPC charts. Here are a couple of blogs to start with:

a   Understanding uncertainty—crime counts and the Poisson distribution.
b   Testing changes in short-run crime patterns: the Poisson e-test.

6   Read Simon Guilfoyle's blogs at www.inspguilfoyle.wordpress.com. Some of his best blogs are:

a   Why binary comparisons are really silly.
b   Weak excuses for using binary comparisons.
c   Stick child's guide to systems thinking.

7   Read Matt Ashby's blogs www.lesscrime.info.com. Some of his best blogs are:

a   Why you can't identify changes in crime comparing this month to last month.
b   Police crackdowns catch few drink drivers.

8   Do you see the pattern yet?

Part III

How Things Concentrate

The Pareto Principle

> If you're Noah, and your ark is about to sink, look for the elephants first, because you can throw over a bunch of cats, dogs, squirrels, and everything else that is just a small animal and your ark will keep sinking. But if you can find one elephant to get overboard, you're in much better shape.
>
> Vilfredo Pareto

The Pareto Principle is commonly known as the 80/20 rule; 20 percent of the causes create 80 percent of the effects, but the Power law distribution on which this principle is based is much more statistically nuanced than that. Even though there are subtleties, this principle can be found in different phenomenon across a variety of disciplines. This principle was first discovered by Vilfredo Pareto. An economist, sociologist, and philosopher living in the 1800s, Pareto was one of the first economists to introduce mathematics into the field. Before Pareto, most universities' economics textbooks were written as philosophical tomes, but he introduced mathematical formulas that accompanied his theories which laid the foundation for microeconomics. The 80/20 rule arose from his study of land ownership in Italy. He found that that 80 percent of the land in Italy was owned by 20 percent of the population—a Power law distribution.

A Power law distribution means that the rate of something is not equally distributed across a population. As you will see in Mental Model #10—Distributions, many phenomena within populations follow the bell curve that we all learned in high school. The person with the lowest grade is the data point at the left of the curve (0), and the person with the highest grade is the data point to the right of the curve (12), and the average of the class is the highest point in the middle of the curve (6) and the overall shape creates a bell. Figure 7.1 on next page depicts a bell curve.

The normal distribution occurs across many different types of phenomena, such as a species' height, weight, and speed. But starting with Pareto, scientists found other types of distributions with natural frequencies that did not fit the normal distribution and although the 80/20 rule was a Power law distribution, when Joseph M. Juran discovered Pareto's work and applied it to the business world and coined the phrase "80/20 rule", it was applied in a statistically simplistic way.

A Power law occurs when there is an exponential relationship between two variables, where a relative change in one variable results in a proportional relative change in the other. For example, doubling *the side* of a square quadruples *the area* of the square, in other words, they are exponentially related to one another. There are many types of Power law distributions, including city populations, computer files, wars, frequency of use of words in

DOI: 10.4324/9780367481520-8

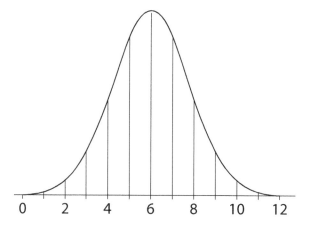

Figure 7.1 An Example of What a Typical Bell Curve Looks Like

any human language (Zipf's Law), people's annual incomes, and number of hits on a web page. U.S. cities are home to 62.7 percent of the population but only make up 3.5 percent of the total land area. Zipf's Law is similar to the Power Law, as the frequency of the use of a word is inversely related to the rank of its use. This means there is a Power law relationship in this book. The relationship is between how often I used a word in this book (frequency) and the percent of the total book it makes up. Typically, the most frequent 150 words used in a document make up 50 percent of the whole manuscript. A Power distribution occurs when the frequency of a phenomenon is not normally distributed but skewed to one side. Applying Pareto's Principle to the business world, if a system or organization needs fixing, then applying efforts to fix the 20 percent that is exponentially related to 80 percent of the problems is the most expedient approach. This method is more effective than focusing quality improvement efforts equally across all aspects of a society, organization, or business. Joseph M. Juran was the first to apply the brilliant precept in Pareto's work when he redis-covered it in the 1940s.

Juran understood that if 20 percent of a cause was exponentially linked to 80 percent of an effect, then by focusing quality management efforts on the 20 percent, variable businesses could get an exponential return on their investment of time, effort, and energy. As such, Juran was the first to apply the 80/20 theory to business management. Juran applied Pareto's idea specifically to production issues. He wanted businesses to focus on the business pro-cesses that generated the most quality issues. He felt businesses would be more effective and efficient if they focused on fixing the 20 percent of causes that created 80 percent the defects. In his experience he had observed the Pareto Principle in business repeatedly, as only a small percent of the causes drove *all* the product defect. Take the case of the Ford Pinto: the gas tank was located in the rear of the car which made it susceptible to rupture and explosion in low impact collisions, but this problem was not the only weakness that made it susceptible. There was a bigger problem, and had Ford focused on fixing that problem, the Pinto might have become the iconic inexpensive 1970s gas-saving vehicle they meant it to be rather than death trap it turned into.

Ford's manufacturing issue that caused 80 percent of the vehicle fires was a design flaw that was not discovered until the deaths, the lawsuits, and the horrible publicity forced them to examine the issue more closely. The gas tank was placed behind the rear axle on the Pinto, making it vulnerable to damage, but what made the Pinto a potential fire ball was the rear axle itself. It was an off-the-shelf component, meaning the rear axle was not made specifically for the Ford Pinto—it was made for the Ford of Europe Capri. The Capri was designed differently than the Pinto. It had suspension arms that were attached to the rear axle with studs. When Ford decided to use the same rear axle for the Pinto it left the studs on the rear axle even though they went unused in the Pinto. When the Pinto was involved in rear end crashes the gas tank was pushed up against the studs and the studs would rip open the gas tank like a can opener. The combination of the rear gas tank placed next to the studs created the deadly combination that led Ford to pay out billions of dollars to families of the deceased drivers and passengers of the Pinto, leading Ford to ultimately discontinue the car. There were several design flaws in the Pinto but narrowing the focus to the design problem that was exponentially related to level of danger for their customer is where they should have been focused. The gas tank was poorly placed, but the rear axle studs were exponentially related to the level of harm.

When applying the Pareto Principle, you should understand that the underlying theory is the Power law distribution. The Pareto Principle demonstrated how there are many things that we scientifically measure where 20 percent of the population make up 80 percent of the outcome—like land ownership, wealth, and city populations based on the Power law distribution. This means that as people accumulate land mass, they pass a threshold of ownership that allows them to exponentially attain more land. It aligns with W. Brian Author's idea of increasing returns—"them that has gets." Once you attain a certain amount, the potential to amass more increases exponentially. The Power law distribution is an exponential formula, while the Pareto Principle simplifies the law into a cause-and-effect business solution. Businesses work at finding the 20 percent of the business process that creates 80 percent of the problem.

The 80/20 rule can be used when thinking about how to change the policing profession by looking at the relationship between city size and police department size. Aaron Clausett from the Santa Fe Institute provides a clear example of a Power law distribution using city size—he examined the 600 largest U.S. cities based on 2000 census data. The average population of those cities was $\mu = 165,719$, but of course New York City and Los Angeles had a population of 8,008,278 and 3,703,000, respectively, which appear to be extreme outliers when compared to the average. To determine if the distribution is normal, one must compare the standard deviation $\sigma = 410,730$ which is significantly larger than the mean ($\mu = 165,719$), indicating this is not a normal distribution. Power law distributions always skew the curve.

Assuming law enforcement agencies employment numbers proportionally reflect the size of their city's population, a graph depicting the number of sworn officers per agency should skew similarly. Heather Prince from George Mason University graphed the number of officers per agency from The Bureau of Justice Statistics 2016 Law Enforcement Management and Administrative Statistics (LEMAS) survey. The graph depicts the right skewed distribution as predicted. Figure 7.2 shows the results.

This resembles a Power law distribution. The LEMAS survey is only a sample of the 18,000 police agencies in the U.S. As such, this graph does not depict all 18,000 agencies, nor does it depict an exact employee number, but only a range of employees. The skewness would be even more pronounced if all 18,000 were represented and each of the departments listed the exact number of officers in their agency. Either way, according to Pareto, if we added up all the officers in all of the police departments in the U.S. we would most likely find that 20 percent of the police departments employed 80 percent of the police. This means if we wanted to create cultural change in U.S. policing, then we should focus our efforts on the agencies that employ the most officers. By focusing policy changes or paradigm shifts on

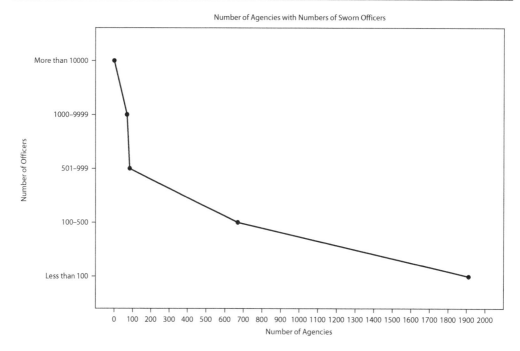

Figure 7.2 Number of Agencies with Sworn Officers based on 2016 LEMAS Survey Data

that 20 percent of police departments, we might be able to achieve the exponential effects of the Power distribution law and influence 80 percent of the outcomes we are looking for. By trying to change every police agency in the U.S., advocates, politicians, and community members are not being as effective and efficient as they could be. The Pareto Principle is just one way of thinking about how to focus your efforts if there is a change in the world of policing that *you* want to see.

This principle has been applied elsewhere in business and other phenomena. For example, some managers have used it to reward a small percent of employees who are producing most of the work, to focus attention on the 20 percent of the customers that create 80 percent of the profit, and to problem solve the 20 percent of the issues that are causing 80 percent of the problems. This concentration of causes also occurs in computer science, for example in programming, 80 percent of the logic of a program can be done with 20 percent of the effort, but the last 20 percent of the logic requires 80 percent of the effort because the last 20 percent is where the coding defects arise. Websites are the same: most website users go to the same pages, meaning 80 percent of your websites go unread, so rather than universally improving content across the website, the improvements should be focused on the content on the most accessed webpages.

The Pareto Principle also applies to studying for exams, 80 percent of the knowledge required to pass a class comes from 20 percent of the effort, but the last 20 percent of knowledge needed to score high marks is where 80 percent of your effort should be. Showing up to class and reading the book contributes to 80 percent of the foundational concepts needed for class, but to achieve high grades a student must understand how and where to focus their efforts. If students do not know where to focus the 20 percent of their studying, it will take them longer to achieve a high mark. When I was teaching criminal justice classes, I would use this principle to help my students focus. Every semester I would ask students if their version of studying consisted of re-reading book chapters, to which they would all nod yes. Then I would ask, when they were studying, were they focused entirely on their studying or would they also text, browse the internet, and/or engage in other distracting activities. Inevitably, most of the classroom would nod their heads. I would explain the difference between feeling as though they were doing "something" to prepare for their test versus actual studying. Human beings like to feel competent, so my students would review the information they already understood. They focused on reviewing the 80 percent in a passive manner. I would explain that by wasting their time re-reading the book and passively ingesting information while distracted (although they would congratulate themselves on the "hours" of studying they did) they were not making good use of their time. If they focused their efforts on extracting the correct information, writing it down, and then working on the concepts they could not understand or remember, they could cut their study time in half and raise their exam scores by half a grade. They were spending 80 percent of their time engaged in an activity that produced 20 percent of their knowledge. I wanted them to shift their focus to the 20 percent and do the hard work that would help them achieve 80 percent of their results. The hard part with humans, as Kahneman has demonstrated, is we like to engage in activities that make us feel competent, we do not like risk when loss is probable, and we naturally fall back on lazy thinking. By focusing on the 20 percent, we can perform at much higher levels, make fewer mistakes, and produce better quality products.

Policing organizations should apply the Pareto Principle to their business processes. It can be used to examine sick time, community complaints, and officer proactivity. Taking a year's worth of data, police could examine which employees generate the highest amount of sick time, complaints, and proactivity. Search for the 20 percent. The goal would not be to punish individuals when examining the data, but rather to evaluate what is happening within the organization and figuring out ways to improve or augment intended outcomes. The goal is to figure out what is contributing to the problem and figure out solutions. If an organization observes that a percentage of employees are suffering the same injuries and ending up having the same surgeries (hip replacements, ACL replacements, shoulder repairs) there might be ways to improve the ergonomics of detectives' desks, officer squad cars, or improve training to prevent injuries. If most complaints are being generated by a small group of officers, is it because they need to improve communication skills (the individual needs attention) or do they work in an area where the citizens are dissatisfied with the police services (the system needs attention) and need better solutions from city agencies? The point of highlighting the Pareto Principle as a Mental Model is to determine what is causing the exponential proportion of outcomes and then concentrating the solutions on those areas. Using the Pareto Principle can be a simple activity to use across many aspects of policing. In fact, this principle has been applied to crime and how crime concentrates which we explore in the next Mental Model.

The Law of Crime Concentration

> Perhaps stability in crime concentration across time is a result of unusual levels of stability of social conditions at microgeographic crime hot spots rather than of trends across neighborhoods or cities as a whole.
>
> Dr. David Weisburd

It seems that every few decades (and lately every couple of years) there are crises in policing that appear to drive change and innovation. More often, however, I think crises drive police agencies into a game reminiscent of Three-card Monte. That analogy hit me recently as I sat on a policing panel with two retired police chiefs and a sheriff of a large Florida county. All three discussed how policing was one of the professions that has changed the most compared to other professions in the last several decades. That discussion led me to really reflect on the way policing handles "change" versus the way in which other professions think about it. For example, the profession of medicine has advanced exponentially in the ability to question prior knowledge, techniques, and practices. Medicine has introduced technology into surgeries, changed the way they teach due to learning about new practices, and changed management techniques to help hospitals adapt to change faster and better to overcome human resistance. These changes occur because medical professionals are always re-examining, re-evaluating, and re-adjusting to create real changes leading to better patient outcomes. Policing, on the other hand, plays Three-card Monte: appearing to make the changes the politicians, the community, and the city councils want, and then accepting the changes only to hide them under the guise of new policies and training, parading them in front of the local media, shuffling them around, and then they disappear right before everyone's eyes. Thus, policing has appeared to have made great changes but, in the end, all things remain the same. When I look at my short career in policing beginning in 1998, we have changed, and yet we have remained the same. We have adopted every captivating technology on the market, yet, when it comes to research that points to better ways to patrol our cities, we remain steadfastly attached to random preventative patrol methods.

That is not to say that change does not occur within policing. Over the last century, policing has evolved from foot patrol to motorized patrol, using telephones to report emergencies, and has shifted to "professionalize" policing. The professionalization of policing was a movement initiated by the advocacy of August Vollmer in the early 1900s after becoming the Chief of Police in Berkeley, CA. He began pushing for better educated and trained police officers. He moved officers into patrol cars and had the first bike patrol, he introduced radios into the patrol cars, and hired university students as officers. He established the

DOI: 10.4324/9780367481520-9

American Society of Criminology (originally called the National Association of College Police Training Officials) to formalize the educational process for officers and to encourage the use of science and research in policing. Vollmer's efforts are largely credited with the move toward the professionalization of policing, and this effort was further advanced by the creation of the Katzenbach Commission in the 1960s.

In 1974, because of the 1960's race riots, a study was designed to test the effectiveness of these random police patrols as a crime prevention method and the results sparked an international controversy about the effectiveness of policing. At the time of the study, the conventional ruling wisdom was if police patrolled large swaths of the city at a time, they would create an "omnipresence." By appearing as though they were everywhere, the police would deter would-be criminals. This approach had been based on two unproven yet widely accepted hypotheses; a visible police presence prevents crime by deterring potential offenders, and the public's fear of crime is diminished by such presence. Thus, routine preventative police patrol was thought both to prevent crime and reassure the public. In the 1970s this strategy was firmly embedded in the overall approach which we now call the Standard Model of Policing. The Standard Model of Policing incorporates aspects other than patrol, but there are several "reactive" behaviors that are patrol-related activities:

- Increased number of police officers
- Unfocused, random motorized patrols
- Rapid response to calls for service
- Follow-up investigations
- General reactive arrest policies.

After race riots diminished, Lyndon B. Johnson convened the Katzenbach Commission, a Presidential Commission focused on studying the state of law enforcement in the United States. Nineteen people were assigned to facilitate the commission and 157 different consultants were brought in to deliver expert testimony on a variety of issues concerning policing—training, education, race relations, use of force, riot and crowd control, and crime prevention. In 1967 after several months of work, the commission released a report titled *The Challenge of Crime in a Free Society*. That report laid out a wide set of reforms for law enforcement agencies of which was "that every segment of the system of criminal justice devote a significant part of its resources *for research* to ensure the development of new and effective methods of controlling crime" (my emphasis). As a result of the President's commission and the call for increased research centered on criminal justice, the Ford Foundation established an endowment to create the Police Foundation (now called National Police Foundation), a private, nonprofit, independent organization dedicated to innovation and improvement in policing. The Police Foundation was established in 1970 and it was the Police Foundation that conducted the first field study of random police patrols.

The Standard Model of Policing was a well-known strategy used for crime prevention in the 1970s, and it was strongly believed that it prevented crime and increased citizens' perceptions of safety. Unfortunately, there was little known about whether those beliefs were supported by the evidence, whether they were true or not. The first step toward finding evidence and examining the truth behind the Model was initiated via the Police Foundation in partnership with the Kansas City Police Department. They applied scientific methods to test a major tenet of the Standard Model of Policing, the effectiveness of random police patrols to reduce crime and increase perceptions of safety. The Kansas City Preventative Patrol Experiment (herein Study) was underway.

The Study divided Kansas City into three geographic sections, each area receiving its own "dose" of police patrol. One area received a "standard" patrol response—officers would answer calls for service and when not on a call would drive around patrolling their area. The second area received a "reactive" patrol response—officers only answered calls for service in the area and did not spend any time driving around the area. They answered a call then drove back to their station. The third area received a "proactive" patrol response—the officers increased the number of random patrols to the area. Each of the three areas contained five patrol beats, totaling 15 beats. The study ran for a year between 1972 and 1973. The Police Foundation completed the evaluation of the study in 1974 and what they found upset the current police paradigm. The Police Foundation website summarized the findings:

> Interestingly, citizens did not notice the difference when the level of patrol was changed. What is more, increasing or decreasing the level of police patrol had no significant effect on resident and commercial burglaries, auto thefts, larcenies involving auto accessories, robberies, or vandalism—crimes traditionally considered to be prevented by random, highly visible police patrol.
>
> The rate at which crimes were reported to the police did not differ in any important or consistent way across the experimental beats. Citizen fear of crime was not affected by different levels of patrol. Nor was citizen satisfaction with police.
>
> "Ride-alongs" by observers during the experiment also revealed that 60 percent of the time spent by a Kansas City patrol officer typically was noncommitted. In other words, officers spent a considerable amount of time waiting to respond to calls for service. And they spent about as much time on non-police related activities as they did on police-related mobile patrol.

The findings reverberated across policing and left many in the field unnerved. Practitioners had long believed that random patrol prevented crime and improved citizen's perceptions of safety. The field erupted in chaos as policing was faced with the dismantling of strongly held beliefs about their true impact on crime. City managers and mayors began reducing their police staffing en masse. One of the retired chiefs speaking on the policing panel ruminated that as a consequence of that Study, Nashville reduced their department from 2800 officers to 1500, leaving them with little capacity to answer calls for service. He felt that although the study results showed that random patrol was ineffective, there was still a minimum level of officers needed to respond to calls for service. Experts in the criminal justice field began advising city officials to reconsider hiring expenditures leading to massive cuts and operating budgets similar to the ones seen by Nashville. The belief that police could deter crime was shaken.

Unfortunately, the belief that police (alone) could deter crime lingered into the 1990s even as crime began to increase. David Bayley wrote in 1994: "The police do not prevent crime. This is one of the best kept secrets of modern life. Experts know it, the police know it, but the public does not know it. Yet the police pretend they are the best defense against crime. This is a myth." Although the findings of the Study were widely disconcerting to the policing profession, it led to great strides in how policing was examined and measured. One such advancement was the increased interest in using theory as a lens for understanding police and their effect on crime and citizens' perceptions of them. One theory that stood out as the best possible explanation of policing's impact was deterrence theory. By exploring underlying theory, researchers could better understand how crime worked and what the police could do that would actually impact it.

Dr. Lawrence Sherman, a prominent figure in policing research, was one of the first scientists to review the Study. There were several glaring concerns that immediately stood out to Sherman. The first concern he identified was that the dose areas were not randomly assigned. This could mean that the Study's outcomes may have been influenced due to neighborhood demographics. Next, he found that the borders of the reactive, proactive, and standard patrol dose areas were adjacent to one another. This caused contamination when officers drove into and out of areas. This research design error led to individual dose areas appearing more similar than perhaps they should have been. A third issue recognized by Sherman was that high crime areas were possibly being compared to low crime locations. The underlying research design problem here, Sherman observed, was the inability to compare outcomes between two areas with similar crime rates. If one area had high crime and another area had low crime and they each received different types of patrols, the type of patrol may not be the reason for no dose effects—it may be because the crime baselines are just too different to observe the effect.

Beyond the research design flaws, Sherman viewed the findings of the Study through the lens of the Pareto Principle as well as the experience of his previous Repeat Call Address Experiment (RECAP) experiment in Minneapolis. The RECAP experiment demonstrated that calls for service were often arising from the same locations. They were not randomly diffuse through the city. He wondered if the lack of crime reduction was not due to police being an ineffective deterrence mechanism but instead due to an ineffective application of the patrol response. Sherman analogized police patrols to medicinal dosing. For instance, if someone were sick with a bacterial infection, they would need to take a specific dose of antibiotics, multiple times a day for several days. If the patient does not take a large enough dose for their body weight, then the antibiotic will not be effective in combating the bacteria. In the case of policing, the Kansas City Experiment showed that increasing officer's presence to a large area did not reduce crime or increase citizens' perception of safety. The dose had no effect on the area, but what if they area was too large, and Kansas City was giving the patient too small of a dose? Would increasing the size of the dose and decreasing the size of the patrol area have different results?

The Pareto Principle argues that for some scientific phenomenon, 20 percent of your causes create 80 percent of the effects and Sherman, using several years of data from Minneapolis, already knew that crime was concentrated at the level of streets and individual buildings. Minneapolis data showed that 3.5 percent of the street segments generated 50 percent of the calls for service in the city, not quite the Pareto ratio, but still an incredible finding. I conducted the same analysis as Sherman in 2011 during a hot spots study I ran in Sacramento, CA and we found that 4.7 percent of the street segments generated 50 percent of the calls for service. Additionally, Pierce, Spaar, and Briggs showed similar results in Boston, and Eck, Gersh, and Taylor found that 10 percent of the places in Baltimore and the Bronx accounted for 32 percent of the robberies, assaults, burglaries, grand larcenies, and auto thefts. These ratios do not reflect the exact ratio of the Pareto Principle but they follow the same principle, a small percent of the streets (cause) are generating a large part of the crime (effect). Applying another analogy to patrol, crime, rather than being like bacterial infection and needing an antibiotic, is more like a cancer in need of a precise approach. Rather than applying chemotherapy to a cancerous area and killing the benign cells along with the malignant cells, police patrol should be focused like radiation and be applied with surgical precision to the areas where crime concentrates. Random police patrols are like chemotherapy—harming good neighborhoods while reducing crime in the bad neighborhoods. Focusing patrols on only the areas where crime concentrates is like using radiation, it focuses on the harmful parts of the neighborhood while leaving the benign parts alone.

Sherman was not sure if the police did or did not influence crime, but he did know that he wanted to find out if the police patrols were applied in a different way, would the outcome be different? Sherman knew from the Minneapolis experiment that calls for service did concentrate in city streets and buildings. Sherman called these areas hot spots while Dr. David Weisburd, another criminologist who came to believe that crime concentrated by street, called them small worlds. Weisburd had walked a beat with the NYPD during one of his first jobs as a criminologist. He realized walking with the officers that they returned to the same streets repeatedly. Just like Sherman, he observed streets with no crime next to streets rife with crime. Sherman and Weisburd partnered to conduct the Minneapolis Hot Spots Experiment to evaluate the effects of increasing patrols in areas where calls for service concentrated.

The Minneapolis Hot Spots Experiment ran for one year between 1988 and 1989 and used a year of data to determine where calls for service concentrated in the city. Sherman and Weisburd used calls for service to measure "hard crime", and "soft crime" and found 110 hot spots in the City of Minneapolis which were randomly assigned to treatment or control groups. Examples of "hard crime" calls were holdup alarms, burglaries, shootings, stabbings, auto theft, theft from autos, assaults, and rape. Examples of "soft crime" calls were audible break-in alarms, disturbances, drunks, noise, unwanted persons at businesses, vandalism, prowlers, fights, and persons down. Random assignments were made within five statistical blocks. The hard crime calls were rank ordered and natural cutting-off points were used for separating the calls into the five statistical blocks. The control area hot spots were given standard random police patrols, meaning the officers were not aware that the areas were designated "hot spots" by the researchers. The study called for the treatment areas to receive three hours of daily patrol at intermittent periods and for random lengths of time. Although the officers increased their time in the hot spots, they did not quite fully achieve the three hours a day by the end of the study.

The important aspect of the study was increasing the amount of time the officers spent in the hot spot and not what they did in the hot spot. The idea was to increase the visibility, not increase the activity. The officers were not told how to police the hot spots, they were just instructed to police the hot spot however they saw fit. Sometimes the officers stayed for several hours at the hot spot, sometimes they drove through, or sometimes they stopped for only a couple of minutes. The target areas were given extra patrol from 11 am to 3 am, seven days a week. The patrol supervisors were given weekly reports based on officer logs to ensure consistent and equal dosage to all the hot spots through the 11 am–7 pm and 7 pm–3 am time periods.

Officer activity and time-on-scene data were obtained through physical observations by graduate students. The students were employed to observe what the officers were doing in their hot spots, how long they remained in the hot spots, and to observe the social activity around the hot spots when officers were present and when they were absent. Observers monitored the control and treatment hot spots to observe citizen activity and officer activity. In the year during the study, observers conducted 6465 blocks of 70-minute observation periods, which generated about 65 observation blocks per hot spot.

What Sherman and Weisburd found from this study was that soft crime and total crime calls diminished anywhere from 7 percent to 16 percent over the course of the year, and for observed disorder there was a 25 percent decrease in the experimental versus control areas. The variation in reduction of calls was due in part to less engagement during the summer when calls for service were high and another period where switching CAD technology caused a glitch in data gathering. Taking this variation into account, they did find that there was a 50 percent reduction in calls for the two months where the integrity of the study was the greatest. The results of the Minneapolis Hot Spots study demonstrated that police did influence crime, and just like focusing your exam efforts on the right type of studying, focusing policing efforts on a small percent of street segments generates the largest effects.

Since Sherman and Weisburd's first randomized controlled trial of hot spots policing, crime concentration has become one of the largest areas of police research with over 65 studies and 78 tests. This culmination of work led Weisburd to writing "The Law of Crime Concentration and the Criminology of Place" for the 2014 Sutherland speech at the American Society of Criminology (ASC) conference. In that article, Weisburd laid out a body of evidence that supports the idea that crime concentrates across geography, within specific crime types, and remains stable across time. He asserted: "This law states that for a defined measure of crime at a specific microgeographic unit, the concentration of crime will fall within a narrow bandwidth of percentages for a defined cumulative proportion of crime." This is just another way of articulating the Pareto Principle or a Power Law, very few areas will generate a large proportion of the crime. He argued that criminology scholars should shift their focus from studying people and begin to study place. Every profession has a life course development with shifts in theory and focus, and during his speech Weisburd argued that it was time for the field of criminology to shift course. Weisburd examined 25 years' worth of articles from *Criminology*, criminology's top-ranked journal, and over the course of that time 66.1 percent of the journal articles used people as the unit of analysis and only 4 percent examined microplaces such as street segments, buildings, or small clusters. Weisburd's call to action for scholars was to shift their unit of analysis from person to place, maintaining that this area of scholarship was ripe for study as there was evidence that the concentration of crime at place mirrored the Pareto Principle and by focusing on these crime concentrations, more could be learned about crime.

During the ASC speech, Weisburd referred to Edward Sutherland, the speech namesake and discussed how Sutherland expressed the need for universal propositions for criminology to become a true science. The formulation of the Law of crime concentration does just that and advances our understanding of crime at place as it is a "general proposition of universal validity." Weisburd examined the universality of the law by analyzing both large and small cities and found similar results across the different geographic regions. Using a convenience sample of small and large cities, Weisburd found that crime concentration was even greater in the smaller cities. The crime concentration in the smaller cities (Redlands, CA, Brooklyn Park, MN, and Ventura, CA) varied from 2.1 to 3.5 percent of the street segments causing 50 percent of the crime, whereas Sacramento and Cincinnati varied from 4.2 percent to 6 percent. He demonstrated that crime concentration occurs universally, which means that analyzing crime by street segments is the best way to determine where to allocate department resources. This universal law is an important milestone in criminology, yet one that is still not universally applied by police departments.

In response to the increased knowledge about crime concentration, the Grand Prairie Police Department decided to examine whether the Law of Crime Concentration applied to their city as it had in so many other cities. The police managers at GPPD understood that Braga, Hureau, and Papachristos had found gun violence was stable and concentrated at less than 5 percent of street segments in Boston and only 1 percent and 8 percent of the street segments generated almost 50 percent of the commercial robberies and 66 percent of the street robberies. They also knew that Weisburd, Morris, and Groff showed that juvenile crime was concentrated in 86 street segments in Seattle. Those street segments generated one-third of all official juvenile crime over a 14-year period. They imagined the success they could have if they focused their limited resources on only 86 street segments rather than the entire city. Finally, they knew that the growing body of place-based research led the National Research Council to state that hot spot policing (synonymous with crime at place) has the "strongest collective evidence of police effectiveness that is now available." Armed with the research on place-based policing, GPPD wanted to explore how the Law of crime concentration applied to them and if them structured a policing strategy around the theory could they reduce crime and calls for service.

Interest in the Law of crime concentration began at an in-service training event conducted by the Law Enforcement Management Institute of Texas. All police executive command staff members in the state of Texas are required to attend this training every 24 months. It was there that I met the executive staff of GPPD and introduced them to evidence-based policing and the research behind place-based policing. It was Deputy Chief Ronnie Morris who wondered if GPPD could build a patrol strategy structured around hot spots rather than beats. He partnered me with his crime analyst Heather Lane to create a beatless patrol quasi-experiment to examine whether a beatless patrol focused on microplaces with high call for service rather than a traditional beat approach to patrol would reduce calls for service and crime more effectively.

Working with Heather was a great experience. She was smart, funny, and a hard worker. One of the first things I have most police departments do when I work with them is to map out their crime and calls for service using three years, one year, and 90 days of data. As Heather began to make the maps, she emailed me: "I am freaking out. All of the maps look the same ... unless that's the point." I emailed her back and said that is exactly the point. I was excited that Heather could already see what the data was revealing and what we know from the research—that crime and calls for service are relatively stable by street segment. Fourteen years of Seattle crime data was examined by street segment in increasing or decreasing trajectories and Weisburd's team showed that crime was a stable phenomenon across street segments. Over the course of the 14 years only 2 percent of the street segments showed an increase in crime. Moreover, in that same study they showed that 50 percent of the street segments generated 100 percent of the crime. The trajectories are difficult to create unless you have a sophisticated statistician, but comparing three years, to one year, to 90 days of data can provide insight as to the stability of a city's crime and calls for service. Similar street segment maps created by the Austin Police Department are displayed in Figure 8.1.

Although it is difficult to tell from this distance, the street segments remained relatively the same. In the Seattle data only 2 percent of the city street segments were increasing in crime, and most of the street segments remained stable whether they were low crime, high crime, or no crime. The stability of crime and calls for service remained relatively the same in the neighborhoods.

In the Grand Prairie study, the executive management had already decided to divide the city in half, making half of the city beatless and half of the city remain in their normal patrol beats. Heather was able to identify the top calls for service street segments in both the treatment side (beatless patrol) and the control side (normal random patrols based on beat) of the city. These street segments were matched based on baseline rates of calls for service and crime. GPPD changed shifts every six months, thus the study began when the shift change occurred, and officers were not told about the study before sign ups. This way there was some reduction in bias as officers were not able to choose the treatment or control area they patrolled. The study ran for six months—the entire shift change period. The results are depicted in Table 8.1:

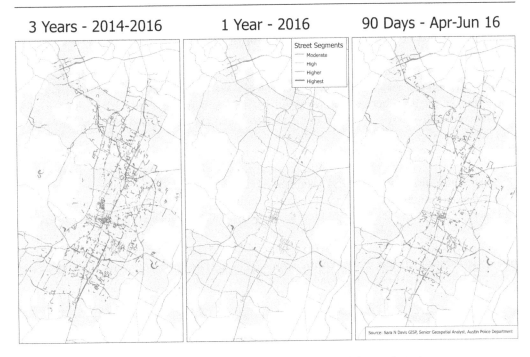

Figure 8.1 Maps of Austin Hot Street Segment for 90-day, 1-year, and 3-year Periods

As you can see, all the treatment areas had a greater reduction for all the variables except Part I crimes. High visibility policing will not reduce crimes that take place indoors thus not all Part I crimes will be affected by a focused hot spots patrol. This is one of the reasons we examined robbery, assault, and burglary on their own, because those crimes are crimes that usually take place in public and can be affected by high visibility policing. Now I am sure you are thinking, wait … what? I thought you said binary percent changes lead to false linear thinking? Remember, here the percent changes were not just comparing a pre/post change in the amount of crime after an intervention. The GPPD study was a scientific quasi-experiment which means we matched the areas based on similar baseline variables beforehand and then used what is called a difference in difference test to evaluate whether the changes in the pre- and post-measures were statistically significant. You do this by comparing the changes over time in the treatment and the control areas and then compare them to each other. If the changes are different enough then they are deemed statistically

Table 8.1 Percent Changes Between the Study Period to the Same Time the Year Before

	Hot Spot Type	July to Dec 2017	July to Dec 2018	Percent Change
Calls for Service	Treatment	11590	10890	−6.0%
	Control	10369	9939	−4.1%
Part I Crimes	Treatment	1334	1052	−21.1
	Control	1372	987	−28.1%
Social Disorder	Treatment	194	150	−22.68%
	Control	94	90	−4.26
Robbery-Assault-Burglary	Treatment	59	41	−30.51%
	Control	26	24	−7.69

significant and you can say that the outcomes occurred because of the intervention rather than by chance if your hypothesis is correct. In the case of the GPPD study we did not find any statistically significant reductions. This could mean that the intervention was not powered enough to see an effect (not enough hot spots) or that the intervention did not work. In either case, the officers involved in the beatless program liked working without the restrictions of the beats better and the executive management observed the officers engaging in more problem-solving activities compared to when they remained sequestered to their own beats.

By focusing police patrols on the areas where crime concentrates, police could reduce patrols to 50 percent of the geographic area and thus could free up police officers to engage in more community policing and problem-solving rather than driving around aimlessly. This approach might reduce some of the community tensions that police agencies are now experiencing. It could lead to a reduction in over-policing, because rather than saturating a whole area, the officers can remain focused on the street segments that really need the attention. Additionally, the next Mental Model demonstrates that besides concentrating on place, the Pareto Principle exists within people too and crime often concentrates among our most prolific offenders—the most ravenous of the wolves.

The Felonious Few

> The folklore of policing has always included an inchoate awareness of high-rate offenders. Police leaders have been provided research that not only supports that fact but demonstrates just how few they really are and how much damage they inflict.
>
> Chief (Ret.) Edward A. Flynn

The concentration of effects is a naturally occurring phenomenon that manifests itself physically, socially, and ecologically in the world. There seems to be no natural phenomenon that is not affected by unequal distribution of cause and effect. This Pareto Principle or 80/20 rule has been observed among the distribution of wealth, the concentration of crime among victims, the market share among firms, the concentration of carbon in the Amazon trees, and even on social media where a small number of Twitter users are responsible for most of the misogyny. Thus, it makes sense that this phenomenon is also found among offenders.

In an article titled, "Sitting Ducks, Ravenous Wolves, and Helping Hands: New Approaches to Urban Policing," Spelman and Eck examined crime concentration across victims, offenders, and places. The article advocated for policing to take a proactive approach to problem-solving, arguing that analyzing local conditions and coproducing a response with the community could reduce crime and fear in the neighborhood. They summarized the extant research into three supporting points for police to create a more focused, tailored, problem-solving strategy:

1 Incidents were rarely isolated; crime and calls for service were as the result of underlying community problems.
2 Crime problems are intimately linked to other municipal problems; they do not occur on islands.
3 Police resources if applied to individual incidents will be ineffective at reducing crime.

While this article was advocating for police to change the delivery of police services from "incident-driven policing" to problem-oriented policing, the main cusp of the article was demonstrating how crime concentrates among victims, offenders, and places. They stated: "These strategies are given a focus by one regularity that seems to hold for crime problems in all neighborhoods: crime is concentrated." If crime concentrates among victims, offenders, and places, then police should focus their efforts on solving the problems there. Without saying it, Spelman and Eck were encouraging the use of the Pareto Principle. Analyzing

DOI: 10.4324/9780367481520-10

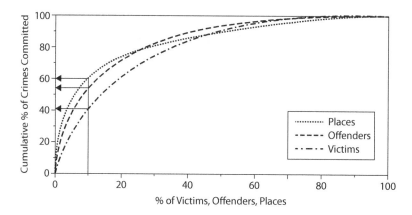

Figure 9.1 Percent of Victims, Offenders, and Places, and Cumulative Percent of Crimes Committed

arrest records and offender interviews they demonstrated that 10 percent of the worst offenders generated 55 percent of the crime, 10 percent of victims are involved in 40 percent of all crimes, and 60 percent of crimes are committed at 10 percent of the places. Crime not only concentrates at place; it concentrates among people. Sherman named this phenomenon The Felonious Few in "The Felonious Few versus The Miscreant Many." Figure 9.1 shows the graph created by Spelman and Eck in the Sitting Ducks article.

The graph was created from arrest records and interviews with offenders. It shows the percent of victims, offenders, and places on the y-axis and the cumulative percent of crime committed on the x-axis. Crime concentrates within vulnerable populations, and vulnerable places, where there is no guardian present. These are the elements of routine activity theory: a victim encounters an offender without a capable guardian to deter a crime from occurring. Applying routine activity theory to the Sitting Ducks proposition, for policing to be effective, their strategy should be to target the people and the places where crime concentrates using a focused, tailored approach.

Eck expanded on his original idea of crime concentration within offenders, in an article with Martinez, Lee, and SooHyun aptly titled "Ravenous Wolves Revisited: A Systematic Review of Offending Concentration." A systematic review (which will be covered in MM #17) is a review of all the research on one topic to determine an overall scientific understanding of the topic. In a systematic review, the researchers describe the level of rigor the studies included must meet. They also clarify how they narrowed their search based on specific criteria, and what studies were excluded if they did not meet the criteria. In the 2017 article, they found 73 studies on the concentration of crime among offenders; 15 focused on the prevalence of offending (the number of offenders within the population), and 27 focused on the frequency of offenders (how many times one offender commits multiple crimes). Only 42 studies had enough data to perform a suitable analysis. When the researchers examined the prevalence studies, they found that 10 percent of the most criminally active people were responsible for approximately 63 percent of crime in the U.S. and 68 percent of the crime in other nations. However, when they examined the frequency studies, they found the most active 10 percent of offenders accounted for approximately 41 percent of crime: that, overall, across gender, age, and nation frequency comparisons 10 percent of the worst offenders caused between 37 and 43 percent of the offending. This was smaller than what would be expected when compared to the 80/20 Pareto Principle. They noted this low ratio occurred when examining the *frequency* of offending across gender, age, and nation (overall), whereas examining *prevalence* within their own population, youths, adults, males, and nations, then between 79 and 83 percent of crime *is* generated by 20 percent of the population. Thus, they stipulate that the Pareto Principle may be more appropriately interpreted in environmental criminology as "20 percent of all individuals in a population account for 80 percent of all crime."

Crime concentration among offenders can also be examined by the amount of harm they cause rather than the raw number count of crime. Two separate crimes do not create the same type of harm to an individual or society. A shoplift is not equal to a homicide or a rape. This means when examining crime concentration among offenders, we should also consider the type of offending. Specialists' (offenders who only commit one type of crime) crime patterns could differ from generalists' (offenders who commit crimes across a broad spectrum of crime). Researchers Liggins, Ratcliffe, and Bland examined the rate of crime concentration over time (2010–2016) among specialists and generalists arrested in Northamptonshire, U.K. They used the Cambridge Crime Harm Index (Cambridge CHI) as measure to determine concentration.

The Cambridge CHI is a tool to classify crime by how harmful it is relative to other crimes rather than comparing crimes using a raw crime count. Counting a homicide and a theft case as equal crime is clearly not a way to examine overall crime occurring in a city or county. By creating a harm index based on sentencing guidelines, and sentencing guidelines acting as a proxy measure of societal values, we can evaluate crimes based on the amount of harm to society rather than crime counts. Harm indexes are covered more in-depth in Mental Model #20—Harm Indexes. The Cambridge CHI used the lowest minimum sentence to create the harm index whereas other crime harm indexes like the California Crime Harm Index (CA-CHI) used the highest maximum sentence, because many of the crimes in the California Penal Code did not have a minimum sentence, only a maximum one.

In the Northamptonshire study, the CHI was used to evaluate the level of concentration among offenders over the course of seven years. The Cambridge CHI was calculated for each offender by totaling the total number of days of imprisonment recommended by English sentencing guidelines in the seven-year period across all years and in each separate year. The offenders were then ranked in a descending order based on their level of harm. Then the proportion of offenders accounting for 80 percent of the total Cambridge CHI scores was calculated in each time period. They found the more diverse the offender was in his crime type, the greater level of crime harm they generated and repeat offenders generated 68.7 percent of all offender-identified crime harm (this data set did not include officer-identified crime). When repeat offenders were "specialists" they only accounted for 22.5 percent of the harm, demonstrating the greater proportion of harm was generated by the "generalist" offenders. Overall, when examining the officer-identified and offender-identified crime harm, 80 percent of the harm came from 7.6 percent of unique offenders. This outcome shows a larger concentration in crime harm (effect) from a small group of offenders (cause) than even the Pareto Principle predicts, rather than 80/20 the ratio, the ratio is 80/8, roughly 8 percent of the offenders in the Northamptonshire region generated 80 percent of the harm to the community.

Recently, harm-focused researchers have begun to examine the victim-offender overlap and how crime harm concentrates among predominant offenders or predominant victims. The study was conducted by Inspector Natalie Hiltz at the Peel Regional Police Service in Canada. Using two years of data and the Canadian Crime Severity Index, she calculated victimization and offending totals across all reported incidents for each induvial involved. Individuals were identified either as first appearing as victims or offenders then tracked for the following 730 days to determine if they were a subsequent victim or offender. There were 27,233 unique individuals that were identified either as offenders or victims of violent crime in the two-year period. There were 17,138 subjects first identified as victims and 10,095 first identified as offenders. Of the 17,138 first identified as offenders, 1,019 were reported as victims in the following two years. Of the 17,138 first appearing as victims, 997 were subsequently reported as offenders. Using the Canadian Crime Severity Index they found that 20 percent of the individuals within the victim-offender population with the highest harm were linked to 71 percent of the overall harm. Hiltz' findings reflects the 2017 systematic review which narrows the Pareto Principle from the 80/20 to being more indicative of a specific population rather than across gender, age, states, or nations.

Analyzing police data to determine the offenders that generate the most crime in the community will help police agencies allocate resources more efficiently. Additionally, targeting offenders for prevention programs that generate the most consistent harm might be a better expenditure of taxpayers' monies. By focusing rehabilitation efforts on the people that need it the most, the community will receive the benefit of the greatest amount of harm reduction. The CHI is an algorithm, using a weighted measure to help predict where the criminal justice system should be focusing its efforts. And if creating a CHI is a too laborious one you could always create a simple algorithm to weight crime by the extent of harm. Homicides could be weighted at 100 while shoplifting could be 1, so that shoplifting is 1 percent of the weight of harm compared to homicide. Algorithms will generally outperform human prediction. By focusing on the Felonious Few, rather than the "miscreant many," police agencies will further reduce the need for over-policing.

The Mental Models in Practice III—Mental Models 7–9

The Pareto Principle, The Law of Crime Concentration, and The Felonious Few

This section of the book espouses the same approach across a variety of issues that impact policing, the Pareto Principle, and the idea that natural phenomena tend to concentrate. This phenomenon holds across several different disciplines besides policing. For policing, it can be a useful tool to examine your department's data and determine if there are problems that concentrate in your city and your agency. Where do violent crimes occur in the city? Is there a small subset of offenders that create most of the harm? Are the victims of certain crimes concentrated in an area of the city or a population (age, gender, race)? Are there issues that concentrate in the department? Does sick leave, use of force, or complaints concentrate among a certain group of officers? If there are areas of concentration in the city or department then focus the agency's administrative efforts on the 20 percent of the people or places that produce 80 percent of the effects. This is where applying a business model like the Pareto Principle to policing can achieve the greatest gains, to reduce crime and calls for service and improve community and officer outcomes, without increasing harm to the community. Here is how to apply Mental Models 7-9:

1 Analyze crime, calls for service, and officer proactivity data separately:

    a   Map out the city data by street segment—intersection to intersection no matter the street length.

    b   Map out the data by three year, one year, and 90 day sets.

    c   Is there any difference between the data sets—look for stability.

    d   Focus efforts on the 20 percent of the street segments that generate the highest calls for service and crime.

    e   Evaluate whether officers' proactivity is occurring on the same street segments where 50 percent of crime is occurring.

2 Analyze arrest data:

    a   List out offenders by number of arrests over the last three years.

    b   Rank offenders from highest frequency to lowest.

    c   Rank offenders from highest harm to lowest harm.

    d   Determine which offenders rank the highest on both lists.

    e   Determine if the offenders who rank high on both lists would qualify as a generalist offender compared to a specialist offender.

    f   Focus diversion efforts on the smallest percent of offenders who are generating the largest percent of harm for the city.

    g   Using a pulling levers approach (carrot and the stick) to reducing recidivism will be your best approach for these types of offenders.

3 Examine the departments' internal data:

    a   Try to determine if there are any 80/20 ratios in the data for complaints, injuries, use of force, or officer proactivity.

    b   Is there an intervention that can be used to reduce or increase behavior depending on what is found?

    c   Determine if there is a particular type of call that generates officer complaints or use of force—are there ways to intervene on those types of calls?

4 Examine any city data that could have an impact on police calls and see where they overlap:

    a   Map the city's fire department and EMS data by street segment and time duration (three year, one year, and 90 day) data sets to determine if the calls concentrate in any way.

    b   Overlap police and fire maps to determine where an intervention might be effective that could reduce calls for both departments.

Part IV

How Things Vary

Distributions

> The statistician knows, for example that in nature, there never was a normal distribution, there never was a straight line, yet with normal and linear assumptions, known to be false, he can often derive results which match, to a useful approximation, those found in the real world.
>
> George E.P. Box

Science and policing are similar in that measurements are a central tenet that drives decision-making, which means measuring correctly is of absolute importance. In science, measurement is king. When scientists write research articles, most of the article is dedicated to what measurements were taken, how they were taken, how many times they were taken, and finally what statistical analyses were performed with those measurements. In policing, measurement is also king; police measure the type and frequency of crime occurrences and the variation between weeks, months, and years (MM#5). What is truly important when interpreting data is understanding the underlying nature of what you are measuring.

In both policing and science, observations are being measured. When the word science is used, it conjures images of people in white lab coats, wearing clear eye googles, and working in a lab to discover the mysteries of physical science. The Meriam-Webster dictionary defines science as "knowledge or a system of knowledge covering general truths, or the operation of general laws especially as obtained and tested through scientific method" (MM#17). On a lighthearted note, according to the very accurate Urban Dictionary, "Any idiot can practice science. It takes a real psychotic genius to pull it off." Although not in a lab, policing also measures observations, counting the number of crimes that occurred before and after a dedicated patrol operation or a POP project to ascertain whether the strategy was effective. Yet what policing misses, that scientists understand and account for, is the number count is not fixed. At the very second a crime analyst downloads the numbers of burglaries that have taken place to date, another might be occurring at the same time and ultimately will not be counted in that moment. More might have occurred, however they went unreported and as a result will not be counted. This can occur in the hard sciences too. Although we know in physics that there is a specific formula for the time it will take a falling body to travel a specific distance, experiments are run on different types of materials, over different distances, using different weights. Even still, when the experiment is conducted again using the same materials, different measurements occur every time. This is not because the experiment is being conducted incorrectly, it is because within every experiment, within every data set, randomness impacts the outcomes.

DOI: 10.4324/9780367481520-11

Science, whether natural, physical, or social is affected by randomness. Randomness is the "noise" within data that obscures the "signal". The signal is what we are looking for in data—it is what we want to interpret to give meaning to the data. Data are dumb, humans must give meaning to data which means we have to understand the difference between the "signal" (information) and the "noise" (randomness or variation). The randomness or variation that occurs in data means that our observations are not the "thing" we are studying, but rather as Salsburg alluded to in the preceding quote, we are studying the distribution of the measurements of the "thing." The distribution of the measurements is the combination of the "signal" and the "noise" and understanding this difference will assist us in understanding and interpreting police data. Understanding and measuring distributions of observations of natural phenomena is what allows us to advance our understanding of the world.

Weight loss is a simple example to think about inherent variation and randomness within observations. Weight loss and gain are influenced by many different variables which include diet, genetic makeup, metabolism, existent or newly developed muscle mass, and an individual's rate of water retention. People get frustrated when they weigh themselves daily and sometimes see an unexplained variation of weight. The weight on the scale is the observed measure, yet that measure has both a "signal" and some "noise." There is variation because of randomness. The dieter could have eaten healthy on a Monday only to find out they weigh two more pounds the very next day. The scale could have been slightly off balance because the tiles are off kilter in the spot where the scale was placed, compared to the day before. Although they ate healthy on Monday, the food was high in fiber or salt which caused water retention. The Monday weight may have reflected a level of dehydration that is no longer present on Tuesday. Instead, if someone weighed multiple times a day, every day for a month, wrote the weights down and did not change anything about their day, a distribution (a range) would start to emerge. If they were, let us say, an average size 160-pound man, they might see that rather than weighing exactly 160 pounds, they range from 158.3 to 162.1 pounds (think of upper and lower control limits). The Salsburg quote at the beginning of the chapter means you cannot measure a "thing" accurately every time like the dieter's weight, but you can measure a distribution of that variable and from that distribution you can describe the probabilities associated with that observation. The "thing" police most want to measure is crime, but like the dieter's weight it's variable. Thus, rather than comparing points in time using raw numbers (binary percent changes), to interpret our data, police should understand and evaluate the distribution of crime. And how data are distributed matters because the variability within data affects our ability to predict outcomes and interpret meaning from the data. It's not size but distribution that matters here. Without understanding how data is distributed around a mean can lead to misinterpretation of the phenomena occurring in the world around us. Howard Wainer in his book, *Picturing the Uncertain World*, called de Moivre's equation the "Most Dangerous Equation." De Moivre's equation provides the standard deviation of the sampling distribution of the mean. He called the equation dangerous because people often do not understand how the equation works and misapply variation to social policy.

Abraham de Moivre was one of the most notable and well-known mathematicians in the 1700s not because he held a lofty position at a university or bank, but because he served as a resident statistician to the gamblers at Slaughter's Coffee House in London. De Moivre's book, *The Doctrine of Chances*, was not only viewed as the gambler's bible but the ideas in his book were the foundation for probability theory. Gamblers would visit de Moivre at the coffeehouse and pay him to calculate the probabilities of winning games of chance. These calculations would take hours to compute by hand. To save himself time, de Moivre created formulas to use for games of chance. The result was his book, *The Doctrine of Chances*. Although a man of his intellect was better suited for academia, he was a Frenchman living in England, thus due to ongoing prejudice against foreigners, he could not gain an appointment at a university. He was finally appointed to the Royal Society of London as a Fellow in 1697 through the support of friends and colleagues who recognized his genius, but he continued to make his living tutoring the well-to-do in math and consulting for insurance companies and gamblers throughout his life. It was his need to make a living that drove his thinking about probability that led to de Moivre's equation—the "Most Dangerous Equation" and the de Moivre—LaPlace Theorem.

The Most Dangerous Equation title arises not because the equation is dangerous in and of itself, but because most people do not understand the equation well enough to interpret real-life data. The equation looks innocent enough on its face:

$$\sigma_x = \sigma / \sqrt{n}$$

De Moivre's equation states the standard deviation of the sampling distribution (σ_x) is equal to the standard deviation of the population (σ) divided by the square root of the sample size ($\sqrt{n}$). What this means is that the variation of the mean is inversely proportional to the square root of the sample size, for example, the smaller the sample size, the greater the variance in measurement. This is what makes the equation dangerous, the misunderstanding of how much influence variance (randomness) has on small data sets. However, Wainer calls it the most dangerous for three reasons:

1   The extreme length of time during which ignorance of it has caused confusion;
2   The wide breadth of areas that have been misled; and
3   The seriousness of the consequences that such ignorance has caused.

Wainer uses several examples in his book to demonstrate the misapplication of cause and effect when examining small data sets. Kahneman's *Thinking, Fast and Slow* mentions one of Wainer's examples—cancer rates by county. Wainer maps out kidney cancer death rates by counties of the United States, showing the counties that have the lowest rates of kidney cancer by decile (lowest percent by 10 percent increments). The counties that have the lowest rates are the counties that are rural, midwestern, southern, and western counties to which he states could be inferred due to clean country living—clean air, water, and fresh food. However, the counties with the highest rates of kidney cancer are also counties that are rural, midwestern, southern, and western counties which could be associated with a rural lifestyle of poverty, reduced access to medical care, high-fat diet, tobacco, and alcohol. Here is where Kahneman's research shows that System 1 is in full force, as it is inept when faced with statistical probability and applies causation when it should not. The rate of kidney cancer is not *caused* by anything, it is a statistical manifestation of having a small sample size. What de Moivre's equation demonstrates is that large variations exist on the outer limits of a population distribution and as a sample size grows, the variability begins to smooth out. de Moivre's equation led to the Central limit theorem and built the foundation for other theories of population distribution.

The Central limit theorem was derived from evaluating the probability of a coin landing on heads over the course of 100 flips. The probability of a coin landing on heads or tails is 50/50 and de Moivre wanted to create a formula that would determine "What is the probability of landing 60 heads when completing 100 coin tosses?" He found that as he increased the number of coin flips (sample size), the shape of the probability distribution approached a smooth curve. Probabilities are the likelihood of an event happening in the future which can be described as a number between 0 and 1, where 0 is an absolute impossibility and 1 is an absolute certainty. Figure 10.1 is a graph of 2, 4, and 12 coin flips and their subjective probabilities.

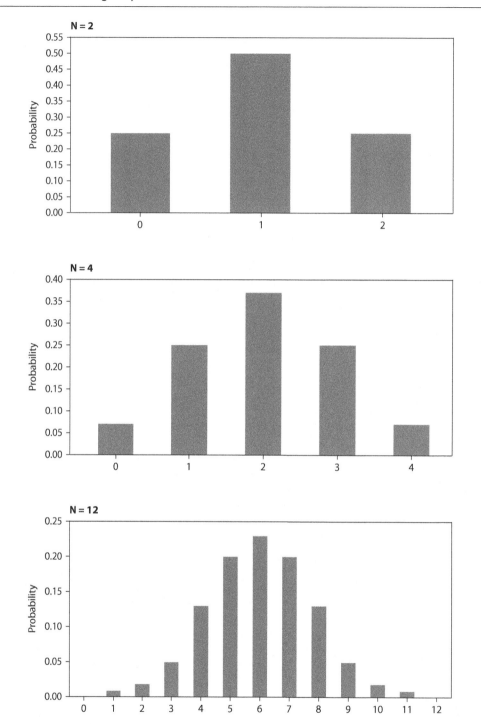

Figure 10.1 Graph of 2-, 4-, and 12-coin Flip Probabilities

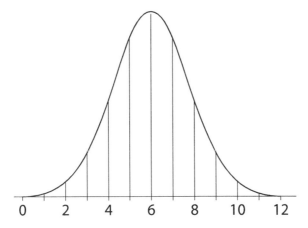

Figure 10.2 De Moivre's Binomial Curve

As the sample size got larger and larger, de Moivre's binomial curve began to look similar to Figure 10.2.

His finding led to the development of the Central limit theorem which states that the sampling distribution of the sample means approaches a normal distribution as the sample size gets larger (no matter the shape of the population distribution), and holds especially true for samples over 30. This builds on his original formula concerning sampling distribution of the sampling means. He understood that if there was a small sample then the variance within that sample could be large, but this meant that the opposite also held, if the sample was large then the variance within the sampling mean would be reduced. As the sample size increased, the variance smoothed out. A sample of crime types exceeding 30 incidents will mirror de Moivre's distribution. We now call this curve the normal distribution or as some of you recall in high school or college, seemingly decades ago, the bell curve. The statistical models of distribution allow us to describe the nature of randomness mathematically which allow for a better understanding of the world around us ... if we apply it.

The discovery of the Central limit theorem and the normal distribution was not only beneficial to the gamblers who frequented Slaughter's Coffee House, but to many different disciplines. The normal distribution occurs frequently in nature, hence the title "normal." The normal distribution was observed in the early 1700s in astronomical observations. Initially, astronomers took these errors as mistakes due to imperfect equipment. The observers and astronomers ignored the errors, and as a result excluded the errors from the data set assuming they were due to human error. Galileo was the first to point out that the errors were symmetrical and small errors occurred more frequently than large errors. It was not until the 19th century that it was discovered that these astronomy errors also followed a normal distribution. Galileo knew that the errors were symmetrical but could not explain why they were symmetrical. Today scientists understand that randomness is inherent in nature, which means all data will contain an element of error and understanding the parameters of these errors is key to understanding the world. Understanding the difference between variation (randomness) and causality is key.

Compare the normal distribution to the skewed distribution of the Power law (depicted in Figure 7.2), another theoretical distribution. The Power law distribution is a right skewed distribution of data in which most of the data points are to the left of the graph with a long, fat tail to the right (positive skew). Not all populations fit a normal distribution which is why it is important to look at your data in several different ways. We observed in Mental Model #8—The Law of Crime Concentration that crime concentrates at place. Crime mirrors the Power law probability distribution geographically but can mirror the normal distribution temporally. Graphing crime and call for service frequency distribution over a year will most likely illuminate the fact that the range will typically fluctuate around the average randomly. This is the brilliance of Petitti's Statistical Process Control Charts, by predicting the "cone of normal" around the crime averages he can keep his executive command focused on problem-solving rather than reacting to short-lived crime spikes. Crime across geography concentrates. Crime across time is normally distributed.

Misunderstanding the variance in data sets becomes dangerous when people interpret this randomness as causality, especially when policy changes follow. Wainer describes how the small school's movement started due to a misunderstanding of how variance works within small populations. When schools were ranked on performance tests small schools out-ranked some of the larger schools on student achievement, thus philanthropists thought that turning larger schools into smaller ones would help with the achievement gap, equating the smaller school size as *causing* the achievement. Yet if one understood de Moivre's equation, they would know this outcome is expected. If smaller schools have a few smart kids it might be enough variance to skew the test scores higher than other larger schools. What the small school advocates never looked at was the other end of the distribution of scores, where small schools also fell, at the lower end of school performance. This occurred for the same reasons, in a small school, a few kids who did poorly on testing could drag down the overall average. Whereas the larger populations smooth out the variance and a few really good or really bad scores cannot skew the outcomes. At the end of the school example Wainer lamented: "Expending more than a billion dollars on a theory based on ignorance of de Moivre's equation suggests just how dangerous that ignorance can be."

Criminal justice advocates and practitioners alike apply causation to small sample variation. The Center for American Progress created a map depicting the rate of gun deaths by state using data from the Centers for Disease Control and Prevention—see Figure 10.3.

The map looks identical to Wainer's kidney cancer map. Wyoming is 6th in the country for the rate of gun deaths with 1016 people killed compared to California at 42nd with 30,703 killed. If using the same causal relationship for cancer or school performance, one would think that living in the country is more dangerous than the big cities of California, rather than this being a result of the variation within a small population.

Policing misinforms itself when it assumes causality from a small data set. Crime data is another phenomenon that follows a normal distribution, and when a small data set, like a week's worth of data, is displayed during CompStat the sample size is not large enough to be representative of the population. As de Moivre's equation has shown, there will be a lot of variation. He demonstrated the variance in a sample increases based on the square root of the sample, which means if you reduce a sample from 100 to 25 you increase the variance in the data (the spread of the data) two times. Reducing a sample from 100 to 25 decreased the sample by a quarter and the square root of .25 is .5 and $1/.5 = 2$. You have *doubled* the amount of error in your sample, now think about a week's worth of data by crime type in a typical city. Most likely there will not be anywhere near 25 incidents of any type of crime which means the sample is not even closely representative of the population. The population in this case is not referring to the number of people living in the city, it is referring to the total number of events of the phenomenon you are observing. For example, if you are looking at a week's worth of data for robberies and there were only three robberies, then

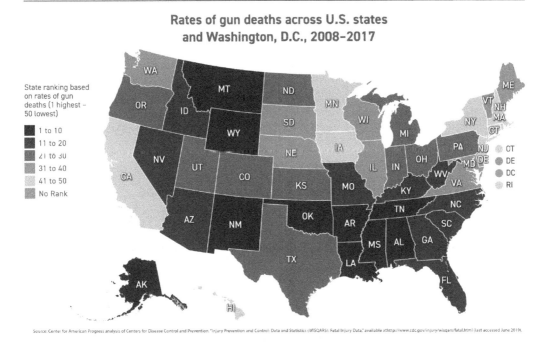

Figure 10.3 Center for American Progress Map of Gun Deaths Across the U.S. Based on Rates

that is the observed sample, but the population is *all* the robberies in the city. Therefore, I would argue that although CompStat was a good step toward making police accountable in the 1990s, it is a dangerous model for police policy today. We understand and know more about our data and statistics today than we knew then. Using small data sets requires a police department to take a small sample of data and extrapolate the results to the greater population. When you interpret small bits of data, you are increasing your chances of observing extreme variations in your data, which may lead to over-policing in areas that already have contentious relationships with their police.

Remember Guilfoyle's study in Mental Model #5—Binary Percent Changes that showed police officers will take binary comparisons, week 1 to week 2 changes, and interpret these changes as meaningful, yet they are only seeing what statisticians call a partially ordered set (a small data set of a larger one). A partially ordered set will contain more errors because it is a smaller set than you see with a larger set, as first observed by Galileo. Smaller sets contain more noise (random variation) because smaller data sets carry more variability than large data sets. De Moivre's equation demonstrates how the sample size is a direct ratio of the variance. The more variance in the data, the more likely your predictions or assumptions based on the data will be flawed. The less data you have, the worse off your predictions will be. The more data you have, the better your predictions will be, and this is due in part to the Law of large numbers, our next Mental Model.

Law of Large Numbers

> I groan when people infer their understanding of policing from the outlier incidents on television. That's like claiming a paint swatch represents the Sistine Chapel.
>
> Dr. Jerry Ratcliffe

CompStat, as we have discussed before, is a management meeting that generally tracks crime by crime type on a weekly, bi-monthly, or monthly basis. CompStat and similar management-type meetings have become a weekly process where executive commanders are expected to make decisions based on the weekly crime data that analysts generate. The expectation is to do "something" if crime is trending up. It was as recent as June 2020 in which Chief (Ret.) Bill Bratton expounded on the virtues of CompStat in an Op-ed in the *New York Times* crediting broken windows and CompStat for achieving a 46.1 percent crime decline in New York between 1990 to 1996 and a 12.5 percent drop in Los Angeles from 2002 to 2006. However, there was and still is much controversy about the crime decline in New York. As many scholars contend that crime was declining throughout the United States and as there are that argue the crime decline in New York was unparalleled. While crime was declining across the country, trauma centers were opening and medical care for violent crime victims was improving. The result was a reduction in the number of homicides. That said, CompStat was a timely innovation that policing needed. In the 1990s police leaders were not held accountable for the crime that was occurring in their districts, bureaus, or beats. CompStat created a paradigm shift in policing that introduced the idea of accountability measures for command staff and that alone was pioneering.

The CompStat format is set up to report weekly crime statistics, differentiating crime between persons and property. From these two categories crime is then broken down into specific crime types, such as Part I crimes—homicide, felony assault, rape, robbery, burglary, vehicle burglary and arson. The example in Figure 11.1 demonstrates how the Austin Police Department displayed their data for their CompStat meetings in 2018 before being trained in evidence-based practices.

APD would compare their current month to date (MTD) data to the same month the previous year (MTD LY) and then generate a percent change to determine if they should be concerned about the level of crime. Agencies that use weekly data will compare the current week to the previous week and/or the current week with the same week the year before. This is the type of reporting we discussed in Mental Model # 5—Binary Percent Changes: comparing pre/post data, or data comparing a specific period of time to another period of time, and determining the percent change in crime. We also discussed how percent changes

DOI: 10.4324/9780367481520-12

Figure 11.1 Austin Police Department CompStat Report for Violent Crime

are influenced by the denominator which makes comparing increasing and decreasing per-cent changes deceiving. Yet his is how the data is depicted at most management meetings.

CompStat-type reporting creates a decision-making environment where decisions will be based on data with too few observations (under 30 will not achieve a normal distri-bution) to truly understand whether crime is actually increasing (special cause) or if the data are just depicting natural fluctuations (common cause) in crime. Kahneman describes this action as attaching a causal interpretation to the inevitable fluctuations of a random process. Humans have a driving need to understand the world, so we attach causality to everything (the "Most Dangerous Equation"). Therefore, we create myths and beliefs so we feel like we can understand and control our environment. Analogous to the flight instructors depicted in Mental Model #3—Cognitive Biases, reallocating police resources based on fluctuations in data parallels the rationale of yelling at pilots after they make an error. Although police presence is increased in an area with an observed crime spike, the resulting drop in crime is not necessarily because of the police presence. Even though one event came after another it does not mean they are causally related and expecting as much is a flawed approach for creating an effective intervention. Mental Model #11—The Law of Large Numbers adds to the explanation about why small bands of data such as weekly or monthly data sets should not be used to make decisions about where to allocate police resources.

The Law of Large Numbers states that as data accumulate, the mean number becomes closer and closer to depicting the mean for the actual population. If you think about it for a moment it makes sense. Consider the bodyweight of everyone in your academy class. If you took the average weight of only your academy mates, how far off the national average would it be? Now take the average of your police department, now your city department, now the city, now the state—as you add data the sample mean weight will come closer and closer to the population mean. This phenomenon is true of all data sets and CompStat data is not immune. Weekly crime numbers are so small in most police agencies that the sample does not accurately reflect the population, yet police executive make resource allocation decisions based on these numbers.

Offense Category	MTD	MTD LM	MTD LY	MTD % Var	YTD	YTD LY	YTD % Var	CR YTD	CR YTD %
HOMICIDE	5	3	2	150%	19	17	12%	17	89%
RAPE	40	50	60	–33%	294	409	–28%	99	34%
BANK ROBBERY	2	3	1	100%	11	19	–42%	10	91%
BUSINESS ROBBERY	14	19	12	17%	131	142	–8%	74	56%
INDIVIDUAL ROBBERY	81	63	40	103%	428	404	6%	118	28%
AGG ASSAULT No FV	100	100	95	5%	654	603	8%	205	31%
AGG ASSAULT FV	112	82	115	–3%	619	707	–12%	382	62%
Total	354	320	325	9%	2,156	2,301	–6%	905	42%

In *Thinking, Fast and Slow*, Kahneman explains that small data sets are misleading as "extreme outcomes (both high and low) are more likely to be found in small than in large samples." This is what makes de Moivre's equation the "most dangerous." Kahneman uses education as an example. Bill Gates funded the small school's movement discussed in Mental Model #10—Distributions when he saw data showing that on average schools with small classroom sizes often had the best grades. If Bill Gates would have looked at the other end of the data distribution, he would have seen opposite, yet equally compelling results. Small schools, like small state populations, often have the worst results—for the same reason that small schools and states have the best results—small samples are influenced by a few outliers which means you will observe them on both ends of the success spectrum. By examining crime in small data sets, police are making decisions based on statistical artifacts, "observations that are produced entirely by some aspect of the method of research." Policing creates its own artifacts in the data because the data sets are so small, they contain randomness, variance, or outliers—whatever you want to call it.

Small data sets can lead to observing radical variation in the data. It can lead to misinterpreting noise (artifacts or random fluctuations) as the signal (the special cause). Expanding the scope of the data, either temporally or by crime type, should lead to less variation in the data and create a truer reflection of what is occurring with crime in the city. This theory is what two curious Australian police analysts decided to test. They wanted to know whether the Law of large numbers reflected itself in better predictive ability for hot spots policing. Hot spots policing is an evidence-based policing strategy that can be a relatively simple policing approach to crime prevention. Crime analysts can determine where crime concentrates in small areas of the city and then police executives can assign officers to patrol the area—simple. This strategy is also extremely complex in that there are multiple tactics the officers can apply once they arrive in the hot spots and there are multiple ways to identify hot spots. Tim Mashford and Scott Davidson, police analysts at the Australian Victoria Police, decided to evaluate the latter issue and conducted a study to evaluate the predictive capacity of different sized data sets for a hot spots policing scheme. Using the assumption that most crime analysts use kernel density estimation (KDE) mapping to locate hot spots, Mashford and Davidson examined both the duration of the data set (varying the number of weeks) and the different parameters the analysts were setting for the KDE (Grid cell size, Bandwidth, Kernel function, and Thematic ranges). Grid cell size is the size of the area the analyst is examining; Bandwidth is the search radius size; Kernel Function is how the points are weighted based on distance; Thematic Ranges is how the output looks; and Input data ranges are the time periods the data sets cover. Mashford and Davidson wanted to examine both the amount of data within different durations and bandwidths that would lead to the best prediction.

Using one section of Victoria, six response zones, and one crime type (vehicle burglary), they ran almost 7500 tests from their 2018 data. They tested multiple bandwidths (150 m, 300 m, 500, and 1000 m), multiple time inputs (2, 4, 12, 26, 39, and 52 weeks) and all the combinations therein—4 bandwidths × 6 time inputs × 6 Response Zones × 52 weeks = 7,488 tests. By varying the data set sizes Mashford and Davidson laid the foundation for understanding how large a data set police agencies should require when making resource decisions. And of course, what Mashford and Davidson found is as the data set got larger and larger, the predictive ability of the set got better and better. As you can see in Figure 11.2, the predictive ability of the data takes a massive leap when moving from 4 to 12 weeks, then another leap from 12 to 26 weeks, then only gets slightly better moving from 39 to 52 weeks of data. Looking at these results, it seems the minimum amount of data that should be used to make resource decisions is 3 months, but that the optimal time is 6 or 12 months.

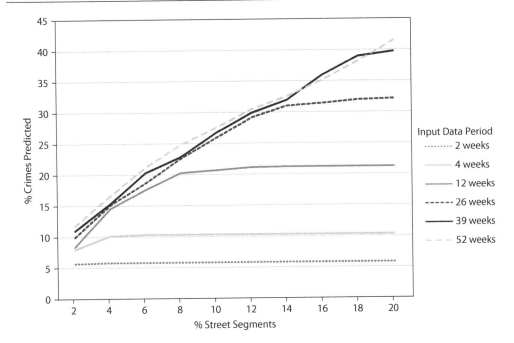

Figure 11.2 Percentage of Crimes Predicted by Area, for Varying Time Input Periods (150 m Bandwidth)

This graph and Weisburd's Seattle study supports examining three years, one year, and three months of data to determine where the problems in a city are located. I typically examine three years of data. This way, if there is one extremely high year or extremely low year, the other year averages out the data. Whether you look at one year or three years, most often crime concentration in a city does not change unless long-term problem-solving has been applied to the area. I encourage crime analysts to generate the one-year and the three-month maps to determine if anything emerged in the last three months that has not been an issue over the last several years. This way police executives can catch any developing issues as they arise.

The best way to evaluate data is to use a year-to-date full annual data set and compare it to a year-to-date prior annual data set. Once the upper control limits and lower control limits are added to the graph, you have got yourself a robust analytical tool, almost as good as Petitti's Statistical Process Control charts. Dr. Jerry Ratcliffe describes this rolling annual data set in his blog, "Year to date comparisons and why we should stop doing them" (www.jratcliffe.net/post/year-to-date-comparisons-and-why-we-should-stop-doing-them). For example, if you want to compare data, then starting in January of 2020 examine data from January 2019 to December 2019 and compare it to January 2018 to December 2018. Then in February of 2020, the month rolls and now examine data from February 2019 to January 2020 and compare it to the previous annual data of February of 2018 to January of 2019. Examine the data from the current annual year and compare it to the previous annual year. As the weeks or months move, so does the data; it is a rolling annual comparison that adds the new month or week to the data set. If you want to read another view as to why year-to-date data should not be compared to year-to-date the previous year, I suggest visiting Ratcliffe's website and reading his blog.

Mashford and Davidson also found that as the data set covered a larger time period, the size of the grid (the area under examination) they needed to predict crime got inversely smaller. This is important as police often react to crime spikes with saturation patrols which

Table 11.1 Victoria Police Optimised Bandwidths
for Varying Time Input Periods

Time input period	Optimised bandwidth
2 weeks	500 m
4 weeks	500 m
12 weeks	300 m
26 weeks	150 m
39 weeks	150 m
52 weeks	150 m

can diminish police/citizen relationships. By analyzing a larger data set, Victoria Police were better able to define their hot spots as you can see in Table 11.1.

Having at least 26 weeks of data as a minimum will achieve the smallest bandwidth possible. Most police departments have access to all their historical data so there is no reason not to examine data over a one-year time period.

The Mental Models we have reviewed thus far offer evidence that some of the data practices police agencies traditionally engage in can lead to System 1 thinking and create biased approaches to resource allocation. Mental Model #11—The Law of Large Numbers was added to provide an understanding of the type of data sets police should be using to support their thinking. Kahneman's book *Thinking, Fast and Slow* devotes a whole chapter to the cognitive bias of small numbers, where he states: "System 1 is highly adept in one form of thinking—it automatically and effortlessly identifies causal connections between events, sometimes even when the connection is spurious." When we use small numbers like weekly or monthly data sets, we are more likely to engage our cognitive biases, see causality when there is none, and make serious errors. The Law of large numbers indicates if we use large data sets, we should be able to make decisions based on the signal (special cause) rather than the noise (common cause).

Regression to the Mean

Excellence doesn't persist; time passes, and mediocrity asserts itself.

Jordan Ellenberg

When a variable is affected by both stable and chance factors, the data end up vacillating around a mean. This fluctuation is known as regression to the mean. Regression to the mean was first discovered by Sir Francis Galton. In the *Lady Tasting Tea*, David Salsburg, describes how Galton's discovery evolved from comparing the heights of men and their sons. When a taller-than-average man had a son, the son was on average shorter than the father. When a shorter-than-average man had a son, the son was on average taller than the father. When averaging data across a population, the height of men would always regress back down toward the average of the population. This phenomenon is true for many things, such as crime and baseball. When crime moves beyond its typical average, eventually it will regress back down toward the mean without any outside influence. Said in another way, when an event occurs outside of an average, the following event that occurs is most commonly closer to the average. This means that when you have the best sports game performance of your life, the game will be followed by a mediocre or slightly above-average game the next time you play. So, relish the current moment, but be sure not to talk smack to the opposing team, because the next time you play, you most likely will not perform to the same level.

Understanding regression to the mean requires an understanding of Mental Model #11— Law of Large Numbers. Small samples possess greater variation than large samples, and large samples dilute the average, so they have less variation. As a sample size increases, the additional data subsequentially bring the overall average closer and closer to the mean of the population. In *How Not to be Wrong*, Jordan Ellenberg describes it this way: "That's how the Law of Large Numbers works: not by balancing out what's already happened, but by diluting what's already happened with new data, until the past is so proportionally negligible that is can safely be forgotten." It's not so much that the large numbers are creating balance, but that the increasing sample size is diluting out the intrinsic variation from a small sample. Examining crime in small slices using weekly or monthly data sets and based on single crime types is like a repetitive exercise in examining small variations in the data as though they were representative of the population. Making decisions based on fluctuations that are most likely due to chance is the reason most police agencies feel as though their time is consumed by chasing data rather than focusing on in-depth problem-solving. Again, there are numerous examples of this issue. Baseball only recently (through

DOI: 10.4324/9780367481520-13

the driving force of the Oakland A's Billy Beane) began to use statistics, rather than their agent's intuition, to drive decision-making. Before then, agents believed in "hot hands," the Cy Young Jinx, and the *Sports Illustrated* effect and some still do.

Baseball statistics, like crime, are influenced by both stable and chance factors. Stable factors include physical prowess, talent, and time spent practicing. Chance factors include the weather, the ability and readiness of the other team, and sometimes interference by fans (see the Steve Bartman Incident). "Hot hands" refer to players, coaches, and fans, believing a succession of sunk shots in basketball means that the player is "hot," which causes the team to respond by throwing the "hot" player the ball more, and then the defense responds to that change by doubling up more aggressively on the "hot" player. Tversky, Gilovich, and Vallone examined scoring patterns of basketball players, and demonstrated there is no such thing as a hot hand. This study, which involved analyzing thousands of sequences of shots, demonstrated that people perceive patterns in randomness. They showed that when people are given a small amount of data (here, a series of sunk baskets), they attribute causality to observed patterns. Slicing crime data into small data sets by week and crime type can lead to this same sort of problem. A small slice of data can lead police to attribute causality. Even though it may be just random variation in the data, if the mind can create a pattern, it will. Using small amounts of data to evaluate baseball players led to one of the media's first observations of Regression to the mean.

Superstitions in sports are often created out of watching players regressing to their natural average abilities. One of the best examples of this was the conventional wisdom developed around the Cy Young Award winners. The Cy Young Award was given to pitchers that journalists deemed the best pitchers of the season. During the 1980s when a succession of Cy Young winners—Steve Stone, Pete Vuckovich, LaMarr Hoyt, Orel Hershiser, Frank Viola, and Guillermo Hernandez—all had horrible follow-up years, it became the common belief among baseball aficionados that the award caused laziness, disillusionment, or some other personal fault of the player that caused them to perform poorly the year after receiving the prize. Toronto Blue Jays radio broadcaster Jerry Howarth called the Cy Young Award the "kiss of death" in his 1986 book, *Baseball Lite*, and so began the belief that the award *caused* the poor performance.

More recently, regression to the mean has been referred to as the *Sports Illustrated* effect. When *Sports Illustrated* features an athlete on their cover, inevitably the next year that player, who was having a great year, tends to follow up with a lackluster performance. *Sports Illustrated* even published an article in their January 21, 2002 issue titled, "The cover no one would pose for: Is the SI Jinx Real?" It is not a jinx. When an event occurs outside of its average (for instance, a really good performance from an athlete over a year), it is usually followed by an event that occurs closer to the average (a lackluster performance over the next year). Think of it this way, any level of play that is an outlier, whether really bad or really good, will be followed by a performance that is closer to a player's normal level of ability. This is just regression to the mean at its finest, rather than the player resting on their laurels or letting fame go to their heads (although, under exceptional circumstances, this might be the case).

Additionally, this issue is supplemented by a form of cognitive bias in which individuals only seem to remember the examples that support their arguments. Sports writers, scientists, and even Wikipedia portray counter examples of individuals who were on the cover of *Sports Illustrated* who had success in the years thereafter—Michael Jordan, Muhammad Ali, Vince Young, and Emmet Smith to name a few. Attributing cause to fluctuations is a typical human reaction. As you have seen in Mental Model #11—Law of Large Numbers and now Mental Model #12—Regression to the Mean demonstrate that we should be cautious in attributing causation to small sets of data and should not be shifting resources in response to any analysis of small datasets.

In most policing organizations, departments tend to react to crime spikes by sending extra police patrols to the areas where the spike occurred, without considering that the crime will most likely naturally regress to the mean. This traditional way of examining crime (through percent changes, binary comparisons, managing by crisis) is flawed, as it leads to resource allocation and policy decisions that result in treading water. Throwing police patrols at a crime "spike" when it may subside on its own is a waste of money, time, effort, and resources. Moreover, it could lead to increasing the community's perception of crime or lead to the deterioration of community relationships if people see the saturation of police patrols as an "occupation." It leads to treading water because those resources could focus on long-term chronic problems, rather than short-term fluctuations.

If we think of police resources as a cost due to the time and effort expended, then allocating directed patrol or assigning a specialized unit to the spike creates a cost. The cost is the number of officers assigned multiplied by how many hours they are assigned to it. If a team of four officers are assigned to the problem for 25 percent of their time for four weeks, that is time they could have spent solving chronic problems in the area or developing community relationships. Remember in MM#6—Second Order Thinking when we discussed if you are moving resources in response to weekly crime data, ask yourself if the problem you are observing in the moment is going to be a problem 10 minutes from now, 10 weeks from now, or 10 months from now? If you are allocating resources to a problem that will no longer exist in ten weeks, then you are wasting resources. There are a few caveats to this suggestion. If you have a band of bad men running through your city committing robberies, burglaries, or other mayhem, then yes, of course you would allocate resources to that problem. A trend or a series is a different type of crime problem. This is not just a spike in crime, but a type of crime you can attribute to a set of specific people. I am talking about crime spikes that are occurring for no apparent reasons other than random fluctuations in data. The only way to discover a random fluctuation is is to figure out what the mean of your data is over a course of time.

Additionally, think about the type of harm you are potentially inflicting on your community by responding to random fluctuations in the crime data. If you respond with a typical saturation patrol or any type of over-policing, you may be setting your agency up for long-term failure through the deterioration of police–community relationships. In fact, police protests and defunding calls during 2020 may have been a result of these deteriorating relationships. We know we need to police high-crime areas, but what is less clear is how to do it in a way that reduces crime without damaging community relationships. In a review of 30 studies Braga, Welsh, and Schnell found that policing social disorder had a moderate effect on reducing crime. When examining moderating factors, community and problem-solving approaches had stronger effects related to the crime reductions than aggressive order maintenance-type strategies. An aggressive order maintenance approach does not appear to be as successful as policing approaches that improve social and physical conditions in a place. Improving a place can improve neighborhood and community relationships. Focusing on individuals can weaken police-citizen relations and may not obtain the crime reductions you are trying to obtain. As suggested in "Race, Place, and Effective Policing," focusing on high-risk places, and high-risk people coupled with a strong commitment to community partnership may be one of the best police strategies for simultaneously reducing crime and improving legitimacy.

As previously mentioned, I recommend mapping crime by street segment to look at the difference in a city's crime at three months, one year, and three years. Police resources should be allocated, and long-term problem-solving should occur, in the areas that have not changed and remain chronic problem spaces. Do not chase the regression down to the mean. Do not follow a crime spike with an intervention. Establish a "normal" level of crime, or average across crime categories and geographic sections of your city, and build in upper and lower control limits and an index that alerts you when crime deviates from the norm.

Creating upper and lower control limits around the average crime can assist police managers in ascertaining when crime is approaching levels where intervention is necessary. Nick Petitti the Director of Business Intelligence of the Rochester, New York Police Department, has created what he calls a cone of normal, upper and lower control limits around the projected crime average. This cone of normal sets parameters for the normal statistical fluctuations that occur in Rochester. The cone of normal flags the data when something abnormal may be occurring to notify command staff that police response may be required. Petitti describes this as moving away from using year-to-year comparison statistics and using a business model of "process control." The goal for Rochester command staff is to compare current crime counts against a benchmark of "normal", rather than the benchmark of the previous year (which may have been very high or very low compared to past years). Understanding your city's averages across crime types and geography can help agencies allocate resources better. Creating a cone of normal can move your police agency away from the traditional model of responding to random fluctuations (i.e., noise) in the data and toward understanding when the data is giving a signal (i.e., a special cause) requiring a response. Figure 12.1 is a graph of citywide assault predicting the number of assaults for the year based on the upper and lower control limits that Petitti created for his police management meetings.

As described by Petitti, the shaded region depicts the statistically expected cumulative range for the year, based on the application of Poisson processes to the year-end center estimate and weekly proportions. Said another way, Petitti is using an advanced statistical method—the Poisson process to predict what number of assaults are the "normal" level of crime based on the weekly averages entered into the model. An easier method would be to

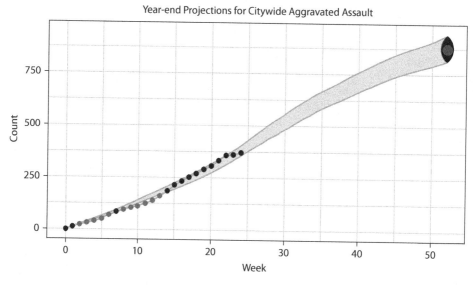

Figure 12.1 Year-end Projections for Rochester PD Depicting the "Cone of Normal"

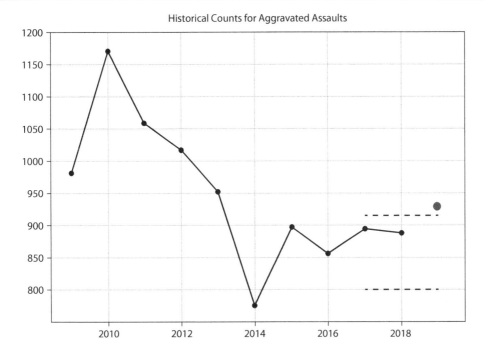

Figure 12.2 Petitti's SPC Chart Depicting Hypothetical Annual Aggravated Assault Totals

use an SPC chart similar to the one shown in Mental Model #5—Binary percent changes. Figure 12.2 displays the same example.

The figure shows hypothetical aggravated assault year-end crime numbers. Using these numbers, you could create upper and lower control limits using one standard deviation from the mean as the limit. Petitti uses two standard deviations as his upper and lower control limits. Which, statistically speaking, is moving executives closer to only shifting resources when crime increases are headed into the less than 5 percent likelihood of occurring. Petitti has asked his police executives not to change their policing strategy until crime has started moving near or past the "cone of normal." This allows his police executives to allocate resources in an effective and efficient way, and to free up time for officers to work on chronic community issues. Understanding regression to the mean therefore frees police executives and city leaders from the current reactive approach to policing that requires police executives to do "something" when observing a weekly crime spike. Using 26 to 52 weeks of data mapped by street segment and using SPC charts as recommended by Simon Guilfoyle and Nick Petitti should help police executives to interpret data more clearly to understand when to do "something" and when to do "nothing."

The Mental Models in Practice IV—Mental Models 10–12

Distributions, Law of Large Numbers, and Regression to the Mean

This section of the Mental Models book grouped together mathematical concepts that build on one another. If you think about the three Mental Models, they are different parts of the same concept. Mental Model #10—Distributions reflects Mental Model #11—Law of Large Numbers—as the sample size gets larger and larger, the distribution more accurately reflects the population, as the sample size gets larger, the distribution is diluted so that the mean (the top of the bell curve) more accurately depicts the mean of the population. When you have a small sample (typically below 30) your distribution will not be a normal distribution, your data will contain a lot of variation, and, if you have a datum that is extremely large or small, the next data point will most likely be closer to the mean. All these Mental Models should guide you to examine larger data sets, find a mean, set upper and lower control limits, and approach sudden resource shifts cautiously. This section advises on applying Mental Models 10-12 in an identical manner as Mental Models 4–6. Here is how to apply Mental Models 10-12:

1 Stop using binary percent change data.
2 Stop using small data sets.
3 Use at least 26 to 52 weeks of data if you are going to compare current time periods to previous time periods.
4 Create Statistical Process Control Charts—compute the average of crime using at least three years of data.

    a Create an upper control limit and a lower control limit using a standard deviation. Nick Petitti in his departmental blog uses two standard deviations which means that you will only be responding to rare crime spikes. I would suggest looking at crime when it increases above one standard deviation. One standard deviation will keep you from reacting when crime is 18.26 percent above or below the average. I think it if is moving toward the high teens it is time to start thinking about intervening tactically.

5 Create Statistical Process Control Charts using the method above for calls for service and for specific crime types.

Part V

How to Determine Causality

Correlation is Not Causation

> Facts are the fundamental building blocks of science but bringing those facts together to have an insight of a certain phenomenon requires a rational, conscientious and creative mind. It's only through rigorous analysis and observation, as well as, creative contemplation, of the empirical evidence, i.e. facts, discovered through decades of research, that we can understand a certain phenomenon.
>
> Abhijit Naskar

Observing a police management meeting is a lesson in understanding how policing developed the bad habit of associating correlation with causation. Most people have heard the statement correlation is not causation by the time they have finished college, the military, or entered adulthood as most have just learned it through word of mouth. This statement is frequently repeated but is often ignored when making decisions. Policing makes this same mistake. Police managers receive weekly data from crime analysts broken down into crime type. During a management meeting, executive managers are required to know what is going on in their areas and then expected to "do something" about it. "Doing something" usually means assigning police resources to the issue and the most common response will be to reallocate some type of patrol resource, whether it be a dedicated patrol through overtime or a directive for extra patrol during a shift. The intervention is regarded as successful if the crime or call for service numbers go down, assuming anyone follows up on the results (often no one follows up at all if the issue at hand subsides). As one commander explained to me, if I see crime going up, I assign officers to the area and then it goes down. The mistake, as you already learned from Mental Models 10, 11, and 12, is assuming a causal link. A caused B: because police officers went to the area (A), crime went down (B). Fluctuation in data is normal. Inserting an intervention in the middle of a random fluctuation (common cause) does not mean the intervention caused the change. This is what is meant when people say that correlation is not causation. Although the timing of the intervention correlates to the reduction in crime, crime is not a linear phenomenon (it will not continue to increase forever). In turn, this means that one cannot be sure the intervention *caused* the crime reduction.

By this point in the book you should understand how randomness affects data and why larger data sets help smooth out this fluctuation. You should understand that cognitive biases will lead you to see patterns in data when there are none and the appearance of successful interventions are often nothing more than regression to the mean. The previous Mental Models laid the foundation for understanding and interpreting data. This Mental Model transitions into understanding causation. Understanding causation will enable you to make

DOI: 10.4324/9780367481520-14

more accurate determinations about what works or what does not when evaluating data and policing programs.

Peter M. Nardi said, "Correlation is a statistical concept that mathematically measures the strength of a relationship between at least two variables." Think about this in the context of policing, most police officers from the rank of officer to the chief want to know if their activity, whether it be traffic stops, pedestrian stops, or searches, are effective at reducing crime and calls for service. To make this simple, the two variables that can be measured easily with administrative data are police proactivity (no matter the type if it is officer initiated) and crime (all crime, not just Part I). If this was a correlational question, then we would ask: how strong is the relationship between increased officer proactivity and crime reductions in a particular area (choosing a geographic area makes this question easier)? In this case, we want a negative correlational relationship. Correlations can have a positive or negative relationship. A negative relationship between two variables means that as one variable goes up, the other variable goes down—for example, as your workout time increases, your body fat composition goes down. A positive correlation means that when one variable increases, so does the other. For instance, crime increases in the summer. This is an example of a positive correlational relationship. As the days get longer and warmer, most police departments see an increase in crime. In the police proactivity example, we *want* a negative relationship between police proactivity and crime, not unlike the workout example. As the officer proactivity increases, crime decreases.

The strength of the correlation between two variables can be determined through linear regression. Linear regression is simply modeling a relationship between two variables on an x/y axis and then drawing a line through the data points that closely fit to most of the points. See Figure 13.1 to observe data points plotted on a graph and Figure 13.2 with the line of best fit running through these points.

You can see how the line running through the data points is trying to create the straightest possible line through all the data—that is the regression line. The correlation coefficient (think high school algebra) designates how strong the relationship is. The formula is $y = mx + b$ where m is the slope of the line or the correlation coefficient and b equals the intercept of the line. If you think back (way back) to algebra, m is just rise over run of the regression line you see in Figure 13.2. If the correlation is an exact correlation (a one for one correlation) then the rise is one unit and the run will be one unit and the correlation

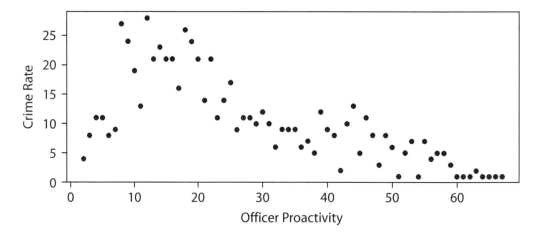

Figure 13.1 Police Officer Proactivity and Crime Rates

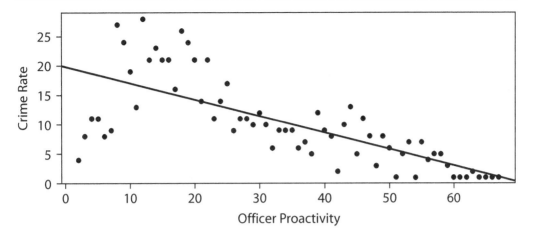

Figure 13.2 Police Officer Proactivity and Crime Rates Depicting a Negative Regression Line

coefficient will be one. Using our officer proactivity example, if the correlation was −1 then for every proactive behavior an officer engaged in, we would see a reduction in crime by one crime.

Correlations can only range from −1 to 1. The strongest correlational relationship you can have is a −1 when it is a negative relationship or a +1 when the relationship is positive. The closer the correlation coefficient is to zero, the weaker the relationship. If the correlation coefficient is 1, then for every instance of officer proactivity, you would observe a subsequent reduction of one crime. This, as we know, is rarely the case in policing. The correlation between most variables in policing and crime will be less than one. What we would like to observe in a policing intervention is a strong negative correlational relationship between officer proactivity and crime, which would be anything above a −.6. The strength of the relationship is segmented into small, medium, and large effects. A small effect is .2 to .4. A medium effect is .5 to .6 and a strong effect is anything above .6. Obtaining an effect size of .2 is typical of most policing experiments due to small sample sizes which makes large effect sizes hard to obtain.

Effect sizes can be calculated for both correlational strength and causal strength. The difference between the two depends on the type of study design and the analysis. Effect sizes can be calculated using a Pearson's correlation coefficient, a linear or multivariate regression model or a student's *t* test. Often a Pearson's correlation coefficient test is performed first to determine if there is a relationship between two variables, to determine the strength and direction of the relationship. If a strong correlation is observed, then a linear regression is performed to determine if there is enough of a relationship that one variable can predict another. To make sure this is clear, the Pearson correlation coefficient tells you there is a relationship between two variables but it does not tell you the direction of the relationship which means you cannot predict which variable is effecting the other. When you are using a multivariate regression model you are examining the relationships between the variables to determine if one variable *predicts* the other. Prediction determines a causal link. As in the case with police officer activity, we want to know how strong the relationship is between officer proactivity and crime, and then we want to determine if the relationship is strong enough that we can determine whether officer proactivity will predict a reduction in crime.

Hot spots policing as a proactive police strategy is one of the most researched patrol interventions in policing and it only has an overall effect size of .132. This finding comes from a 2019 meta-analysis conducted by Braga and colleagues in which they reviewed 65 studies with 78 tests, but small effect sizes in policing can produce large outcomes. The Sacramento Hot Spots study I mentioned previously that I conducted in 2011 achieved a statistically significant reduction in Part I crime and calls for service while only having a small effect size.

The study was a simple one. We randomly assigned 21 high crime and call for service hot spots to receive 15 minutes of high visibility policing—treatment (car parked in a visible spot with overheads turned on) and 21 hot spots received the standard patrol model of policing—control. The study was run for 90 days and the officers averaged about four visits a day. At the end of the study we found a 25 percent reduction in Part I crimes and a 7.7 percent reduction in calls for service when comparing 2011 to the same time period in 2010 in the treatment hot spots versus the control hot spots. The raw difference was a reduction of 35 Part I crimes and 75 calls for service in 2011 compared to the same period in 2010 in the treatment versus control condition. That is a reduction of approximately ten Part I crimes a month and 25 calls for service a month, for an hour a day of preventative work. Additionally, I found a small negative effect in the relationship between officer's street checks (proactivity) and Part I crimes $r = -.206$ which was statistically significant at the $p < .01$ level, and a small negative effect in the relationship between officers issuing traffic citations (proactivity) and Part I crimes $r = -.281$ and at the $p < .05$ level. The relationships were not statistically significant for calls for service. This means there was a small gain between some of the enforcement activity and Part I crime reductions, but I could not tell with any surety that the call for service reductions had a correlational link to the specific officer proactivity. Unlike medicine, where a small effect size might demonstrate low efficacy of a treatment for improving an individual's outcome, in policing a small effect, if the correlation is in the correct direction, prevents multiple victims from suffering. Therefore, understanding the difference between correlation and causation is vitally important.

Correlation seems like a simple Mental Model, but it is deceiving. If we have learned anything in the last 30 years, it is that humans are not good at innately understanding statistical data to make decisions. We tend to rely on heuristics and biases when interpreting data. We think we are using System 2, but we are really letting System 1 guide our thinking. Correlation is an actual mathematical formula. To determine correlation properly, an advanced statistical analysis needs to be conducted to compute the correlation coefficient. People repeat the mantra "Correlation is not causation," yet police examine weekly data as though there is a causal relationship between crime and their prevention efforts, when in actuality no one has done the minimal analysis to determine if there are correlational effects between the two variables. We tend to use data to support our beliefs, rather than using data to examine our beliefs. Even though we know "Correlation is not causation," in policing, causal statements using anecdotal or correlational data are commonly presented in management meetings. Take the following quote from a management meeting:

> The majority of marijuana grows in the North area have been in sector Xray (fictitious sector). Prior to the start of the Marijuana team, we had spikes in robberies, weapons, shootings, and assault crimes. As of the middle of this year we have seen a decrease in all those categories. The Marijuana team has had a positive impact.

This example demonstrates either an *inability* or potentially an *unwillingness* to understand how police activity affects crime. I only throw in the term "unwilling" because it is easier to make a causal statement like this than it is to take the time to think deeply about all the potential causes of crime spikes and reductions. Thinking deeply requires one to examine their theory—A causes B— the marijuana team (A) caused a reduction in four different crime types (B). Even without thinking too deeply, attributing the creation of a new team to crime drops across four crime types seems to be a fairly miraculous cure. This is where we make our mistakes in reasoning. We attribute one variable as the cause of the other and ignore the multitude of other variables that can also influence the outcome. Instead of accepting the flawed reasoning, the question should be asked: "How do you know that? How do you know that the marijuana team *caused* the crime drop?" Talking through how you are making sense of your data is an important component to understanding what crime data is telling you. Taking a step back and thinking deeply about the marijuana statement one can see that the speaker is turning a correlational statement into a causal statement. Further examination of the statement is required. Asking "How do you know that?" or "How do I know that" helps to understand whether you are making a correlational or causal statement.

One area that police executive managers do not have control over is the public's improper use of statistics on social media. Social media is another forum where policing statistics are thrown around and correlation and causation are confused. It makes it difficult for policing to allocate resources effectively and efficiently when the public can use social media as a forum to advance inaccurate information and advocate for more resources, programs, or projects. For example, Advance Peace, a gang intervention program run outside the City of Sacramento's oversight, was given credit for reducing gun homicide in Sacramento, California on Twitter in 2019. The tweet read:

> We must focus on ending the cycle of gun violence in our urban communities. South Sacramento experienced a 43 percent decrease in gun homicides compared to the 4-year average before @WeAdvancePeace was implemented. This is only the first step.

This statement has several red flags that critical thinkers should detect immediately. The first is the Advance Peace program which has been implemented throughout Sacramento, not just South Sacramento. What does the data from the North area look like? If Advance Peace was the causal link to a reduction in gun homicides, then the whole city should experience a reduction in gun homicides. The North area should be observing decreases if the program is working. Why was this data left out? Why choose to compare this year to a four-year average? Did including that fourth year get the percent drop the evaluator wanted to see? Would a three-year or five-year average not have the same results? When people post causal statements such as these, the same questions such as "How do you know that?" "How do you know that Advance Peace was the cause?" should be asked. Currently, the City of Sacramento has been experiencing a massive increase in homicides due to a gang war that is going on in the city, yet there are no tweets attributing this as a failure of Advance Peace.

Another factor in determining the difference between causal statements and correlational statements is thinking about all the variables that influence an outcome. The tweet focuses on gun homicide, yet medical care is a big factor between someone surviving a gunshot wound and dying from a gunshot wound. Were there improvements in the last four years for the medical care in the area or ambulance response times that would improve chances of survival? If the goal of the Advance Peace program is reducing gang violence, then the shootings and other violence should also be going down, not just gun homicides. Gang activity bleeds well beyond homicides. Furthermore, the Sacramento Police Department had been making efforts to reduce gang and gun violence at the same time as Advance Peace through officer proactivity, peace walks, and investigating gang cases. These variables could have also contributed to the decline in homicides. Without a counterfactual (the outcome that would have occurred had there been no intervention) there is no way to determine that the Advance Peace program is the variable that *caused* the 43 percent decrease in gun homicide in South Sacramento. Even running a multivariate regression analysis (an analysis that determines the strengths of the correlations of a variety of variables to an outcome) on the reduction of gun homicides to Advance Peace efforts is limited. The regression analysis would be incorrect without knowing all the societal variables that contribute to gun homicides.

To create an accurate regression model, the model requires all the dependent variables that influence the independent variable to determine the strength of the correlation. In the example of gun homicide, a multivariate regression analysis would be inaccurate without taking the police department efforts into consideration. Without knowing how many hours officers were engaged in proactive patrol, investigative follow-up, community engagement, or any activity that would deter gun homicide, the regression model would be flawed. Researchers would also need to consider other factors that contribute to gun homicides—the availability of guns per capita, gun laws in the state, socioeconomic demographics, literacy, and so on. Police researchers' understanding of why crime occurs and what deters crime is still limited, thus regression models in criminology will always contain error to some extent. Weisburd and Petrosino examined tests of empirical criminology that took place between 1985 and 2005 and found that criminological theory only explains about 10 to 20 percent of the major causes of the outcomes of interest. Regression analysis as a method of determining the effectiveness of crime prevention measures will be unreliable until criminological theory can explain over 50 percent of the variance. Weisburd and Petrosino elaborated:

> Regression models cannot take into account measures that are not accounted for or measured incorrectly and adjust outcomes for them. If one purpose of multivariate modeling is to inform public policies, a model that omits relevant factors will lead to inappropriate policy recommendations.

If researchers do not know or understand all the relevant factors, then regression modeling is a weak statistical method for building crime prevention methods.

The arguments presented above are the reasons why scientists say "Correlation is not causation." A strong correlation coefficient is still not causation. A comparison group that did not receive the intervention (control group) is needed to make causal links between policing interventions and crime outcomes. If you do not have a comparison group (a counterfactual) you do not know what would have occurred, had you done nothing. Regression to the mean reveals itself in the comparison group; if there is no intervention, and crime goes back down to the average then the intervention was not the cause. It can be determined if the changes were due to the intervention or merely by chance by comparing the outcomes of the intervention group to the non-intervention group and this is what Mental Model #14 explains at greater length.

Causal Inference

Testing of police practices with controlled comparisons can show what works for whom, what doesn't, and what is most cost-effective.

Dr. Lawrence Sherman

At the scene of a crime or during an interview, police take pride in knowing good evidence when they see it. Police leaders should be just as careful in collecting evidence about whether police strategies have the effects they intend and cause the results they are observing. Data naturally fluctuates. There is a signal (special cause) in data indicating what is important, and there is noise (common cause) in data that distracts attention from the signal. In policing, it is imperative to know the difference. Police want to know if crime prevention interventions have an effect on reducing crime, if they improve citizens' perceptions of the police and their perceptions of safety, and if the interventions cause harm. We want to be sure that the crime reductions we are prepared to take credit for happened because of our policing, rather than from other factors. Francis Galton demonstrated this fluctuation in data by examining human height. He discovered that whenever we study a variable that is affected by both stable factors and factors influenced by chance, the ratios in question have a tendency to wander about an average. Since crime and calls for service are variables that have both factors (stable and chance), determining whether police interventions have large enough effects to shift the numbers from the mean (up or down) requires us to compare a control group to a treatment group to rule out the "by chance" element of the data.

In Mental Model #12—Regression to the Mean, the marijuana team statement was used as an example for looking at the difference between correlational and causal statements. Without a comparison group, it is difficult for the police department to interpret the data attributed to the marijuana team. Although the captain gave a list of crime types that declined after the marijuana team had been formed, it is impossible to know whether the marijuana team alone *caused* the reduction in robberies, weapon offenses, shootings, and assaults. There are several variables that could have contributed to the crime declines. For instance, what was patrol staffing like? Were there other teams doing any proactive activity in those areas? Were the homicide or gang teams incapacitating high-rate offenders? Without knowing (and holding constant) every other variable that could have contributed to the declines, there is no way to be sure the crime reductions were not merely regression to the mean (MM#12), or that there are no other variables that contributed to the reduction of crime. A comparison group, a control group, or a counterfactual is needed.

DOI: 10.4324/9780367481520-15

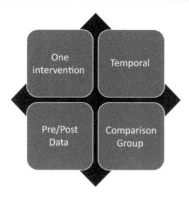

Figure 14.1 The Four Elements for a Causal Relationship

In science, when two variables change in relationship to each other, there are four requirements for deeming the relationship causal rather than correlational—there is only one intervention, the intervention occurs before the outcome (temporal requirement), there is pre/post data, and there is a comparison group—see Figure 14.1.

The first step in finding a comparison group is to find a similar area. To determine how influential the marijuana team was, the comparison area would need a comparable base rate of robberies, weapons crimes, shootings, and assaults, and marijuana grows. Then compare the X-ray average crime drop (before and after the intervention) to the comparison area, let's call it Zebra. If the average crime drop is substantially larger in the X-ray sector compared to the Zebra sector, this is now one step closer to deciding that the marijuana team caused the drops in crime. One very simple way to evaluate a treatment and control group is to use the ABC Spreadsheet from the www.reducingcrime.com website. The spreadsheet uses pre/post data from a treatment area and a control area to calculate how much better (or worse) the treatment area did on average compared to the control area.

As noted previously, it is important that a chosen comparison group has a similar baseline as the treatment group for the outcome you are evaluating. For example, if a police agency assigns a new team (like the marijuana team) to an area to deter drug crime, then the comparison area should be a similar-sized area that is experiencing comparable levels of drug crime as the treatment group. If the treatment area (A) is three square blocks and has roughly 30 drugs crimes a month, then the comparison area (B) should be approximately three square blocks in size and have 30 drug crimes a month. To get even more granular, you could examine the types of drug crimes that occur in the prospective locations. If area A is made up mostly of drug sales, and area B mostly experiences drug possession crime, then another part of the city might be a better match. Additionally, it would be beneficial if the two areas were homogeneous in other respects, such as geography, demography, and number of residences versus businesses. Two areas may have equivalent crime base rates, but other important dissimilarities may not be comparable, thus it is vital that the control group be as similar to the treatment group as possible. For example, testing an intervention in a residential area against a comparison business area may be problematic, as the types of people the areas attract differ, and the areas are differentially affected by variables such as time of day and day of week. When testing an intervention on people, the same rules apply. The chosen comparison groups should not only have similar baseline outcomes before an intervention, but they should also have an analogous population. It is important to note that field experiments are not perfect and often studies are limited by what presents itself in the location. The goal is to get the treatment and control areas as homogeneous as possible. While dissimilar baselines weaken the level of rigor of the research, experiments remain more rigorous than observing pre/post-binary percent changes.

This book in many ways has been leading up to this Mental Model. Without understanding how brains work, how they lead humans astray, and the underlying mathematics, understanding the importance of a comparison group for determining causality would be difficult. Mental Model #13—Correlation is Not Causation explained why correlational models are poor models for explaining criminological theories or predicting criminal behavior. Weisburd and Petrosino suggested in their article "How Well Do Criminologists Explain Crime" that randomized controlled experiments can provide unbiased estimates of the effects of the variable of interest. Having a comparison group keeps data from being misinterpreted as a special cause rather than a common cause. Randomizing whether a unit of analysis (person, place, or thing) is allocated to the treatment or the control group reduces researcher bias. In the next section I use Critical Incident Stress Debriefings (CISD) as an example of why comparison groups are important for understanding causality.

Many police departments use CISD as a tool to prevent Post Traumatic Stress Disorder (PTSD) among police officers who have experienced a critical incident. CISD is a psychological intervention used to assist officers in dealing with the physical or psychological outcomes associated with exposure to trauma. PTSD can be a common outcome for individuals exposed to daily trauma. Created in the 1980s by psychologist Dr. George Everly and Dr. Jeffrey Mitchell, a firefighter/paramedic to combat PTSD among officers exposed to daily trauma, CISD involves a "specific, 7-phase, small group, supportive crisis intervention process." The process is extensive and can be found at www.icisf.org. Briefly, it involves meeting with a therapist and the individuals involved in the traumatic incident and follows these seven steps:

1 Introduction: Participants introduce themselves.
2 Facts: Participants share their account of the event.
3 Thoughts: Participants share their first thought after the event.
4 Reactions: Participants share how the event impacted them emotionally.
5 Symptoms: Participants share any physical or emotional reactions they are having to the event.
6 Coping: Participants create a coping plan.
7 Follow-up: Participants are asked if they would like to talk about anything before the session ends.

In 2000 Mayou, Ehleers, and Hobbs designed a randomized controlled trial to understand the effects of a CISD on traffic accident victims' PTSD symptoms. The study tracked the victim's PTSD symptoms using the Impact of Event Scale (IES), Brief Symptom Inventory (BSI) and qualitative interviews. The IES determined how strongly the event impacted each victim. The BSI determined the number and strength of each PTSD symptom the participants were experiencing. The IES and the BSI were administered after the traffic accident, but before and two times after the debriefing intervention. Four-month and three-year post-test intervals were chosen to examine the immediate and long-term effects of CISD. Participants were grouped into high impact groups and low impact groups based on the IES results and then randomly assigned to receive psychological debriefing (treatment group) or to receive no intervention (control group).

As noted earlier, having comparable control and treatment baselines is important when examining causality in an experiment. In the above example, the IES was used to determine whether the traffic incident mildly or greatly impacted the study participants. Comparing a participant who was greatly impacted to a participant who was mildly impacted would have led to inaccurate outcomes. Importantly, the highly impacted participant may show greater improvement than the mildly impacted participant, as the mildly affected participants' gains would appear small compared to the effects for highly impacted participants. In addition to assessing victims' high versus low impacts, the researchers took into consideration eligible participants' injury levels and hospital stay lengths. As patients entered the hospital and agreed to participate in the study, they were randomly assigned to receive either no intervention (control group) or a psychological debriefing (treatment group).

It is important to recognize that psychological debriefings differ across research projects. When comparing two different research articles on a topic, it is important to determine whether various parameters of the study are the same. For instance, comparing whether the interventions are the same, whether the studies measure the same outcomes, whether the definitions of the interventions are the same, and so on? The definition in one study does not always mean the same concept in another study. In the traffic accident study, Mayou et al. described psychological debriefing as a patient receiving an hour-long psychological counseling within 24–48 hours after their traffic accident. The intervention included "reviewing what occurred during the accident, the encouragement of emotional expression, and initial cognitive appraisal of the traumatic experience." Treatment participants were provided with information about potential psychological responses to the event. The impact of the event on the patient was measured 24 hours after the event but before the intervention, four months after the intervention, and then three years post-intervention. Figure 14.2 demonstrates the effects of the intervention on the high impact group.

As you can see, the high impact patients' symptoms improved after four months and continued to improve after three years. This is what pre/post data often looks like in policing interventions in the sense that crime (i.e., outcome variable) is increasing, police intervene, and then crime declines. But remember that analyzing data in this simplistic form results in a correlational rather than a causal relationship. To imply that a psychological debriefing *caused* an improvement in PTSD symptoms, a comparison group is required. In other words, the study needs a counterfactual that demonstrates the PTSD effects for participants who did not receive intervention.

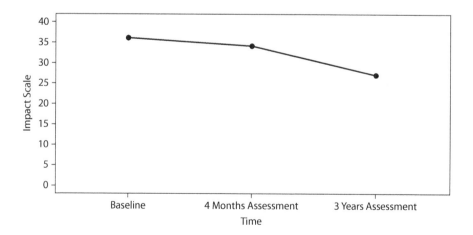

Figure 14.2 CISD Treatment Effect of High Scorers

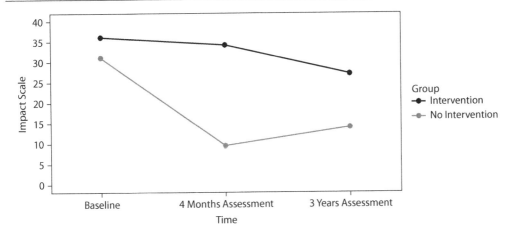

Figure 14.3 CISD Treatment Effects of Intervention and Non-intervention High Scorers

Figure 14.3 shows the outcomes for high impact patients who received no treatment (the control group), together with the treatment group. Once the outcomes of the comparison no treatment group are paired with the outcomes of the treatment group, a very different story emerges. The control group participants, who did not receive a psychological debriefing, had a large reduction in symptoms at four months compared to the treatment group. Thus, doing nothing appeared to be more effective than doing "something" (i.e., intervening). And even though the control group's PTSD symptoms increased between the four-month and three-year post-test, their scores remained significantly lower than the treatment group three years after the intervention. e.e. cummings said it best:

here is the deepest secret nobody knows

(here is the root of the root and the bud of the bud

and the sky of the sky of a tree called life; which grows

higher than soul can hope or mind can hide)

and this is the wonder that's keeping the stars apart.

the secret my dear is the **importance of a comparison group for understanding causality**.

Well maybe e.e. cummings did not actually write that last line in his famous poem, *i carry your heart with me (i carry it in)*, but if he was writing a love poem to a police pracademic, this is how it would have ended. A causal link between the intervention and the outcome cannot be attributed to the intervention unless there is an understanding of what would have happened had you done "nothing" instead of "something." In science, this is "nothing" (i.e., no intervention, no treatment). The counterfactual, or the group that received "nothing" models the regression to the mean (MM#12). It shows how the data randomly fluctuate when there is no intervention, and what the noise looks like. The light grey line in Figure 14.3 demonstrates how the PTSD symptoms of participants in the control group regressed to a normal level after a duration. Their symptoms appear to have abated naturally. They spiked immediately after the accident and lowered to normal levels (regression to the mean). This phenomenon sometimes occurs in the realm of crime and policing. By the time

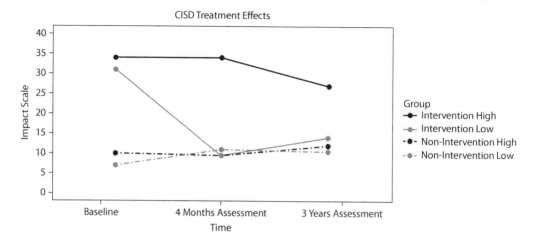

Figure 14.4 CISD Treatment Effects of Intervention and Non-intervention of High and Low Scorers

the police recognize a spike in crime and respond to it, crime may already be regressing back to its natural level. Assuming the crime reduction was *caused* by the intervention rather than regression to the mean is a common error in logic.

Proper evaluation of a program, intervention, or practice requires a comparison group to account for regression to the mean. This is done by comparing the mean of the treatment group to the mean of the control group. If the treatment group difference is large enough from the control group, it will meet a statistically significant threshold. Without a comparison group, a causal assumption is limited. Figure 14.4 shows the outcomes of the four study groups: high impact with treatment, high impact with no treatment, low impact with treatment, and low impact with no treatment.

When comparing the low impact groups to each other the psychological debriefing (i.e., treatment) group shows a greater immediate relief of symptoms in the four months after the intervention, but after three years, the control group shows a small improvement over the treatment group. Observing all four groups together demonstrates the need for equivalent comparison groups at baseline. If the high impact group had been compared to the low impact group, or the high impact with no intervention (i.e. control) group had been compared to low impact with intervention (i.e., treatment) group, it would look like the psychological debriefing was a successful intervention. Figure 14.5 demonstrates the importance of having similar comparison groups at baseline by displaying comparisons of the high impact control group and the low impact treatment group.

Comparing groups that are not similar at baseline will give misleading outcomes. The group starting at a higher level will often show the greatest improvement because that group is already primed to achieve some improvement. Not only is a comparison group needed for causality, but similar baselines are needed as well.

Mental Model #14—Causal Inference builds on the elements of Mental Models #12—Regression to the Mean and #13—Correlation is Not Causation by demonstrating the importance of both to establish causality. A comparison group is needed to account for regression to the mean. Although some scientists might argue that statistical analysis has become advanced enough to determine causality using regression modeling, criminologists do not understand all the variables that contribute to crime yet, and experimentation remains one of the few ways to establish causal links between police activity and crime.

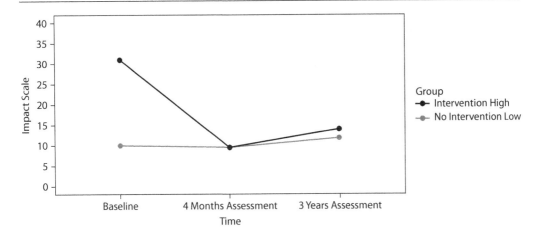

Figure 14.5 CISD Treatment Effects of Intervention Low Scorers and Non-intervention High Scorers

CompStat was an innovative management tool in the 1990s, but now that we understand policing and crime much better than we did before we can use this knowledge to more effectively and efficiently deploy resources. We know, for instance, that crime is stable across people, places, and property. We know that small data sets have greater variance than large data sets. We know that there is no such thing as a "hot hand." We know there is regression to the mean and that without an adequate comparison group, constantly chasing data spikes to rapidly deploy personnel and resources will be an ineffective use of taxpayers' monies. Mental Model #15 begins with discussing new ways of thinking about collecting, analyzing, and depicting data to ensure that police executives are spending their time, efforts, and energy effectively, and are ultimately achieving departmental goals.

Bayesian (Probabilistic) Reasoning

> Bayes is all about probabilities and how these are dynamically moving just as life is around you. It helps you think rationally about the best things to do; it doesn't promise "facts" or everlasting solutions, simply because in an everchanging world with highly diverse contexts it can be misleading to search for "static and universal truths."
>
> Dr. Ken Pease

For police leaders looking to advance 21st Century Policing, the theories of Thomas Bayes have a promising future for the policing profession. Business has embraced his Mental Model for many years and advances in machine and artificial learning have integrated them into the mainstream. New challenges in moving from traditional, reactive law enforcement strategies toward focused, tailored, proactive problem-solving are providing an ideal opportunity to integrate proven structures for the way the policing profession balances demands and problems. From the Age of Reason, also known as The Enlightenment (17th and 18th centuries) came many of the modern intellectual and philosophical movements that inspired these Mental Models and statistical theorems. This thread of thought connects Descartes' "I think therefore I am," to Newton's *Principa Mathematica*, David Hume, Kant, Adam Smith, and The Reverend Thomas Bayes.

Mental Model #15—Bayesian (Probabilistic) Reasoning is based on the theories of Thomas Bayes, another famous statistician (who was really a reverend) living in the 1700s. Like de Moivre, Bayes faced discrimination not for being a foreigner, but for being the wrong religion. Bayes was a Presbyterian and as such he was not allowed to attend the University of Oxford or Cambridge. He had to travel to Scotland to attend the University of Edinburgh to attain his education. He returned to England and spent his life as a minister but was fascinated by mathematical problems and dabbled with them on the side. He wrote and published only two works while he was alive: one mathematical and one theological. Yet, Bayes' most famous work was published posthumously, after a friend of his, Richard Price, found the essay and brought it to the Royal Society of London's attention. The work was titled "An Essay toward Solving a Problem in the Doctrine of Chances."

Bayes' Theorem presented in the article framed by Price, applied to situations when determining the probability of event (A) occurring was "conditional" on the previous event (B). From this paper you could mathematically determine the probability of the previous event (B) from the probability of the current event (A). This was how statisticians determined that lung cancer was linked to smoking. Researchers could not randomly assign smoking to children, but they could compare the probability of lung cancer in a group of smokers to non-smokers. They could statistically show that the probability of lung cancer was increased

DOI: 10.4324/9780367481520-16

in the population of smokers. Shifting away from probability in the form of a mathematical formula to how we think, Bayesian reasoning means to update our beliefs based on new information and by doing this we get closer and closer (although never achieving) to a 100 percent ability to predict a future event. This is different from the coin flipping problem, where the probability of obtaining a head or tail is exactly 50/50 every time, because one flip of the coin does not affect the next flip. Bayesian reasoning centers on events that have an impact on the next event occurring. If A happened, then what is the likelihood of B occurring? Or if B occurs first then what is the likelihood of A occurring? In the context of crime, for example, Bayesian reasoning sounds like this: if a house was broken into on street A, what is the likelihood of another burglary occurring on the same street at house B? This is not predictive policing, as "predictive" implies you can predict when and how something will occur. Bayesian reasoning is probabilistic reasoning, thinking about how likely something is to occur. Reviewing burglary research, a burglary committed at one home increases the likelihood of the neighboring houses being broken into over the next few weeks—this is Bayesian reasoning. It does not mean with 100 percent certainty a neighboring house will be broken into; it means that the likelihood of it occurring has increased.

Bayes' theorem is easy to compute as it uses addition, subtraction, multiplication, and division, but it is not something that we innately apply in our heads when deciding. Often, we fall back on our heuristics of how we think the world *should* work rather than evaluating the probabilities of something occurring. I attended a counter bias training class where officers were presented "shoot/don't shoot" video scenarios. One of the scenarios involved a man with a gun at the park. When the officers arrive on scene there is a man sitting at a picnic table with a gun near him. As the officer begins to engage with him, the man stands up, starts yelling about how "they made him do it," and grabs the gun. The man is upset, waving the gun around. The officers involved in the scenario at this stage typically point their weapon at the man while trying to de-escalate the situation. In the middle of the scenario a "Good Samaritan" comes out of nowhere, tackles the man, disarms him, then points the gun at and begins yelling at the man in distress. The officer now has two men, the original distressed man on the ground still yelling and screaming, and the Good Samaritan who is yelling and pointing the gun at the distressed man. The officer must decide how to react. The scenario ends with the Good Samaritan shooting the distressed man and it is at this point that most of the officer involved in the scenario shoot the Good Samaritan. Although I was observing on the course, students still asked what I would have done. I said I would not have shot the Good Samaritan either, but only because I was weighing the probability of injury versus non-injury. The class looked at me quizzically. I explained, if I shoot the Good Samaritan then there is a 100 percent probability that someone is going to be injured. If I wait and see what happens I have a 50 percent chance no one will be injured. There is a 50 percent chance the Good Samaritan pulls the trigger and a 50 percent he does not. My probability for no injuries is higher if I do not shoot. Basing decisions on probability rather than emotions is more likely to get the correct outcomes most of the time; although you must understand *how* probabilities work to recognize how to apply them in life otherwise you can have disastrous results.

One of the most famous cases of misapplied probabilities occurred during the trial of Sally Clark. Clark was a solicitor in the U.K. who had two babies who died tragically of Sudden Infant Death Syndrome (SIDS) within two years. She was subsequently arrested for murder, as no one could believe that two children could die of the same syndrome within such a short period of time. When the babies died, both were solely under her care. During the trial, the prosecution called on an expert witness, Sir Roy Meadow, a Professor of Pediatrics, to testify on the likelihood that two children within two years could die of similar causes. Meadow relied on simple math to determine the likelihood, evaluating the probability of the babies dying as a separate event—like a coin flip. Using the rate of cot death of babies raised in non-smoking, middle-class homes, he stated there was a 1 in 8,523 chance of a child dying of SIDS. If two children died of SIDS in the same home this increased the likelihood to:

$$\frac{1}{8,523} \times \frac{1}{8,523} = 1/72,641,529$$

Treating the events as though there were separate events produced a 1 in 73 million chance that two SIDS deaths would occur within the same household. Meadow multiplied the two probabilities. Although it is still unknown why SIDS occurs, we do know from research that genetic disposition often leads to analogous health outcomes among siblings. Rather than treating two SIDS deaths as independent events, they should have been treated as events dependent on each other; the likelihood should have been estimated using Bayes' Theorem. To set up the equation the probability question would be framed as: what is the likelihood of baby 2 dying of SIDS now that baby 1 has died of SIDS? Bayes' Theorem is

$$P(A \mid B) = P(B \mid A)\, P(A)/P(B)$$

$P(A \mid B)$ is the conditional probability that A happens given that B already happened;
$P(B \mid A)$ is the conditional probability that B happens given that A already happened;
$P(A)$ is the probability of A happening;
$P(B)$ is the probability of B happening.

To determine the probability of something occurring based on past events, you would multiply the likelihood of B happening given that A already happened by the likelihood of A happening on its own; then divide this equation by the likelihood of B happening on its own. Thus, to determine the probability of having two babies die of SIDS under Sally Clark's care, you would have to know the probability of a baby boy dying of SIDS in a middle-class, non-smoking household and the probability of it occurring twice. The question should have been what is the likelihood of baby 2 dying after baby 1, then the equation would be:

$$P(2 \mid 1) = P(1 \mid 2)\, P(2)/P(1)$$

In a later paper, Hill found that the likelihood of a second SIDS death increases four- to five-fold after the first death. Thus, instead of

$$P(2 \mid 1)\ \frac{1}{8,523} \times \frac{1}{8,523}\ \text{the equation would be}\ P(2 \mid 1) = \frac{\dfrac{5}{8,523} \times \dfrac{5}{8,523}}{\dfrac{1}{8,523}},$$

which would not be a 1 in 73 million chance, but a 1 in 7 chance both babies died of SIDS. When this likelihood is compared to the chance of two children being separately killed by their mothers, which is a 1 in 9 chance. Two double SIDS cases are rare, rarer still are two homicide cases. Clark's defense team did not pick up on the statistical error, but thankfully the Royal Statistical Society did and wrote a letter to the crown outlining why the statistical reasoning was incorrect bringing the inaccuracy to light. Clark's defense team appealed the ruling, including the statistical error in the first appeal, and was denied. It was not until evidence was discovered that the second baby actually died of a bacterial infection that Clark's guilty ruling was overturned. Sadly, from the loss of two children and the stress of the trial, Clark died of unintentional alcohol poisoning seven years after the trials began. Bayes' Theorem states that your predictions must be updated by prior dependent events and in the Sally Clark case having a previous child die of SIDS is a prior dependent event.

Bayes' Theorem is not only important in criminal cases, but it is also important to crime analysis. The most common measure of crime and police effectiveness is the Uniform Crime Report (UCR) and the National Incident-Based Reporting System (NIBRS) which is an index of major crime categories. Government and news reporting rely on year-to-year and month-to-month binary comparisons using this state and federally mandated data. During the COVID-19 pandemic, the media would run stories about how crime had dropped in the months during the stay-at-home orders compared to the same months the year before. Matt Ashby, a retired U.K. police officer, turned intelligence officer, turned Professor of Crime Science at University College London, attributes "throwing out information" as another reason why we should avoid doing month-to-month or week-to-week comparisons. In his blog, he cites two media articles where the newspapers point out a 22 percent drop in violent crime in San Jose, CA and the overall drop in crime in Scotland. (On a side note, I call this "no-duh research", no-duh crimes decrease in number as people are staying home more often, and most criminals do not break into houses when people are actually in them.) Ashby's first point in his blog that doing month-to-month comparisons "throw(s) away useful information." The useful information is the information that updates your probabilities.

Ashby's blog covered five different arguments for why comparing month-to-month data is not useful. To make his first point he used public homicide data from Atlanta and plotted them on a chart. He visually depicted how homicides changed from 2016 to 2017. His chart is displayed in Figure 15.1.

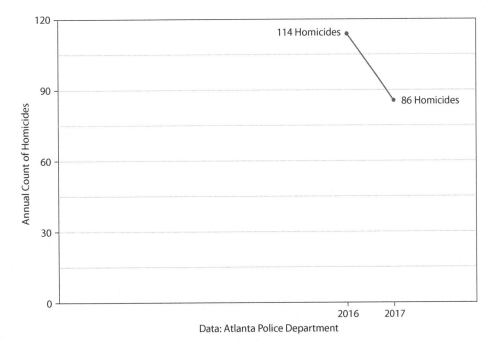

Data: Atlanta Police Department

Figure 15.1 Atlanta, GA Homicides from 2016 to 2017

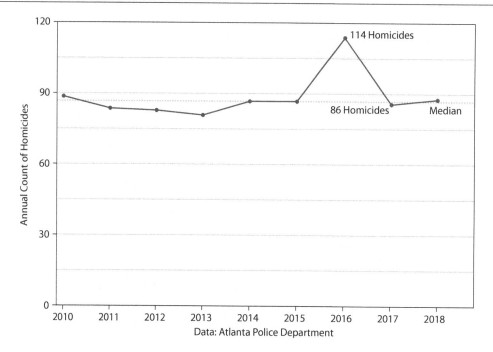

Figure 15.2 Atlanta, GA Homicides from 2010 to 2018

The drop looks amazing! Homicides dropped 25 percent over the last year. Atlanta PD's prevention efforts must really be paying off, right? Then Ashby adds the data from the previous five years. Figure 15.2 shows the data from the previous five years. Now the 25 percent year-to-year comparison does not look all that great anymore. Ashby argues that by doing month or year data sets compared to the previous month or year data set, you are throwing out important data. You need to look at the change in the data in comparison to the rest of the data. Ashby gives an example of the same 25 percent homicide decline during different data trajectories in Figure 15.3.

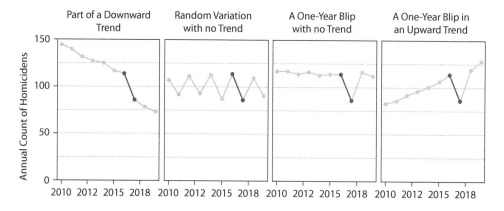

Figure 15.3 Examples of the Same 25 Percent Decline in Homicide During Different Data Trajectories

Examining the 25 percent decline in homicide means something different for each of these data sets. Bayesian reasoning means that you update your thinking (predictions) based on the newest information. The information *prior* to the newest information is still relevant. If someone lives in an area that carries a 10 percent probability of their house being broken into and a house on their street is burglarized (which now statistically increases the chances of being broken into by 75 percent), they should not ignore the 10 percent historical probability *or* the newest 75 percent probability. Both numbers should be considered when determining probability. Unless both numbers are considered you will be "throwing out information."

Dr. Ashby demonstrated how leaving out previous data can make a month-to-month change in crime look good, but once the context of the preceding year is added, the reduction is not as great as it seemed. How crime data is displayed is important, as displaying it one way versus another can influence System 1 thinking and create bias. A common practice in CompStat is to show the number of crimes that have occurred since the beginning of the year compared to the same time frame the previous year: for example, comparing the January to March 2020 number of homicides to the January to March 2019 homicides. Besides the lack of Bayesian reasoning using this method, it also ignores the Law of Large Numbers (MM#11), Regression to the Mean (MM#12), and False Linearity (MM#4). If there is a relatively large increase in the number of homicides at the beginning of the year it does not mean that homicides will continue at that pace and keep increasing linearly for the rest of the year (remember Matt Kemp). As data is added every month, the average starts to smooth toward its natural mean by diluting the variance in the small data set. The additional data dilutes the noise, so you can differentiate the signal from the noise. Comparing year-to-date data sets to the previous year data sets is essentially comparing noise to noise and the interpretation of it is meaningless. Bayesian thinking would argue that the March to December 2019 data was left out, thus the data for the rest of 2020 was meaningless. These Mental Models intersect in many ways because the fundamental reasoning beneath each one relies on many of the same principles.

Bayesian thinking should not only be applied to crime data but can be applied to police work itself, although only in a specific way. In an East Midlands Police Academic Collaboration (EMPAC) blog, "Bayes Theorem and Policing", Dr. Ken Pease argues that Bayesian thinking closely aligns with the fundamental nature of policing itself. He states:

> Bayes is all about probabilities and how these are dynamically moving just as life is around you. It helps you think rationally about the best things to do; it doesn't promise "facts" or everlasting solutions, simply because in an everchanging world with highly diverse contexts it can be misleading to search for "static and universal truths." Policing knows this already, so I believe there is potential here for "real-world" use.

In this blog he compares Bayesian thinking to academic thinking or experimental thinking, arguing that in policing, police officers do not have time to wait for the results of an experiment, they rely on experience thus Bayesian is better. Pease's argument assumes two mechanisms: first, that police officers are updating their thinking when encountering new information and, second, that there is feedback from which to update your thinking. There is a huge difference in applying Bayesian thinking in crime analysis and applying it to patrol-type activities as Pease suggests, and that is the lack of a feedback loop for police officers.

To update our thinking with new information we *must* have a feedback loop and in policing, like many professions, there is no feedback loop. For example, when officers respond to a call for service for a dispute between neighbors, they handle the call as they see fit. There is no feedback loop for the officer to know if the dispute remained resolved (it may not but they no longer call the police), whether the citizen was satisfied with the level of service, if the relations between the neighbors improved due to the officer's efforts, or if there was a return call for service (unless the officer checked the computer automated dispatch (CAD) system). If there is no feedback as to a person's actions, then they cannot update their thinking. Pease related Bayesian thinking in the field to experiential learning: "the aspiration is to become less and less wrong in the light of experience rather than reach truth by comparing two or more ways of doing something (which in any case will drift over time after the evaluators have left)." Pease was diminishing the need for a counterfactual in the development of officer expertise. Two researchers (one I have mentioned before, Kahneman, a non-believer in intuition, and one I have not, Dr. Gary Klein, a believer in professional intuition) co-developed a research project to answer the question whether certain professions developed intuition over the course of their careers. At the end of their collaboration, they did not come to the same conclusions as Pease.

To become "less and less wrong" in a profession's understanding of their craft, there must be a way to confirm if their thinking is becoming more and more correct. In *Thinking, Fast and Slow*, Kahneman discussed his skepticism of accurate intuition. In his many years of studying human thinking and decision-making, he repeatedly observed how easily humans relied on heuristics rather than logic when making decisions. Kahneman was not sure that humans would update their previous heuristic with new, accurate information. He thought they were more likely to update their thinking by creating a heuristic. Counter to Kahneman's belief in human intuition was Klein's. Klein studied how people made decisions in demanding, real-world situations called Naturalistic Decision Making (NDM), and he strongly believed in the idea of intuition. His book, *Sources of Power*, discussed how intuition is really recognized experience. Because the two psychologists had such opposing views to how human intuition manifests itself, they decided to work together to figure out when human intuition is effective and when it is not. They decided to answer the question: "When can you trust an experienced professional who claims to have an intuition?"

Professional expertise has long been criticized due to experiments revealing that some "experts" were no more likely to make an accurate prediction than a novice which Kahneman calls the illusion of validity. There were studies that showed college students with no psychology training were just as effective at helping people as psychologists with extensive training. Trained psychologists were understandably upset about the study, but those studies began to establish the idea that predicting human behavior is quite difficult. The divergent views of Klein and Kahneman caused them to take over a year to flesh out their research idea. In the end, they agreed on one principle: that the confidence people have in their intuitions is not a reliable guide to their validity. Many police officers justify their actions using their intuition. Based on Klein and Kahneman's research this confidence may be misplaced. As they began their research, Klein and Kahneman decided that there must be two conditions present to acquire skill: (1) An environment that is sufficiently regular to be predictable and (2) An opportunity to learn these regularities through prolonged practice. If these conditions were satisfied, then intuitions were likely to be skilled. Predictability requires a feedback loop. To gain expertise in something, people need a cause and effect—a feedback loop. Someone takes an action (cause), and they see an outcome (effect). In policing, police often act (arrest, cite, interview, de-escalate) and do not see the subsequent effect (reduction in crime, speeding, or social disorder, or find out if someone was lying or not), or they do not get the opportunity to observe the counterfactual.

Intuition without predictability (there is little predictability in policing) leads to flawed intuition. As Kahneman himself states: "Claims for correct intuition in an unpredictable situation are self-delusional at best, sometimes worse." In policing, there are some instances of immediate feedback loops to develop intuitive skill, such as communication. When interacting with the public, police often get immediate feedback on their communication skills through observing how a citizen reacts. Does the citizen relax, get angrier, or shut down? A police officer can learn different ways of dealing with the public, because the feedback is immediate, but what the officer cannot determine is the pattern of communication that works overall for different people. This requires evaluating data to a macro level and the human brain is not capable of remembering every interaction, every contact, and every variable over hundreds of stops, which means officers are left with only heuristics and biases.

Police cannot develop accurate intuitive skills for decision-making on calls for service that involve arrests, citations, mediations, or warnings as there is rarely a feedback loop on these types of calls. These same inaccuracies were discovered in the medical field with radiologists who also never got feedback on their diagnosis of tumors on X-rays. Without being told if they were correct or not in their observations, their diagnosis of anomalies never got better. Even when they were shown the same X-rays they had previously evaluated as "normal" or "abnormal", they contradicted themselves 20 percent of the time. Without a feedback loop, expertise does not increase with experience. Just like the radiologists in Kahneman's book who never received feedback on the accuracy of their diagnoses, officers often do not see the effects of their decision-making (there is no feedback loop), thus the effects of their actions are not "quickly evident." To learn from field experiences the outcomes need to be "quickly evident." Police need a feedback loop. Many police practices, policies, and best practices are based on untested assumptions which means it is unknown whether they are true or not.

There are better ways than best practice to build a profession. Pease advocates for Bayesian reasoning over experiments stating policing cannot wait for experiments to tell policing whether an intervention is effective or not. Sherman and Weisburd would advocate for experiments to create causal links between practices and outcomes. Klein and Kahneman might advocate for police departments to create a feedback loop to build expertise in the field. I think there is a way to infuse all types of research and feedback loops to build better, more effective policing practices than simply using best practices and it is the intent of this book to give you the tools to do that.

The Mental Models in Practice V—Mental Models 13–15

Correlation is Not Causation, Causal Inference, and Bayesian Reasoning

This section of the Twenty-one Mental Models book reviewed three ideas central to policing data—Correlation is Not Causation, Causal Inference, and Bayesian (Probabilistic) Reasoning.

Here is how to apply Mental Models 13-15:

1 Think about how your agency is presenting their data. Do you still do binary comparisons? Change your CompStat model to present data as suggested by Ratcliffe, Ashby, Petitti or Guilfoyle.
2 When implementing a policy, practice, or program pilot the program.
3 Figure out the unit of analysis—is it a person, group, or place?
4 Whatever the unit of analysis, find a comparison group that has similar baselines.
5 Determine outcome measures. Is it Part I crimes, social disorder, mental health calls, etc.?
6 Run the pilot for six months or a year before analyzing your data.
7 Using Ratcliffe's ABC spreadsheet input your pre/post data from the intervention areas (or individuals) and the control areas.
8 Determine if the policy, practice, or program is effective use of police resources.
9 Check your assumptions and update your beliefs based on updated information – do not throw out pertinent data.
10 Create as many feedback loops as possible for your police officers.

    a Give citizens the ability to comment on their experience of an officer's service.
    b Review body worn camera video with officers so they can observe where their body language did not match their verbal communication.
    c Review body worn camera video with officers so they can observe where they could improve officer safety. Football coaches review video footage with players all the time, why does policing fail to take advantage of that opportunity?
    d Give officers time to follow up on calls for service to determine whether the problem they responded to has been solved.

Part VI

How to Think Scientifically

Peer Review Your Perspectives

Some years ago I was struck by the large number of falsehoods that I had accepted as true in my childhood, and by the highly doubtful nature of the whole edifice that I had subsequently based on them. I realized that it was necessary, once in the course of my life, to demolish everything completely and start again right from the foundations if I wanted to establish anything at all in the sciences that was stable and likely to last.

Rene Descartes

Peer reviewing your perspectives means to check your opinion, views, and assumptions by examining where you got your information from to determine if it came from a credible source. Did your information come from empirical studies, academic journal articles, or books written by academic experts? Even before I was introduced to evidence-based policing, as a field training officer, I would teach trainees to verify their sources of information. I did this because I came to believe that there were many "cop myths," beliefs passed from one cop to the next without ever verifying the veracity of the information, floating around in the field. Often when I would hear a cop myth, I would ask: "How do you know that?" and inevitably they would answer: "Officer Smith told me." My response would be the same every time—did you check the general orders, the case law, or verify the information yourself? And the typical response was, "No." At the time I was drilling the practice of verifying information into my trainees' heads, I was focused on the laws and general orders we were bound by, rather than research. I wanted my trainees to make sure they developed a robust understanding of what they could and could not do by law and our general orders. I would tell them; you *do not* want to be the person involved in a search that you did not have the legal right to conduct. Always be sure of your legal standing! The problem is we often accept, believe, and share information without verifying the veracity of it first.

One of my favorite stories that illustrated this point happened early in my career. I arrived on scene to a call that was already in progress. When I got to the house, the suspect was in custody sitting in the living room. Officers were in the other room searching the house for evidence. I approached the officer in charge and asked: "What can I help with?" He said: "You can help with the search." I responded: "Sure no problem." As I followed the officer into the other room to help with the search I asked: "What's the exception to the warrant requirement that allows for the search?" He responded: "Exception to the warrant requirement?" I said: "Yeah—you know, our authority for conducting a search in someone's house." He said: "Oh yeah, it's a continuing search." I looked at him and said: "What's a continuing search?" He said: "You know when you start a search and then you

DOI: 10.4324/9780367481520-17

continue it." I stopped and said: "Wait. What?" He looked at me and repeated: "You know when you start a search based on an arrest, and you continue the search. We're continuing our search." I looked at him and said: "Yeah, that's not a thing. You need an exception to the warrant requirement to search a person's house." I went over all the exceptions to a warrant requirement with him. I told him: "Yes you can search the area around where you arrested him (reach, lunge, and grab) and you can search him, but you cannot search the entire house without a warrant."

I had seen this many times before where officers take a legal exception from one area and apply it to another. It is not that officers are corrupt or ignorant, it is just that in policing there are so many laws and exceptions to remember, officers will sometimes confuse different rules of law (especially when they are new). We also pick-up practices from each other without questioning where they originally got the idea or information. Looking at the circumstances, I could tell that the officer was confusing "fresh pursuit" which allows an officer to search for a fleeing suspect in a house *without* a warrant, with being able to search an entire house after an arrest. One exception allowed when you are in fresh pursuit is "a continuing investigation" and, looking back, I think that was the legal exception the officer was taking from one aspect of the law and applying it incorrectly. He was thinking because the investigation was ongoing, he could continue his search. I explained that a "continued search" is not an exception to the warrant rule. If we wanted to search the house, we would have to get permission or a warrant. No matter what you are doing in life, before adopting information as true, check on the accuracy of the information.

It is also vitally important to peer review solutions adopted and promoted by others, especially solutions deemed "best practices." Before I understood what evidence-based policing was or how to test my theories, I was the proud creator of two, yes that's right, two California POST best practices for recruiting. I created the Sacramento Police Department's (SPD) Female Fitness Challenge and the Community Recruiter Program. POST included both programs in their recruitment and retention best practice guide and the Community Recruiter Program was featured in the International Association of Police Chiefs magazine, *Police Chief*. The Female Fitness Challenge was a 12-week fitness program that kicked off with timing the women in the physical agility test during a day-long recruiting event and documenting their starting weight. After the initial event, the women would participate in an hour-long workout once a week with SPD female officers. At the end of the 12 weeks, the women were once again tested on the physical agility course to see if they improved their times, their physical ability, and re-weighed if they changed their physical body mass. The program was intended to recruit more women into SPD. The Community Recruiter Program was an educational program that trained community members on the requirements to become a police officer so they could recruit officers from their communities into SPD. We never collected data from either of these programs and never attempted to determine if we achieved our goal of increasing SPD's diversity. I know for sure we did not receive any new recruits from the community recruiter event. We recruited two women over four years of running the Female Fitness Challenge and anecdotally we heard some women applied because it made SPD appear more female friendly than other agencies in the area, but we had no evidence to support those assumptions. Yet without any evidence of effectiveness, both programs were deemed "best practices" for recruitment and retention by California POST. Even at the time, before I knew what evidence-based policing was, I understood the term "best practice" in policing was meaningless. "Best practice" in policing means "common practice." It is a practice that one agency shared with another, then another, then another, until enough agencies were doing it to call it a "best practice."

I realized I had missed an opportunity to learn so much more about recruitment and retention once I understood the value of testing my assumptions. I could have changed the Female Fitness Challenge from a "best practice" into an evidence-based practice. I just did not have the knowledge at the time the opportunity presented itself. As Dr. Cynthia Lum from George Mason University says: "Good science is just good planning." It is the structure and the planning that take an idea from a "best practice" to an evidence-based practice, and that structure begins by testing our assumptions.

Throughout this book, I explain the statistical and psychological reasons why some of our approaches to policing are flawed, yet logic and reason is not typically what changes our minds. Usually, it is a story or anecdote that resonates with us personally that shifts our thinking. The story that resonated with me was about Dr. Richard Cabot and Dr. Joan McCord. It made me question every assumption I ever made about policing, the criminal justice system, and human behavior. Their research has spanned almost seven decades now. It was one of those research stories that when I finished reading the first article on the study, I thought to myself, I *know nothing*! Then I began reading the next article that was written about their work and then the next. Their work arose out of testing a common assumption in the criminal justice field and proper planning, two things that, given a little effort, policing could easily do more consistently.

The interesting thing about this work was that Cabot and McCord never met. Cabot's study started in 1939 the same year he passed away and McCord was only nine years old. McCord's work started years later in 1956 when she was awarded a grant to examine the long-term effects the study participants. Two people separated by decades, linked through one of the first randomized controlled trials conducted in criminology, and one of the few to span decades. The study was called the Cambridge-Somerville Youth Study and it was borne of Cabot's work as a medical doctor in the Cambridge-Somerville area of Massachusetts. The area was highly populated with low socioeconomically situated factory workers. He observed young boys from this area getting into criminal trouble early in their lives and incrementally progressing to more serious crimes as they got older. The Massachusetts Reformatory had an 80 percent recidivism rate for juveniles at that time and Cabot felt that punishment was not having the intended effect. Cabot hypothesized (as many people have) that if someone would intervene at an earlier age to create a positive influence, maybe the juveniles would be prevented from entering the juvenile justice system. Cabot thought if the boys had a counselor, positive after-school and summer activities, and access to resources (medical and psychological aide) they would be less likely to get involved in criminal activity. He wanted to prevent delinquency using positive interventions rather than react to delinquency using punitive ones. His logic (and others) at the time was the boys are engaging in criminal activity, so they must be engaging in criminal activity because they do not have a role model to teach them socially acceptable behavior. A role model will give them an example of what to do, activities will keep them out of trouble, and tutoring will help them in school. A counselor (role model or mentor) could assist with all these concerns and would possibly keep them out of the criminal justice system. The logic model looks like Figure 16.1.

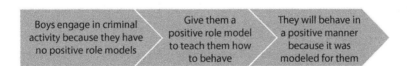

Figure 16.1 Logic Model for Cambridge-Somerville Study

The assumption here is that the individual requires the intervention, not the institutions, the families, or the socioeconomic structures that are in place. The other assumption is that access to resources and outside positive activities will keep kids out of criminal activity. This assumption stems from the belief about "idle hands" make for the devil's work. Thoreau said it well: "The devil finds work for idle hands." The assumption underlying the research was, if you give a child a mentor to teach them how to behave like civic minded citizens, and you fill their time with positive activities, then they will have less time and be less inclined to engage in criminal activity. He knew punishment was not working so he wanted to try something new. The commendable thing about Cabot was he subjected his theory to a rigorous peer review, in this case the gold standard of review—a randomized controlled trial. The rigorous study design he created laid the foundation for future evaluations for decades to come and with it McCord's unanticipated discovery.

By using a randomized controlled trial, Cabot designed a study that minimized the risks of confounding factors influencing the results. A randomized controlled trial is a study where participants are randomly assigned to receive the intervention (treatment) or no intervention (control). The structure of a randomized controlled trial is shown in Figure 16.2.

After a sample of the population is assigned to treatment or control, has received either the intervention or no intervention, they then are followed up for a specific duration to compare the outcomes between the two groups—this is essentially the basic format of a randomized controlled trial. Apart from the differing interventions, the two groups are treated and observed in the same manner. Additionally, the outcomes measured at the end of the study are identified at the onset of the study to avoid any statistical manipulation after the fact. As such, randomized controlled trials are considered the gold standard of science; it holds all the variables constant except for the one being tested.

Cabot took his study one step further than most of the current research surrounding delinquent children. He wanted to overcome the bias inherent in other studies that only targeted children who were involved with the criminal justice system. To avoid this bias, Cabot included "difficult" (boys prone to delinquency), "average" (boys exhibiting a normal amount of delinquency), and "zero" (boys not prone to delinquency at all) boys in his sample. This sample aptly reflected the total population rather than just concentrating on the hardest cases. Furthermore, the boys were matched to another participant who was similar in age, socioeconomic status, religion, geography, grade in school, and then randomly assigned to the treatment or control group. The control groups only had contact

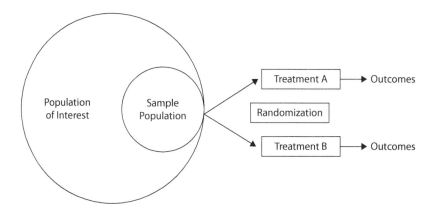

Figure 16.2 The Basic Structure of a Randomized Controlled Trial

with a researcher for data-gathering purposes. The treatment group boys participated in the intervention on average for five years. The children assigned to the treatment group were appointed a counselor to provide them "regular, friendly attention," basically a mentor.

Mentoring as an intervention is one of the most utilized solutions for a "performance" problem we use today. Although it was not called mentoring when Cabot first established his program, it was called character development instead. The intervention he created for the Cambridge-Somerville study was comparable to juvenile mentoring programs that are in existence today. At that time, the field of social work thought that children who displayed delinquent tendencies needed early intervention to avoid a life in the criminal justice system. It was believed that through developing a child's spiritual powers, physical capacities, mental abilities, and emotional security, children would attain better social development and it would loosen their delinquent tendencies. The study's intent was to develop the "whole" child. The counselors were to meet with the boys once a week, provide academic tutoring, attend to any medical or psychiatric needs, and refer them to summer camps, YMCA, boy scouts and other after-school activities. The hypothesis was that by giving the boys the support they needed to develop strong character it would act as a prophylactic to delinquency.

Sadly, Cabot died the year the study went live. He did not survive to see the outcomes of his well-designed, well-thought-out study. When the data was analyzed at one- and three-years' post intervention, researchers found that there was no difference in school adjustment, psychological testing, and the number of offenses committed. In fact, the three-year post intervention data showed that the treatment group committed 264 offenses compared to 218 by the control group. Law enforcement and social workers might view this as a failed experiment because the intervention did not "work." However, equally important is research that demonstrates what does not work. Research provides information that would not have been realized otherwise, and it helps us to build our understanding of the world. And this is where the story of Dr. Joan McCord and the lasting power of randomized controlled trials truly begins.

The genius of the Cambridge-Somerville study was not only the idea that a longitudinal study (a study conducted over many years) is pivotal in understanding juvenile delinquency, but that it was a randomized controlled trial. The random assignment allowed researchers to evaluate the effects of the intervention even after a long period of time. In hindsight, this was fortuitous as when the one- and three-year follow-up results came back with unsupportive findings, they hypothesized that the positive effects of the intervention might not manifest themselves until later in life. It is parallel to taking your children on a trip around the world in their teens, knowing that they will not care in the moment, but maybe it will affect their life choices in the future. Power and Wittmers hypothesized the same when they observed the lackluster results. It was these initial speculations about the latent effects of the study that allowed McCord to get funding from the Cabot Foundation to design a comprehensive follow-up study ten years after the original intervention. What she found was completely startling, even to her.

Examining social programs requires meticulous collection of data and long-term follow-up. Social scientists understand that life course development does not remain stagnant throughout life. Individuals go through many different developmental periods which require examination of the effects of a social program not only in the moment of completion, but years later to determine the entirety of the effects. This is what McCord wanted to understand about the Cambridge-Somerville study, the long-term effects. The two previous evaluations examined the crime outcomes, psychological health, and adjustment to school with unsupportive findings. Now that these young men were adults, McCord wanted to see if the intervention effects finally manifested themselves when these young men reached their 20s. Once again, she noted null findings, no statistical difference between the group of men participating in the treatment and the men who were left alone. This was the third study on these group of young men to find the same outcomes—no difference.

McCord was not easily swayed, and she was a meticulous researcher. Her ideas around social research and policy centered around finding objective measures of data rather than self-reporting data. As she stated in an interview, some of her earliest work as a research assistant was coding women, reporting on their behavior toward their children. She reflected in the interview that reporting our own behavior is a poor measure, as we tend to report as the person we view ourselves to be rather than the person we are. McCord's understanding of human behavior and research design gave her an understanding of how valuable the Cambridge-Somerville study was. The study allowed her and her fellow researchers to conduct rigorous evaluations of the program over the participants' lifetime, but she also understood through her earlier research with mothers and self-reporting that in the 1950s she did not have the means to evaluate the program in the manner she wanted. She was limited in many ways by her access and ability to analyze data. It was not until the 1970s that she realized that newly invented computers were powerful enough to analyze more than just a few objective outcomes of the men. If she could locate the men who participated in the study, she could expand the list of outcomes and examine whether the study influenced other areas of their lives. It was now almost 30 years after the study ended and she knew this was not going to be an easy task.

The men who participated in the study were now in their 40s, well into living their lives and making decisions that may have moved them out of the area. Finding all these men was a task that she was up for and she was not going to allow her research to be anything less than perfectly meticulous. As her son related in a Freakonomics podcast, her dedication to rigor was so great that when one of her graduate students reported that one of the subjects was dead, she asked: "Do you have a death certificate?" The response was: "Well no, but all his relatives say he is dead." Her response was to keep looking for him until they found a death certificate. Ultimately the subject was found and when he was asked why everyone kept saying he was dead, he responded that his family was ashamed of him for going to prison. Rather than telling people he was in prison, everyone would say he was dead. Due to McCord's meticulous record keeping and the fact that 80 percent of the men still lived in Massachusetts, she found 98 percent of the men who participated in the study and then set to gathering objective information (rather than self-reported information) about their lives to determine the long-term effects of Cabot's experiment.

In her 1978 study, the objective measures went beyond the initial narrow metrics that Cabot intended to observe. McCord wanted to examine outcomes along a wide range of factors—factors that determine overall quality of life. She evaluated objective measures for death, crime, mental and physical health, alcoholism, job satisfaction, and marital satisfaction, six additional measures beyond offending. She understood that recidivism was not the only outcome metric that could be influenced by Cabot's mentoring program. She knew participants could potentially recidivate but have better outcomes when it came to marriage or job prospects. Research has shown that many people age out of crime. McCord wanted to determine whether the mentoring program had taken root over the course of the young men's lives and improved their outcomes in their 40s. Surprisingly, this is not what she found. The men in the treatment group on average, had occupations with lower prestige, higher blood pressure or heart trouble, were more likely to commit two or more crimes, had more symptoms of alcoholism, had higher rates of mental illness and arrest, and died on average five years younger than the men in the control group. The men who received mentoring were worse off than the boys who received nothing.

McCord was thorough in her research; she knew some would argue that these findings had nothing to do with a treatment program the boys went through in their youth. As such, she analyzed the intensity and duration of the treatment to determine if it corelated with outcomes. She evaluated the dose of the treatment like a medical doctor would evaluate the potency of a dose of a drug. She compared the amount of "dosing" the boys received and showed that the boys receiving two doses of summer camp were 10.0 times worse off compared to the boys that received no summer camp. As the intensity and duration of the program increased, the negative outcomes for the boys increased. She had several hypotheses about why the treatment group was worse off than the control group, but the only hypothesis that stood up to scrutiny was that the intervention "raised the expectations of the boys" and when those rewards did not manifest themselves after the intervention, they became disillusioned with life. The intervention, rather than improving the boys' lives, had an iatrogenic effect, and made them worse off. Testing the benefits or backfire effects of criminal justice interventions, no matter how logical they may seem or how many good intentions people may have, will remain unknown unless there is rigorous evaluation. As McCord put it: "Unless social programs are evaluated for potential harm as well as benefit, safety as well as efficacy, the choice of which social programs to use will remain a dangerous guess." Policing assumptions need to be peer reviewed. The assumptions on which police base community interventions may not be correct. There are still police agencies engaging in practices that have research that demonstrates their ineffectiveness and/or backfire effects (DARE, CISD, and Scared Straight).

After reevaluating the Cambridge-Somerville study, McCord understood all social interventions should be tested no matter how good the initial intentions. She realized that our assumptions about the world were not always correct and became famous for uncovering backfire effects in criminological studies. Her work culminated in an article titled "Cures that Harm" which reviewed five different criminal justice interventions that had backfire effects. She demonstrated that court volunteer programs, which are common in many U.S. courts, were iatrogenic. Once again, the assumption was that individual intervention would lead to better outcomes. When one of the programs was finally evaluated, it was found that those who received assistance from volunteers ended up committing more crimes than those who did not receive assistance. Another program with backfire effects was a group interaction training. This training focused on developing the social skills of potential delinquents by giving them opportunities to discuss their issues with positive role models. An evaluation of the program demonstrated that for middle school-aged children, there was no effect, but for high school-aged participants misbehavior and delinquency rates increased. Peer-reviewing studies is how policing knowledge should be developed rather than trading "best practice" from agency to agency. Replicating programs without understanding whether they work and if they have been evaluated can be damaging to your communities. One of the most famous programs McCord reviewed in her "Cures that Harm" article was the Scared Straight program.

Scared Straight was a program for first-time offending juveniles that began in the 1970s. As part of their probation or instead of a jail sentence, juvenile offenders were required to visit an adult prison to show them the atrocities of prison firsthand to deter them from future offending. The underlying theory of programs such as Scared Straight is deterrence theory. Program advocates and others thought that realistic depictions of life in prison and presentations by inmates would deter juvenile offenders or children at risk for becoming delinquent and from further involvement with crime. The fundamental assumption of this program was that experiencing fear in the present about their offending would prevent them from offending in the future (remember how "present you" and "future you" work?).

Scared Straight was adopted throughout the United States and several different countries, was assumed to be effective, and claimed an 80 to 90 percent success rate. It took 20 years before some researchers began to question the validity of the professed results and a randomized controlled trial was conducted to evaluate the effects of the program. The assumption was fear was an effective deterrent, thus no one studied the program. When the first randomized controlled trial was run, half the juveniles were assigned to a Scared Straight intervention and half the kids were assigned to the control group with no intervention. When the outcomes were evaluated after the intervention, the researchers found that the juveniles in the treatment group were more likely to be arrested than the control group. One of the participants from the original Scared Straight documentary raped and murdered his neighbor only two years after the documentary aired. He was not convicted until his DNA was matched during a cold case investigation in 2005. Although this is an extreme example from this intervention, when comparing the outcomes from the treatment group to the control group the researchers demonstrated that in this case, doing "nothing" was better than doing "something."

This is one of the fundamental points of this book, to examine the underlying assumptions about policing, crime, and what works. Peer reviewing your assumptions is not just about sources of information, it is also about your basic beliefs when it comes to policing and crimes. As you have read beginning with Mental Model #1—System 1 and System 2, human brains are flawed. The way we acquire and access information is based on efficiency rather than accuracy. If we want to police our communities in the safest, most efficient ways possible, we need to test our assumptions, test our practices, test our policies, and test our programs. Otherwise we may be increasing harm rather than increasing benefits. Dr. McCord dedicated her life to shedding light on harmful criminal justice practices. Yet, Scared Straight programs, mentoring programs, and court volunteer programs exist to this day. Policing must peer review their practices, policies, and cultural assumptions and make sure their existing structures reflect current empirical knowledge.

The Scientific Method

I apologize for being so old fashioned, but I believe the scientific method is alive and well and will remain so, regardless of amounts of data. Data will be astonishingly more plentiful in a few years compared to the current era which will then be seen as a period of data dearth. We will still need the scientific method to make sense of data.

Dr. John Ioannidis

Policing, especially after 2020, is a profession that must understand its practices in an empirically comprehensive way. Police should be scrutinizing their strategies and practices and examining them scientifically. Too often, police executive decisions are made based on the current political climate, the desires of city leadership, or the media who all drive practices they assume will be good for the community with little or no empirical evidence. By now you should have developed a solid understanding that implementing social interventions without testing means that policing is one of the very few professions allowed to experiment on their communities with no oversight. Police departments can implement interventions or programs with the best of intentions, all the while not understanding that although their intentions may be good, the outcomes could be negative. This is how the U.S. and other countries ended up with Scared Straight programs intended to reduce juvenile recidivism, but those programs increased recidivism instead. Understanding the scientific method and how to develop a rigorous research design will help you implement interventions in a way that will help you better understand what is going on in your communities.

When I teach courses on evidence-based policing, officers will often tell me that they cannot run experiments like I do because they do not have a PhD. They argue they do not have the training. I always tell them, our earliest scientists did not have PhDs, they had a natural curiosity about how the world works and tried to figure out how to use observation and experimentation to create understanding of natural phenomenon. I also tell them I did not have a PhD either when I ran my first experiment. I just wanted to know if there was a better way to deploy patrol to reduce crime and calls for service without adding extra work. Although I did not have my PhD, I did have good mentors who helped me with my research design and answered my questions along the way—Dr. David Weisburd, Dr. Cynthia Lum, and Dr. Chris Koper from George Mason University. Dr. Cody Telep, who was a graduate student at the time, assisted with the data analysis. Doing field research requires good planning, oversight, and a systematic way of gathering observations.

DOI: 10.4324/9780367481520-18

The scientific method has been used by plenty of people who did not have PhDs. Using the scientific method only requires the desire to understand how the world works, the willingness to systematically gather data, and figuring out how to set up a way to test your hypothesis.

Sir Francis Bacon was the first to describe a scientific method as using inductive reasoning and observations as a way of understanding the phenomenon in the world. Today the scientific method as described by the Khan Academy is a six-step process:

1   Make an observation.
2   Ask a question.
3   Form a **hypothesis**, or testable explanation.
4   Make a prediction based on the hypothesis.
5   Test the prediction.
6   Iterate: use the results to make new hypotheses or predictions.

The scientific method in its most basic form is collecting data in a systematic way to test a null hypothesis, rather than a hypothesis. This gets confusing for some because this approach disproves a theory rather than proves a theory. The public gets weary of "science" changing their stance on a particular topic. It is not that "science" changes its mind, it's that science never "proves" anything. If the nutrition scientists said eggs were not good for us five years ago, and now they say two eggs a day are fine, then do scientists really know what they are doing? The answer is yes for two reasons: first, science is never static because our understanding of the world grows as we develop new ways to evaluate the world, and second, because we are testing a "null" hypothesis rather than a hypothesis, science is never proving anything, only disproving.

To understand the null hypothesis, just think of the opposite of what you hypothesize will happen and that is your null hypothesis. Take for instance hot spots policing, if you want to test the idea of a hot spots program reducing calls for service, then your null hypothesis would be something to the effect of: when comparing hot spots patrols to standard patrols there will be *no difference* in calls for service between the two areas. Looking at Figure 17.1, the null hypothesis step would be generated at the same time your hypothesis is generated.

A null hypothesis is typically some type of *no difference* statement. This means if you find a statistically significant difference between the calls for service for the two areas then you know it was as a result of the hot spots intervention rather than another variable and you reject the null hypothesis. You disproved the idea that there would be no difference between the two areas. You are not "proving" hot spots works, you are disproving that it does not work.

Developing a hypothesis and the resulting null hypothesis is only one of the steps of the scientific method and sometimes the easiest. We all have beliefs about how the world works and as police officers, we definitely have beliefs about how crime works, how people behave, and what type of interventions will work to reduce crime, calls for service, and recidivism. Just pick one of your beliefs about policing or crime and you have a research question. The harder part is matching the correct research design to the question. Depending on the research question, you may have to reach out to an academic for some help. Research designs are not intuitive, but once you learn how to set them up, they are not that difficult. The difficulty lies with matching the question to the design, and then performing the analysis to understand the outcomes. Additionally, some research designs are more rigorous than others and when peer reviewing your assumptions (MM#16) it is good to know where

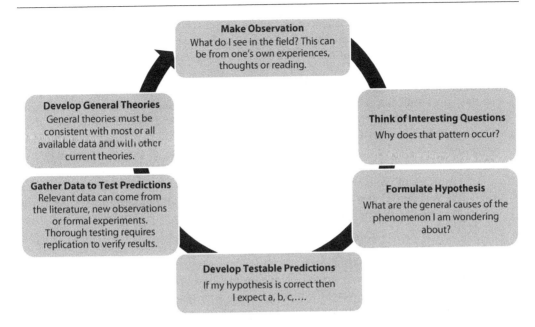

Figure 17.1 The Scientific Method

studies fall in their level of rigor. Thankfully, a group of researchers created the Maryland Scientific Methods Scale as a framework to rank the different levels of research rigor.

The Maryland Scientific Methods Scale (MSMS) is a ranking matrix that was first presented in a Congressional report titled "Preventing Crime: What Works, What Doesn't, What's Promising" and was officially titled the MSMS in a 2002 book *Evidence Based Crime Prevention*. The scale was used to evaluate how criminological interventions differed in methodological quality. The scale translates the recommendations made in the 1979 book *Quasi-experimentation* into a numeric scale and reflects the medical model's Hierarchy of Strength of Evidence for Treatment Decisions which is reviewed in Mental Model #18—Evidence-Based Practice. *Quasi-experimentation* was written by Cook and Campbell to explain why some research methods are better than others. The book outlined the numerous internal validity issues which appear in research designs when there are no comparison groups and a lack of randomization. As you will recall, Mental Model #14—Causal Inference explained the need for a comparison group to link causality between variables.

The MSMS was an attempt to turn the *Quasi-experimentation* tome into a framework that could be easily applied to the field. As such, the MSMS ranks research methodology on a scale of 1 to 5, with 1 being the lowest scoring research methodology beginning with correlation (MM#13).

1 After intervention measures (cross-section, one time);
2 Before–after measures, no control (over time);
3 Before–after measures, comparable control conditions (no controlling for multiple variables);
4 Before–after measures, comparable control conditions controlling for variables (similar baselines);
5 Randomized controlled trial (random assignment to treatment and control groups).

Remember, correlation is not causation which is why correlation is at the bottom of the scale and ranked as a 1. As the numbers increase, the causal link becomes stronger and stronger. As stated on page 12 of the "What Works" Congressional Report,

> In order to reach level 3, a study had to employ some kind of *control or comparison group* to test and refute the rival theory that crime would have had the same trend without the crime prevention program (the counterfactual); it also had to attempt to control for obvious differences between the groups, and attend to quality of measurement and to attrition issues. If that comparison was to a more than a small number of matched or almost randomized cases, the study was given a score of "4". If the comparison was to a large number of comparable units selected at random to receive the program or not, the study was scored as a "5", the highest possible level; random assignment offers the most effective means available of *eliminating competing explanations* for whatever outcome is observed.

The MSMS interprets the ranking through a causal lens. Research that hints at two variables being associated is nice, but correlation only means that two variables change in conjunction with each other, there is no way of knowing if one variable is *causing* the other variable. Policing wants to know how to cause changes in crime, not how increases in crime are linked to summer temperatures. Correlation typically only looks at data at one point in time, comparing two variables to each other using a statistical procedure such as a Pearson's product-moment correlation coefficient, Spearman's rank correlation coefficient, or linear regression.

Before and after studies are ranked at Level 2 because they are a touch better than merely correlating data. A before and after study starts to demonstrate that if there are changes in the data after the intervention, then the intervention may have caused the changes. Although, before and after data does not account for regression to the mean (MM#12). Without a comparison group, there will be no way to be sure if the data is just regressing to its normal average rate or if the intervention caused the change. When the control group (no intervention) is compared to the treatment group and there is a statistically significant difference between the two before and after averages, then it can be assumed that the difference between the two is not because of regression to the mean. The outcomes are because of the intervention.

Before and after studies with a comparison group are ranked at Level 3 or 4 depending on if the treatment and the control group are similar at baseline. The dependent variable of the treatment group should not be statistically significantly different from the control group at baseline. This was reviewed in Mental Model #14—Causal Inference when examining the baseline of traffic accident survivors. That study was a Level 5 study because of the randomization, but if we took out the randomization then the study would be ranked at Level 4. The researchers matched the high impact treatment patients with high impact no-treatment patients. Now, if the high impact patients were matched to a low impact patient without any randomization the study would be ranked a Level 3. If the baselines were not similar, if the dependent variables were statistically significantly different, then the study would be ranked a Level 3 on the MSMS and if they were similar then the study would be ranked a Level 4.

To analyze the baseline data for statistical significance a Student's t-test or t-test would be used. A t-test is a statistical test that evaluates a hypothesis by comparing two means. The numerator is the difference between the two means—the signal and the denominator—and the noise is the standard error of the mean or variance of the sample. If there is large variance in the sample compared to the population then the standard error will be high and there is less likelihood of finding a statistically significant difference between the treatment and control groups. Think of variance this way, if you were examining BMI and your sample of people were brand new police recruits and the population was the whole police department, the recruit BMI sample most likely would have low variance compared to the whole population of the department. The recruits just graduated from the academy hence they are at the top of their game and physically fit. Now, if you made half of the recruits eat a high protein diet and the other half eat a high carb diet, to determine which diet was better and if there was a statistically significant difference between the two group's final weight then the p-value of the t-test would be smaller than .05. If you recall the normal distribution from Mental Model #10—Distributions, you will remember that with most phenomena the data will create a normal distribution, meaning the average rates will center around a mean and the outliers will be at the tail end of the distribution in the 3rd standard deviation of the curve.

When examining small data sets rather than a normal distribution it is called a t distribution: as a small data set gets larger and larger the distribution progresses closer and closer to a normal distribution. When comparing the two means of the recruit's weight, they will be deemed statistically significantly different from each other if the observed value of his weight falls into the 3rd standard deviation. Figure 17.2 shows the 3rd standard deviation is where very unlikely observations fall.

In the case of a level 3 study, if the baselines are drastically different from each other it reduces the study's internal validity, which means you cannot say conclusively that the independent variable *caused* the dependent variable. If the baselines are similar and the means are statistically significantly different from each other, then you are starting to reach a threshold of being able to observe the actual signal through the noise and now you are able to say more confidently that one variable *caused* another. In policing, we are looking for causation not correlation. If you are going to allocate resources to a particular program, policy, or practice, then you want to make sure you are achieving the intended effects.

Finally, the randomized controlled trial gets the gold star as a Level 5 study because randomization helps with internal validity issues, especially bias. With a retrospective study where a researcher is evaluating a program that was already conducted, to get to a Level 4 on the MSMS the researcher will have to find a comparison group with similar baselines for the dependent (outcome) variable. This requires the researcher(s) to choose the areas,

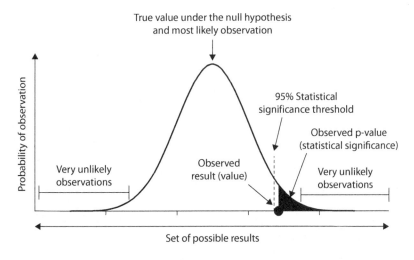

Figure 17.2 A Depiction of Where an Unlikely Observation will Fall on a Normally Distributed Curve

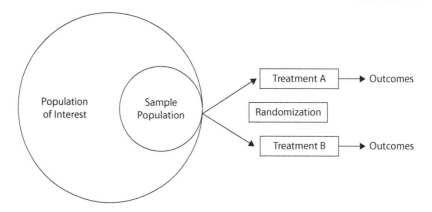

Figure 17.3 The Basic Structure of a Randomized Controlled Trial

people, or things to compare which introduces bias. Whenever bias is introduced into a study, the internal validity is reduced. When participants, places, or things are randomized by a computer, it removes this bias.

A randomized controlled trial is a study where the participants are randomly assigned to one of two or more interventions. A sample of the population of interest is assigned to treatment (intervention) or control (no intervention), systematically observed for a period of time, and then the average outcome measures of the two groups are compared. Other than the intervention, the two groups are treated identically. The structure of a randomized controlled trial (RCT) is depicted in Figure 17.3.

The assumption is the randomization will average out any variability between the two groups. If you are studying a weight loss intervention with a group of 200 people, 100 people are assigned to the intervention (treatment) and 100 people will be left to their own devices (control). The 200 people will represent the population, they will be people of all ages, weights, and physical ability. The assumption behind RCTs, is that on average the same number of people who are a 25 BMI will be assigned to the treatment and control side, as would a 24 BMI or 23 BMI. The randomization averages out the variability between the two groups, but you should not take this for granted. A t-test should be performed to determine that there is no statistically significant difference between the two groups at baseline.

The Portland Police Bureau performed t-tests when conducting a randomized controlled trial on community engagement patrols in crime hot spots. Ninety 500-foot × 500-foot grids were identified in the City of Portland as high call for service areas, 30 were assigned to a two 15-minute dose of community engagement, 30 were assigned to a four 15-minute doses, and the control group received a standard patrol response for a 90-day period. In this case, because there were three groups to compare rather than two, an Analysis of Variance (ANOVA) rather than a t-test was performed to determine if there were any differences at baseline. They were able to determine that there were no differences at baseline which meant their study was off to a great start to demonstrate causality, but sadly by the end of the nine-month period both the two and four dose areas did not show any statistically significant differences in the treated areas compared to the control areas. This is why it is so important to test your ideas, because good intentions do not always lead to good outcomes. The idea of community engagement was just that, a good idea.

Policing still engages in "best practices". Police implement practices based on what other organizations are doing because it sounds like a good idea or sometimes because they face pressure from outside the organization. McCord spent her life conducting research to demonstrate that criminal justice social interventions may be doing more harm than good. The police officer's duty is to the community which means policing should have an empirical understanding about the programs they implement in their communities. The only way to have this type of understanding is to use the Scientific Method to test hypotheses about what works and what doesn't in policing. Once these programs, policies, and practices have been tested and shown to have empirical support, only then should they be practiced and only then can they be called evidence based

Evidence-based Practice

It all comes down to expectations. If we believe that things are often complicated and our knowledge is always incomplete then the EBP approach is helpful and satisfying. If we believe that absolute truth and definite proof can and must be established by looking at all the 'facts' then this approach feels rather pointless.

Dr. Rob Briner

I have heard people argue that "evidence-based" has several meanings depending on who you speak to, which has always intrigued me as evidence-based is a term that emerged from medicine; thus, I have always believed it has specificity. If you Google "evidence-based" you will get almost a million hits, but just because someone decides to infuse their perceptions into a definition does not mean that it has multiple meanings. It only means that many people do not understand its origins or its application. I analogize this misunderstanding to the idea that there are various meanings to the word elbow. If someone redefines it to mean the inside part of where the forearm and upper arm meet, rather than the outside does not make it accurate. Elbow has a universally agreed upon definition. Sometimes over the course of cultural adaptation a new meaning of a word will develop, but in the case of "evidence-based" it still does not simply mean using data as so many believe it does. As I said, redefining language for your own personal interpretation does not make something true. Thus, this section will describe what evidence-based means, where that definition came from, how it was translated into evidence-based policing and what adopting evidence-based policing means for our profession.

Stating something is "evidence-based" means you are applying both expertise and science to an individualized problem. Dr. David Sackett, one of the founders of evidence-based medicine (EBM), defined it as "the conscientious, explicit, and judicious use of current best evidence in making decisions about the care of individual patients." Dr. Sackett, one of the founders of EBM, was a mischievous prank-playing rebel doctor who was willing to take on the outdated paradigms of 1967 medicine. He started a clinical epidemiology and biostatistics department in a small, relatively unknown school in Canada called McMasters where EBM was born. In 1967 McMasters had recently opened a medical school and was looking to expand its internal expertise. They did not follow the typical medical school model of lectures, examinations, and students with backgrounds in biology and chemistry. They accepted students with backgrounds in anthropology, literature, and psychology and teaching was based on problem-based, self-directed learning, with evaluations based on

DOI: 10.4324/9780367481520-19

tutorial performance. McMasters was a rebel institution looking for renegade doctors making it the perfect fit for Sackett.

The culture of McMasters allowed Sackett to challenge the medical field's practices at the time, which Sackett felt were often based on hunches, intuition, and personal experience. Instead Sackett used what he called a "critical appraisal" for evaluating interventions. Critical appraisal, as explained by Dr. Guyatt, was the idea that some evidence is better than others (think of the Maryland Scientific Methods Scale) with opinion ranking at the very bottom. If Dr. Sackett were alive today, opinion would be ranked next to, Facebook, TikTok, LinkedIn, or any other social media form, where people spread ideas they learned from their friend's cousin's neighbor's best friend, who said things like she knew someone who got breast cancer from antiperspirant. Critical appraisal meant examining a patient's symptoms and then examining the research literature to determine the best intervention empirical research had to offer. If faced with multiple, sometimes conflicting research studies, then Dr. Sackett's definition of critical appraisal meant that the more rigorous research study was chosen. This meant there needed to be a method to rank the quality of research.

Before evidence-based medicine was even a term to be defined, Sackett and Busse created a table to reflect Sackett's idea of critical appraisal in a book chapter titled "The Philosophy of Evidence-Based Medicine." Figure 18.1 derived from their book chapter is reminiscent of the Maryland Scientific Methods Scale discussed in Mental Model #17—The Scientific Method. That is because this article was the first attempt at ranking scientific literature and the MSMS was adopted from Guyatt and Busse's model.

This hierarchy has two types of studies not included in the MSMS, Systematic Reviews, and n-of-1 randomized controlled trials. The definition of a systematic review is in its name. A systematic review means systematically reviewing all the current research on a topic, even

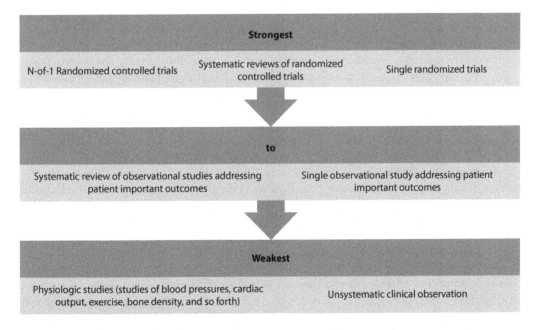

Figure 18.1 Critical Appraisal Ranking Model

the research in the gray literature or literature that did not make it into an academic journal. When reporting on a systematic review, the researcher will describe how they searched the literature, what search terms were used, how many studies they found, and then define how they decided to include or eliminate a study from the analysis. This creates a systematic approach. All the studies are reviewed in totality to determine whether the overall outcome demonstrates the efficacy of the intervention as one study does not make an intervention evidence-based.

Another type of systematic review is a meta-analysis. A meta-analysis is a mathematical approach to a systematic review. New statistical methods have allowed statisticians to aggregate the effects of all the studies on one topic and determine the intervention's overall effects. An effect size is a number that tells us the magnitude of a phenomenon and ranges from 0 to 1. Dr. Jacob Cohen, a psychologist and statistician, laid the statistical foundation for conducting meta-analyses and created a ranking system for effect sizes, which remains true today. A small effect size is .10, a medium effect size is .30, and a large effect size is anything over .50. He stated,

> The terms "small," "medium," and "large" are relative, not only to each other, but to the area of behavioral science or even more particularly to the specific content and research method being employed in any given investigation … In the face of this relativity, there is a certain risk inherent in offering conventional operational definitions for these terms for use in power analysis in as diverse a field of inquiry as behavioral science.

Cohen's work was foundational to meta-analysis studies because by analyzing the effect sizes of all the studies on a particular treatment/intervention, we can understand if an intervention is effective overall. The efficacy of an intervention is determined by analyzing the effect size of each study against the sample size of the study. For example, hot spots policing has been the topic of several meta-analyses. The most recent hot spots meta-analysis included 65 studies based on 78 tests. Anthony Braga and his co-authors reviewed all 78 tests and weighted the effect sizes to determine the overall effect size. They found a small effect for hot spots policing reduced crime outcomes in treatment areas compared to the control areas.

Another type of study Sackett included in the initial critical appraisal hierarchy that is not included in the MSMS is n-of-1 trials. N-of-1 trials are mainly conducted in the medical field. The trial's sample size is one person. These trials rigorously evaluate the effects of a treatment on a single individual. They are conducted with only one person because in medical trials, people with comorbidity—patients presenting with two or more simultaneous medical conditions—are excluded from randomized controlled trials. When conducting randomized controlled trials, the goal is to isolate variables to determine the effects. If a study is testing the efficacy of a drug, therapy, or other prescriptive treatment, then having participants with various comorbid presentations would reduce the researcher's ability to causally link the intervention's effect to the outcome. This is where n-of-1 trials take place: if a patient has anxiety, depression, and insomnia, and if a doctor wants to determine the best medication for that patient to improve their outcome, the Dr. could run an n-of-1 trial. N-of-1 trials are usually a challenge-withdrawal design, which means taking a medication for a set period of time (A) and then withdrawing with no medication for a set period of time (B). The challenge-withdrawal looks like -A-B-A-B-A-B for the duration that is needed to determine efficacy. By experimenting with the medication through use and disuse, keeping rigorous track of outcomes, and evaluating the outcomes objectively, the doctor can determine how effectively the medication is working for the patient. S/he can monitor how it affects the patient's anxiety, depression, and insomnia all at once, whereas

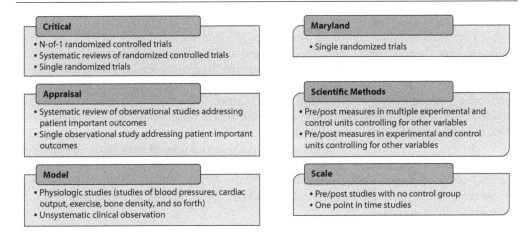

Figure 18.2 Critical Appraisal Scale Compared to the Maryland Scientific Model Scale

this cannot occur with randomized controlled trials if all the participants have different types of comorbidity. N-of-1 trials have not been used in policing which is why we do not see it ranked in the MSMS. Although, I believe if we treated communities or areas like the medical field treats an individual, police could perform n-of-1 studies on a community to determine what interventions work the best to reduce crime and calls for service while creating the least possible harm to the public.

Examining the medical model's critical analysis hierarchy and the Maryland Scientific Methods Scale we can see how the MSMS attempted to create something similar, a framework for criminologists, police, and policy makers to apply to their decision-making process when utilizing interventions. Figure 18.2 depicts the critical analysis hierarchy and the Maryland Scientific Methods Scale next to each other for ease of comparison. Although the critical appraisal framework and the MSMS are not exact replicas, it is apparent that EBM was beginning to develop from the critical appraisal hierarchy and the MSMS was translated from those efforts.

Sackett believed in critical appraisal of both the research literature and of one's knowledge because he knew medical doctors were relying on their training and expertise which was out of date within two years of graduating medical school. Also, their experience was only based on the patients they treated which was usually a small, biased sample. For people to understand his passion for critical appraisal, Sackett would often tell the story of President Washington's demise as a way for people to understand his passion for critical appraisal.

The first President of the United States developed a throat infection or a case of epiglottitis while out riding his horse in the cold. Epiglottitis is a condition, where through injury or infection, the epiglottis (the flap in your throat covering the windpipe to prevent food from entering your lungs) swells and blocks your windpipe, potentially asphyxiating you. When Washington fell ill, he believed in the current medical knowledge and asked his overseer to let his blood. He thought the bloodletting would improve his condition and he would be better by the morning. Instead, he woke with a fever and felt worse, leading to his personal physicians being summoned. After his physicians examined him, they agreed with Washington's methodology and bled him again.

Bloodletting was a practice that had begun some 1600 years earlier. Hippocrates derived the idea that women's menstruation was the body's way of ridding itself of disease, therefore bloodletting would also rid the body of disease. Consequently, the practice of bloodletting began. For centuries physicians believed the body consisted of four humours, blood, phlegm, yellow bile, and black bile and to be disease free the humours had to be in balance. Blood was considered the most important, thus if one got sick, physicians believed the blood inside the body had stagnated and had to be let. When retelling the story of Washington's case, Sackett liked to explain that it was known from early 100 B.C. that the intervention for epiglottitis was a tracheostomy, creating a hole in the trachea to insert a tube to bypass the inflammation and get air to the lungs. Physicians at the time, both during 100 B.C. and 1799, learned through apprenticeship, which meant their learning was limited by what their predecessor knew. In this case, Washington's doctors thought bloodletting was the best course of action because that is all they had ever been taught. He died December 14, 1799, just 21 hours after getting sick from riding his horse in the cold after his physicians (who had sworn an oath to do no harm) let almost 40 percent of his blood. Good intentions do not equal good outcomes.

Sackett would tell that story to highlight the fact that at the time of the President's demise, doctors knew of a better approach for epiglottitis, but Washington's doctors did not because medicine was not standardized, and as a result each doctor used the method they learned as an apprentice. Interventions were not tested; they were passed on, generation after generation, doctor to doctor, without anyone thinking to test bloodletting for efficacy—except for one. Jan Baptista van Helmont completed his doctorate in medicine in 1599, 200 years before President Washington succumbed to his throat infection. He called his medical education "senseless prattle," feeling as though he was sold ideas about medicine that were never proven. He felt so strongly about the lack of evidence supporting medical decisions that he challenged the "Humorists" to a randomized controlled trial, although he called it a contest, he understood the basic need for randomly allocating treatment and having a comparison group. The James Lind Library translated van Helmont's original document where he threw down the metaphorical gauntlet at the zeitgeist. The documents show that Van Helmont did not just propose a contest, but put his own money on the table to demonstrate the seriousness of his beliefs. His contest proposed they treat between 200 and 500 patients and take turns alternating interventions—his method (A), then bloodletting (B), then his method (A), then bloodletting (B), otherwise known as A/B testing. Van Helmont offered 300 Florins if the Humorist's had fewer funerals than he. In addition to the money, he offered the greatest prize of all: "For I swear that if you win I shall happily abandon my evil opinions and hereafter enter fully into your doctrine." He offered to believe them. He offered to abandon his opinion because he believed in the pursuit of truth over his personal beliefs. If they had fewer deaths than he did, he would have empirical evidence. He would have cause and effect. He vowed to let evidence drive his opinion. No one took him up on his challenge. Instead, bloodletting was passed from physician to apprentice for centuries without testing whether this intervention was effective or not (as were most interventions at that time), which is why medicine only began helping humanity rather than hurting it within the last 70 years.

In 1967, when Sackett accepted his new post, in all likelihood he did not realize he was among a group of men that would create a paradigm shift in medicine that would help physicians heal and cure more people than it ever did before. Before the 1950s, medicine harmed more than it healed. However, with the discovery of sulfa, penicillin, antibiotics, drugs for blood pressure, hormonal imbalances, and breakthroughs in major surgical procedures, hospitals, as described by Atul Gawande in his book *Being Mortal*, became a place to be cured. Between the period of 1946 and 1966 with the passage of the Hill-Burton Act, 9,000 hospitals were built in the United States. In those 20 years, hospitals proliferated but controlled research in medicine was just starting.

When Sackett was starting his new job at McMasters, randomized controlled trials had only been used in medicine for a little over 20 years, but like van Helmont he was a pursuer of truth. The truth he pursued was to teach medical experts that they should be relying on the best research available *and* their clinical expertise. In addition to creating the clinical appraisal hierarchy, he participated in a series of articles in 1981 titled "How to Read Clinical Journals" which outlined his thinking about how to digest research. Those journal articles laid the foundation for the idea of EBM. A decade later one of Sackett's mentees, Gordan Guyatt, in an article with other McMaster's colleagues, coined their critical appraisal efforts—evidence-based medicine. This article was titled "Evidence Based Medicine: A New Approach for Teaching the Practice of Medicine." This article was followed by a new article series: *The Users Guides to Medical Literature*. This series appeared in the *Journal of the American Medical Association* (JAMA), and also outlined EBM. The new series "vividly separated issues of risk of bias (termed 'validity'), understanding the results, and deciding on their applicability issues," which were less clearly defined in the critical appraisal series. This series had much more "emphasis on the results and applicability steps". Results and applicability have been the main focus of EBM ever since. The reasoning behind focusing on results and applicability was that a finding discovered in a laboratory might not manifest itself the same way in the field.

In "Evidence-Based Medicine: What It Is and What It Isn't," Sackett defined "best evidence" as "clinically relevant research …" and he defined clinical expertise as "the proficiency and judgment that individual clinicians acquire through clinical experience and clinical practice." EBM is the application of research to the practice of medicine; it is *applied* research. Relatively soon after Sackett published his article on what EBM is and isn't, Dr. Larry Sherman translated the idea of EBM into the idea of evidence-based policing. On a plane ride home from a restorative justice conference in Australia, Sherman read *Demanding Medical Excellence* by Michael L. Millenson. The book outlined a method for making the medical profession accountable. At the time of its publication, many doctors were still using tradition and common practice when recommending medications or interventions to their patients rather than what was recommended by medicine. They were not in the practice of examining the research literature before recommending interventions. In some ways, it was not the fault of the individual doctor but of the politics and culture of the profession. EBM was still relatively new in 1997 when the book was first published and acting on the best research available was not part of the medical culture. Assessing the landscape at the time, Millenson stated: "In other words effective change cannot come about because an individual actor vows to do things differently. It is the system in which physicians, nurses and others work that needs to change." It was within these pages that Sherman began to see a framework for how policing could systematically approach problems.

I met Sherman in 2010 while I was on a Fulbright Scholarship working with the London Metropolitan Police Service. My foray into evidence-based policing and thinking about policing in a whole new framework was a serendipitous accident. I was out on maternity leave when my new captain called me at home to ask me to attend a symposium hosted by California POST on the recruiting pipeline. I had previously been in the recruiting unit, and at the time my captain called, I was the sergeant overseeing our high school magnet and school resource program. Both my captain and my lieutenant were new to the unit and did not feel as they knew enough about the magnet program to attest to its usefulness. I reluctantly agreed to go leaving my almost three-year-old and my four-month-old home with my husband to attend the symposium. It was there that I met Jim Bueermann who was the police chief of Redlands, California at the time. In my bio, he had read that I was heading to London for my Fulbright the next January, and during the symposium he approached me and said he wanted to talk to me about it later. At dinner that night, out with the group from the symposium, I sat next to Jim. He told me about evidence-based policing, explained the outcomes of different research findings, and asked me if I had ever heard of Dr. Sherman. I told Chief Bueermann that I had never heard of Sherman or evidence-based policing before and being a 12-year police veteran who prided myself on staying up to date on case law, I was disappointed in myself that I had no idea there was a whole field of research in policing. By the end of the night, Chief Bueermann asked if I would like the University of Cambridge to be my host university for my Fulbright and in my head, I was like, "Hell yeah!" but instead I said "Yes, please." And just like that, Chief Bueermann offered to write a letter to Sherman and pitch the idea. At the time, I did not realize it, but I was making the fateful decision to follow the white rabbit and the University of Cambridge was to be my Wonderland.

At the time of my Fulbright in 2010, Sherman was running a master's course in Applied Criminology and Police Management for working police executives. The course met three times a year, two weeks at a time. After Chief Bueermann wrote his letter, Sherman invited me to attend one of the sessions with the Master's students. This was my introduction to evidence-based policing. During the sessions, Sherman would meet with me to make sure that I was understanding the courses and to discuss evidence-based policing. It was during these meetings that I got to understand the meaning of evidence-based policing and how Sherman began thinking about how to police differently many decades before he read *Demanding Medical Excellence*.

Before Sherman was a professor at the University of Cambridge, he was a conscientious objector of the Vietnam War, and when the draft came up, he was 74th on a list of 365. To avoid being drafted into the war, he took a fellowship at the Mayor's office in New York. Having an interest in civil rights, Sherman thought he was going to grow up to be a politician or an attorney, but his path, like mine, took him down a road that led him to policing.

One of the pivotal moments for Sherman and his views on policing took place during the fall of 1970. Sitting alone at the Mayor's office during a Jewish holiday, Sherman took a phone call from an Officer Blood telling him that the city's jails had been overtaken by inmates. Numerous jails experienced uprisings over poor conditions, unreasonable wait times for bail hearings (in some instances, defendants were waiting over 12 months to get a hearing). The Mayor at the time was John Lindsay, who was known for his civil rights advocacy and for walking the streets of Harlem and Brooklyn to meet with his socioeconomically disadvantaged constituents. Lindsay believed in the rights of human beings and equality for all. Rather than using force immediately, Lindsay entered into negotiations with the prisoners, while a young Sherman assisted with arranging bail hearings for prisoners, trying to bring the riots to a peaceful resolution. Through Lindsay's negotiations, the inmates released all the hostages, control of the jails was regained by correction officials, and the riots ended. Sherman observed this outcome compared to that of the Attica Prison Riots which occurred a year later. Governor Nelson Rockefeller's negotiations failed, and he decided to use force to regain control. In the process of reclaiming the prison they killed 39 people—29 prisoners and 10 hostages. The difference between the two hostage situations in Sherman's eyes was the differing approach to crime and justice—punishment versus procedural justice and Sherman was on the side of justice.

After working in the Mayor's office, Sherman transferred his fellowship over to the police department, where Chief Patrick Murphy assigned him to track the implementation of the neighborhood police teams' program. In addition to the neighborhood policing teams, Sherman worked on several projects for Murphy and ended up in the planning and research division working under Anthony V. Bouza who was an inspector at the time. Bouza formed a strong bond with Sherman and when Bouza took over the investigations unit he had Sherman come work for him. Sherman would work undercover as a civilian complainant, going to police stations to lodge a complaint to see if the precinct Captain would accept it. On most days, he would be thrown out of the precinct. Under Bouza's mentorship, Sherman's work on these topics led him to believe that there must be a better way to lead police reform.

Seeing the deep-seated issues between the police and the community, Sherman realized the criminal justice system required change. Rather than going into politics or becoming an attorney, he decided to continue his education and became a criminologist. He completed a diploma in criminology from the University of Cambridge in 1973 and then an MA and PhD in sociology from Yale in 1974 and 1976. After graduation, Sherman began studying the effects of policy on police behavior, crime concentration, and performing randomized controlled trials of police patrols. Sherman had maintained his relationship with Bouza, and in 1980 when Bouza became police chief of Minneapolis, Sherman had access to a police department where he could conduct research and have the support of an innovative chief. The relationship led to several influential studies in policing, beginning with the 1984 Minneapolis Domestic Violence Experiment. The study on domestic violence arrests was one of the first randomized controlled trials to test the effects of policy on policing outcomes. The study examined police responses to domestic violence randomizing by color-coded folders whether the officer would make an arrest, offer "advice" or mediation, or tell the offender to leave the house for eight hours. At the end of the study, the findings were summarized as "arrest is best" which led states to mandate that police *shall* arrest for domestic violence offenses citing the study as evidence of reducing recidivism.

Sherman's work with police departments early in his career was foundational in his understanding of how crime manifests. Analyzing data in the early 1980s from the Minneapolis Police Department led Sherman to discover that many of the calls for service were repeats. The same addresses generated call after call after call, leading him to believe that not all areas of the city needed a police presence, maybe just certain areas of the city needed an increased presence. Then in 1989 Sherman, Gartin, and Buerger published an article titled "Hot Spots of Predatory Crime: Routine Activities and the Criminology of Place." That seminal article demonstrated that 50 percent of the Minneapolis calls to the police were generated from 3 percent of the city's intersections and places. This was the first step in a series of foundational research articles that supported Weisburd's Law of crime concentration (MM#8). It was a major paradigm shift at the time. Until that article, criminologists studied people as a unit of analysis rather than places. This finding—5 percent of city street segments generated roughly 50 percent of the calls—was replicated across several different cities in countries across the globe, and as described in Mental Model #8, has now become Weisburd's Law of crime concentration.

Both Sherman and Weisburd had early field experiences that influenced their thinking about crime, for Sherman it was working closely with NYPD and Minneapolis, and for Weisburd it was accompanying NYPD community police officers on their walking beat. Completely outside of each other's influence they were both arriving at the same conclusion. For Weisburd, the idea of crime concentration started while he was walking the beat with the NYPD community officers. He realized that officers returned to the same parts of their beat over and over again. Rather than patrolling "bad neighborhoods" he realized they patrolled bad "places." Weisburd began thinking about how crime existed in "small worlds," rather than large neighborhoods. Which made him wonder if there was a better approach to patrol than random patrol policing. It was during this time in their careers that Sherman and Weisburd met.

Weisburd had obtained a faculty position at Rutgers University, and they were searching for a visiting distinguished professor the same year he began his tenure. The Dean of the School, Ronald Clarke, asked Weisburd to serve on the search committee. When the two senior professors assigned to assist with the interviews did not show up, Weisburd was left to do the interviews and make the decision by himself. Sherman was one of the interviewees. Knowing he and Sherman both shared the same mentor, Weisburd called Albert Reiss, Jr. to ask him what he thought about offering Sherman the position. Reiss told Weisburd that Sherman would be a fantastic addition to Rutgers. Weisburd nominated Sherman for the position, and Dean Clarke, knowing the two researchers had similar interests, decided that one of Sherman's prime responsibilities would be to work with Weisburd.

Sherman and Weisburd were both immensely interested in examining the effects of police patrols on crime and calls for service, especially in areas where crime and calls for service were concentrated. When Sherman started at Rutgers, he was already running the Minneapolis Repeat Call Address Experiment (RECAP) experiment and calling the places with repeat calls for service "hot spots." Weisburd's "small worlds" and Sherman's "hot spots" focused on the same idea, that small areas of a city generated the most crime and calls for service. And they wondered if focused police patrols in hot spots could prevent crime and reduce calls for service better than random patrols. At that time, the common belief among the media, academia, and even some police chiefs was the police could not effectively prevent crime. This ideology developed out of the failure of the Kansas City Preventative Patrol Experiment to show reductions in crime from increases in police patrols. It was also perpetuated in books like *Police for the Future*.

In *Police for the Future* David Bayley wrote:

> The police do not prevent crime. This is one of the best-kept secrets of modern life. Experts know it, the police know it, but the public does not know it. Yet the police pretend they are society's best defense against crime.

This belief started when the Kansas City Preventative Patrol Experiment (reviewed in MM#8) found that routine police patrols did not prevent crime or increase citizen's feelings of security. The study examined whether increased police patrols would reduce crime and improve citizen's perceptions of security. The findings drove the ideology of that era, which was police could not prevent crime, but Sherman and Weisburd were not sure that point of view was accurate. By diffusing the patrols throughout the entire city rather than focusing on the "hot spots" or "small worlds," Sherman and Weisburd hypothesized that the Kansas patrols were not effective because they were not properly focused on the areas where crime concentrated. This led Sherman and Weisburd to devise the Minneapolis Hot Spots study (discussed in Mental Model #8—Law of Crime Concentration). This study was one of the first randomized controlled trials to test a patrol intervention.

Simultaneously, as the Minneapolis Hot Spots study was occurring, Weisburd was conducting a similar study with 56 Jersey City drug hot spots to determine the effects of increased police patrols on drug and prostitution calls for service. This study showed inconsistent results with decreases of narcotic activity in some hot spots where activity was the highest but not in all hot spots. These seminal studies built a model for Sherman and Weisburd that has continued throughout their career, a model of using the outcomes of applied research (RCTs) to drive police practice and policy. Both Weisburd and Sherman understood that like medicine, randomized controlled trials were the only way to determine causality in the field. Without a comparison group, there was no way to understand whether the intervention *caused* the outcome. And while both Sherman and Weisburd have contributed to the diffusion of evidence-based policing across the globe, it was Sherman that first put the idea of evidence-based policing into print.

Reading the book *Demanding Medical Excellence* was the pivotal moment for Sherman. Millenson gave a framework for holding the medical establishment accountable. He covered topics like the cost of care, medical culture, and the idea of EBM. Sherman saw the value of what an evidence-based framework could bring to the policing profession. *Demanding Medical Excellence* explained the idea of EBM and how the medical field was making advances in medical care through applying research to patient care, but as with any paradigm shift it was not an easy road to forge.

Convincing doctors to use research to drive practice was, as Millenson said, like "herding cats." In his book, he told story after story of research that was known in the field by the researchers but was not applied in the field at all or until decades later. One of the doctors Millenson highlighted was Dr. Scott Weingarten, who at the time of the writing was the Director of the Los Angeles Cedars-Sinai's Medical Center for Applied Health Services Research. His primary job was to "inform fellow physicians that the way they practice medicine seems to deviate from the scientific literature," to make sure clinical practice followed scientific evidence. Cedars-Sinai wanted to ensure their doctors were applying the current known rigorous scientific findings in practice. Weingarten adopted the McMasters Hierarchy of Evidence and expanded the scientific grading system from A-C to A-E to review the piles and piles of scientific articles lining his desk in order to organize them into clinical pathways for the physicians at Cedars-Sinai. He created a system to ensure evidence-based practices were being followed. Reading about Weingarten and Millenson's ideas on how to hold the medical field accountable, Sherman realized it was an outline that policing could follow.

When Sherman's flight landed at Heathrow, he had already decided that policing could follow the same framework as the medical field and began summarizing the idea of evidence-based policing. He began by giving a lecture on "Evidence-based Policing" and writing an article of the same title for the Police Foundation (now the National Police Foundation). The article was published in their "Ideas in American Policing" series. He described evidence-based policing as "the use of the best available research on the outcomes of police work to implement guidelines and evaluate agencies, units, and officers." This is the definition most people commonly refer to when they discuss EBP. Still, Sherman went on to describe it more robustly further down in his paper, stating:

> Evidence-based policing is about two very different kinds of research: basic research on what works best when implemented properly under controlled conditions, and ongoing outcomes research about the results each unit is actually achieving by applying (or ignoring) basic research in practice. This combination creates a feedback loop (Figure 18.1) that begins with either published or in-house studies suggesting how policing might obtain the best effects.

Feedback loops (MM #15) are needed for Bayesian reasoning. Without a feedback loop, experts have no way of systematically improving outcomes. Sherman was applying the same ideas to policing that Millenson discussed in his book. He understood what Sackett, Guyatt, and Weingarten were trying to do when they developed EBM. Police officers are like medical doctors. The police officer's job is to service the public so rather than creating an outcome desired by a patient, they should be focused on the public. Police should understand if their interventions *cause* the desired outcomes (reduced crime, disorder, and social harm). To improve police practice, police need a feedback loop to learn from those outcomes. Theory and laboratory testing are one thing but testing interventions in the field is the *only* way (according to Sackett, Millenson, and Sherman) of understanding if the interventions truly achieved the expected outcomes.

Field research has disproved many experience-based theories, especially in policing. When I say experience-based theories, I mean when we take our individual experiences and develop a theory about how humans work. Scared Straight was run for 35 years before a randomized controlled trial demonstrated that it increased participants' rates of recidivism. Practitioners thought by showing juveniles their potential future they would quit committing crime. Future consequences rarely reduce current behaviors, which is why dieting is so hard. DARE has had multiple field experiments that have revealed the programs shortcomings and sometimes adverse outcomes. However, this program is still alive and well in many police departments across the country. Critical Incident Stress Debriefing (CISD) was debunked in the field of psychology over a decade ago as an ineffective tool against PTSD, but police agencies across the U.S. still use this as an intervention after a critical incident.

Field testing has also indicated what works. Hot spots policing is one intervention that has been shown to have moderate effects for reducing crime, calls for service, and specific types of crimes (drugs, prostitution, theft, etc.). Focused deterrence, using a carrot and stick approach (opportunities and punishment), has proven to be an effective method of reducing violence. Introducing home health visits for socioeconomically disadvantaged persons reduces child abuse and neglect, violence by children later in life, and domestic violence between parents. Many psychological issues stem from poor parental bonds, and the health visits before a child turns two helps establish stronger bonds, which reduces a lifetime of negative effects. Probation officers trained in core correctional practices were 13.7 percent more effective at preventing their offenders from reoffending than untrained probationers.

Being evidence-based indicates a practice was tested in the field and has shown positive outcomes. There are evidence-based practices that work in many professions: medicine, education, social work, and public health, to name a few. Sherman, along with Weisburd, understood that field testing police practice was a fundamental requirement for policing policies. And although Sherman wrote the first article on evidence-based policing, as Guyatt first coined the phrase even though it was Sackett who created the framework, Weisburd has been just as influential in the development, implementation, and diffusion of evidence-based policing.

The Mental Models in Practice VI—Mental Models 16–18

Peer Review Your Perspectives, The Scientific Method, and Evidence-based Practices

Mental Models 16–18 is about understanding and testing your assumptions. Policing has many assumptions, ones we created ourselves and others that were passed to us from the academy, field training officers, supervisors, or other officers. Our assumptions come from everywhere. It is our duty to our communities to understand whether the policing practices we engage in are based on credible sources or "best practices." It is also our duty to test our practices to make sure they are the most effective and least harmful to our communities. Here is how to put Mental Models 16–18 into practice:

1. Write down all your assumptions about policing on the left-hand side of a piece of paper.
2. On the right-hand side, write down how you learned that information.
3. If you do not know where you got the assumption from, see if you can find empirical research that supports your belief.
4. Create another column and if your assumptions are based on research, write in the third column what the level the research design reaches on the MSMS.
5. The chart should look something like Table 16.18.1.

Table 16.18.1 Example of Chart for Listing Assumptions and Empirical Support

Assumptions	Source of Information	Empirical Support	MSMS Rank
Hot spot policing does not displace crime			
Mentoring is an effective tool for helping women to get into specialty units			

Part VII

How to Make Decisions

Targeting, Testing, and Tracking

Knowledge is very clearly not the same as action.

Michael L. Millenson

Sherman's original definition of evidence-based policing has stayed consistent over the course of the last several decades, but it was not until 2013 that he outlined a strategy for applying it. Sherman's work with police agencies over several decades led him to realize that although he had given policing a definition of evidence-based policing (EBP), he had never really outlined a strategy for applying EBP. It was one thing to understand that research *should* be applied to police practice, but *how* you applied it to police practice is a different animal. It was knowledge versus practice. As such, in 2013 he created a method for applying EBP to the field. He called it Triple T—Targeting, Testing, and Tracking. *The Rise of Evidence-Based Policing—Targeting, Testing, and Tracking* explains how to apply EBP by (1) Targeting the problem at hand, (2) Testing an intervention, and (3) Tracking the outcome.

The science author Brian Clegg has said in his book, *The First Scientist: A Life of Roger Bacon*, that Bacon had "mathematics as a foundation, an openness to consider information without bias, and an understanding of the need to communicate ... (and) the true essential that would turn natural philosophy into a science." That final component was experiment. Police too should recognize the importance of understanding the fundamental workings of the natural world, because how, when, and where police are deployed has effects, positive and negative, on society. Clegg went on to state that "he (Bacon) was so convinced that it was necessary to go beyond the unthinking acceptance of authority as a source of knowledge and to the practical" ... "Therefore he who wishes to rejoice without doubt in regard to the truths underlying phenomena must know how to devote himself to experiment." Most police slogans, mission statements, and tag lines make some type of statement about protecting and serving, thus it is only right that police have a clear understanding of what police behaviors are linked to those outcomes. If police are to protect and service, based on Bacon's foundation of knowledge, without experimentation, police cannot be sure their practices are generating the effects they desire, for experience alone "does not make a conclusion certain." Without a strategy to employ the scientific method, policing is left to intuition, tradition, and best practice. This is what Sherman's model of Targeting, Testing, and Tracking offers, a strategy to determine whether police practices are working (obtaining the goals the organization desires). Sherman's model like the First Scientist, Roger Bacon argued, includes experimentation.

DOI: 10.4324/9780367481520-20

Some have called the Targeting, Testing, and Tracking, or Triple T strategy, a repackaged form of the Scan Analysis Respond Assess (SARA) model, but SARA was never meant to be a scientific approach to policing issues. SARA was built on a model of binary comparisons. During the scanning process officers used their experience or administrative data to determine if there was a problem in an area. Analysis suggested looking at what other agencies were doing to combat a similar problem or creating a solution that felt right. Responding meant doing "something" to solve the problem. Rarely did the "A" of SARA get completed, as this would require assessing the outcomes to see if the issue had improved. In policing, success is often based on anecdotal evidence of an area superficially looking better, crime statistics regressing to the mean, or everyone just feeling good about what they did for the community. The female fitness challenge I created was never evaluated to determine if the female applicant pool increased or if it improved women's chances of passing the physical fitness test. Without knowing about EBP I completed an SAR. I never knew how many female applicants we actually had before the challenge and I never checked how many applicants we had after. I just knew that my supervisors liked the program. I was named employee of the quarter for it. The department received positive media coverage and it was recognized as a best recruiting practice by California POST. Although SARA may seem similar to the Triple T strategy on the surface, it was never meant to be a strategy for scientific assessment. It was instead designed as a Problem-oriented Policing (POP) strategy. On the other hand, Triple T was conceived specifically as a scientific strategy designed to implement EBP so, while SARA and Triple T appear similar, they are clearly not the same. Sherman describes the Triple T strategy as:

1   Police should conduct and apply good research to target scarce resources on predictable concentrations of harm from crime and disorder.
2   Once police choose their high-priority targets, they should review or conduct tests of police methods to help choose what works best to reduce harm.
3   Once police agencies use research to target their tested practices, they should generate and use internal evidence to track the daily delivery and effects of those practices, including public perceptions of police legitimacy.

Targeting

Targeting the problem requires proper use of your crime data. As we have discussed previously in Mental Model#10—Distributions, small data sets potentially have wide variations which means examining crime data week by week or month by month will most likely result in a data set that is too small to be useful. I recommend that police departments have their analysts pull nine sets of data for three time periods, three years, one year, and 90 days. Then I have them map the call for service data, crime data, and officer proactivity data for those periods by street segment. Remember how crime analyst Heather Lane performed this task she emailed: "All the maps look the same ... or is that the point?" This was exactly the point. I have suggested that agencies perform this exercise for two important reasons. The first is to see where their problems concentrate and the second is so that they can see that many of the problem areas remain unchanged from year to year. If they determine that the 90 day map is similar to the three year map, it then allows them to understand that they can slow down and consider solving problems rather than reacting to weekly binary percent changes. Without this insight, executives tend to rely on the very small data sets of weekly data and find themselves merely chasing fluctuating data, responding to noise rather than the signal.

When examining your data for concentration, besides places, do not forget to examine people and property. When it comes to the Mental Model#7—Pareto Principle, we have learned that many things concentrate in nature. In policing, this means there are hot people, hot places, and hot property. This concept could even be extended to a list of the top offenders in a given city. This principle has been used in medicine, where high utilizers of emergency services have been identified to determine whether there are better suited interventions to provide treatment and care to replace the expensive use of services like the emergency room. In policing, a crime analyst could look at the top offenders for social disorder problems, for burglaries, or other offenses that could be proactively prevented. This principle would not only apply to offenders as hot people but could also be applied to people identified as crime victims. Over the course of my career, I have seen Asian families targeted for home invasions due to the belief that they keep their savings hidden in the house rather than in a bank. Sex workers are another group of victims that could be targeted as well as the elderly. Recently, Inspector Natalie Hiltz in the Peel Police Department in Canada has looked at the overlap between victim and offender harm. She found that offenders that were victims in the two years previous to their offending generated 2.7 times as much harm to society than offenders that were never victims. Whether the hot person is a victim or an offender, the point is to determine whether the crime is concentrating in a particular group of people so that an appropriate response can be considered.

Crime can also concentrate in things. During the 2007 recession, many police departments saw a rapid uptick in metal theft. Construction sites and schools were being targeted for the copper wiring as the price per pound had skyrocketed. Many agencies did not approach the copper theft problem directly but chose to target the recycling companies by rapidly putting into place city ordinances that required recyclers to be able to verify where the copper had come from. This prevented the recycler from accepting stolen copper. When property becomes portable and small, there is a tendency for increased theft, as we have seen over the last two decades with computers and phones. One good example of using a Triple T strategy for a hot property problem was using a "Code 2" vehicle lights intervention conducted by Captain Jason Potts at Vallejo PD to deter theft from autos.

During the holiday season, the City of Vallejo would see an increase in their thefts from autos at their local mall. To reduce the number of thefts, Captain Potts worked with BetaGov, a nonprofit dedicated to helping criminal justice institutions perform rapid-cycle randomized controlled trials, to test a strategy of intermittently patrolling the mall with their "Code 2" lights on (blinking red and blue lights). The intervention aimed to answer the question of whether being highly visible would deter would-be thieves from breaking into vehicles. The officers were randomly assigned to patrol the mall with a "lights on" or "lights off" condition. The study took place at the mall over the 34-day holiday season. Officers would receive their assignment at the beginning of shift to engage in a "lights on" or "lights off" patrol. At the end of the 34-day period BetaGov analyzed the data and determined that there were less auto thefts and auto burglaries during the "lights on days" than the "lights off" days. Although it is common to have theft issues from parked cars, directing officers' patrol strategy and what they would do during their shift was something new. Traditionally, between calls for service most police officers can patrol the way they want, where they want (if they stay within their beat), how they want, and because over time officers' habits have developed into an independent contractor mindset, officers tend to dislike having their patrol activity directed. As much as officers may disagree with having their patrol activities managed, direct oversight of patrol officers has been shown to reduce crime, calls for service, and the use of force. Achieving these benefits, however, first requires

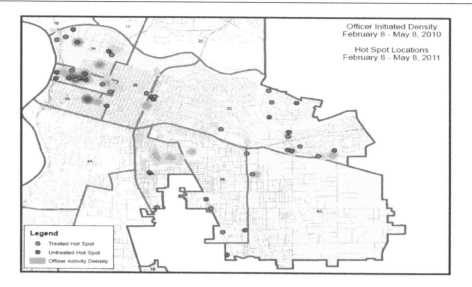

Figure 19.1 Sacramento Police Department Hots Spots Maps Depicting Officer-Initiated Density

an understanding of where your officers are patrolling and what they are doing when they are there.

Mapping officers' proactivity just like crime can reveal a lot about a police organization. By examining where officers are conducting their proactive engagement, managers can begin to understand if their officers are choosing to police in the areas where problems are occurring or if they are policing in areas where it is easy to catch a stat. When the Sacramento Police Department mapped out CFS hot spots and then layered it with the officer's proactivity in preparation for the Sacramento Hot Spots study they could see that officers were not always policing in the problem areas—see Figure 19.1.

By failing to manage an officer's proactive engagement, police agencies open themselves up to over-policing in some areas without seeing additional crime reduction gains. Officers believe they know their beats. They will say that a good cop knows where the crime is, but they do not work all shifts, all days of a week, every week of the year. This means that although beat officers may have a general idea of the problems in their area, they do not know everything about their area. Additionally, as you read in Mental Model #1—System 1 and System 2 thinking, their minds are not computers so they cannot retain the massive amount of information they are receiving the way a computer can. Their minds will access data based on the heuristics—ease of availability, saliency, and emotional attachment. The findings of the Sacramento Hot Spots study demonstrated that this phenomenon existed in their organization, a finding that was replicated by colleagues in other countries as well.

Ellie Macbeth, a business improvement coordinator for the Police Service of Northern Ireland, along with her Cambridge advisor Dr. Barak Ariel evaluated officers' ability to predict crime hot spots by asking officers to note them on a map (waymarkers) and then compared their predictions to crime reports and displayed both on maps. She showed that officers were poor predictors of where crime was occurring and going to occur. They predicted false positives almost 100 percent of the time—97 percent to be exact. These false positive areas were locations where the officers thought crime was occurring, but it was not. This finding was so significant that Malcolm Gladwell highlighted their research in his book, *Talking to Strangers*. This study was replicated with New Zealand officers and they too only demonstrated a 12 percent accuracy at predicting hot spots. The Sacramento Hot

Spots study, New Zealand study, and Ellie's work demonstrate that leaving officers to decide where to police may not be the best patrol strategy. When targeting a problem, executive managers need to know where crime is occurring, what types of crimes are occurring, how often they occur, and what their officers are doing about it. Managers need the numerator (crimes or calls for service) *and* the denominator (officer activity) to get a good grasp on what is going on in their city. Without both, police executives' understanding of what is going on in their community will be drastically limited. Once executives have all the information and gain an understanding of what their target is, then they can take the next step in the Triple T strategy and test an intervention.

Testing

The intervention depends on the problem. Is the problem burglary, robbery, drug dealing, theft, or some other type of social disorder? Only once the problem has been identified should executives begin to look for an intervention. When officers are at this stage of problem-solving I usually refer them to the What Works Centre's Crime Reduction Toolkit (https://whatworks.college.police.uk/toolkit/Pages/Welcome.aspx). The tool was created by the U.K. College of Policing which was formed in 2012 to advise policing in the U.K. and Wales. It is the professional body that "provide(s) those working in policing with the skills and knowledge necessary to prevent crime, protect the public, and secure public trust" (www.college.police.uk/About/Pages/default.aspx). The tool ranks interventions that have been tested for efficacy and efficiency in an easily navigable format.

The greatest aspect of the Toolkit is how user friendly it is. A training course is not necessary. Getting to the website is all the knowledge needed. Down the left side of the table there are filters to click on to narrow down the types of interventions displayed. It can be narrowed down by level of impact (what intervention works best), the focus of the intervention (prevention, diversion, or reoffending), the type of problem (burglary, robbery, drink driving, etc.), the target population (adult, young person, child, or place), and the other factors involved (drugs, alcohol, or gangs). Once the search is narrowed down the table mode will display the interventions in a list format. The table will indicate if the interventions were effective or not by displaying an icon next to the intervention.

The Toolkit's icons range from ✓✓ to XX, with ✓✓ indicated the greatest efficacy and XX indicating a backfire or harmful effect. The intervention's efficacy rating is based on a thorough review of the empirical literature. In addition to efficacy, the Toolkit also explains how the intervention works (the theory behind the intervention), where it works (particular places or people), how to implement the intervention (the strategies employed), and how much it cost to implement. The Toolkit is a great starting place to find potential interventions, but nothing says an original idea cannot be tested. Just remember that testing is important, because even though some of these interventions worked in some areas does not mean that they will work in all areas. You must test the intervention, hence the strategy of Targeting, Testing, and Tracking. After testing, data will need to be tracked to determine whether the intervention is having the expected outcomes and continue to track even after the intervention shows positive effects.

Tracking

When Sherman speaks of tracking, he is not speaking of binary comparisons as depicted in a typical CompStat or managers' meeting. This is most widely implemented with the introduction of a comparison group which allows you to understand what would have happened if nothing was done. If we do not know what would have happened had there been

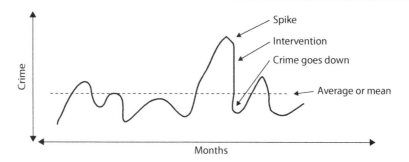

Figure 19.2 Hypothetical Crime Spike Followed by an Intervention

no intervention, then we cannot say that the outcomes were because of the interventions—Mental Model #14—Causal Inference. The reason a comparison group is needed is to make sure that the pre/post data is not just regressing to the mean. The figure above shows where police interventions commonly take place. Often by the time police notice crime has hit a high point, and then deployed an intervention, the spike is receding back to the norm. The spike could be regressing to the mean but without a comparison group there is no way to know if the intervention *caused* the crime drop. Figure 19.2 depicts a hypothetical spike followed by an intervention.

Binary outcomes, pre/post data or this week compared to last week, as explained by Simon Guilfoyle in Intelligent Policing, "tell us nothing about long term trends. They do not aid us in predicting the future." Additionally, small data sets potentially have wide variations which means you can be interpreting noise rather than a signal. As Donald Wheeler said: "While all data contain noise, some data contain signals, before you can detect a signal within any data set you must first filter out the noise." Having a counterfactual to compare data helps untangle the signal from the noise.

Choosing a comparison group can be done a couple of ways depending on the type of intervention. You can randomly assign people, places, or times to a treatment or control group or you can choose the people, places, or times to receive treatment or control. Just remember if there is not random assignment, bias will be introduced to the study and you cannot be as confident that your intervention *caused* your outcomes (MM#14). I have police colleagues who randomized the day of treatment for their experiment; in one study officers wore body cameras on some days but not others. In another study officers visited hot spots nine times a day on one day and only three times a day on others, randomizing the number of visits. Randomizing the days of intervention is not a perfect fix due to contamination issues, but not a bad approach when in a pinch.

Sherman suggests tracking not only crime data, but also police activity. In his Triple T paper, he suggests using the powerful tool of GPS to determine where officers are engaging in police activity. In the Sacramento Hot Spots study, we used GPS from the officer's squad cars to determine how much time they spent in a hot spot and how many times they visited the hot spot. One cautionary note however pertains to the computing power needed to accurately analyze GPS points: although the study was small as it was only in two districts and lasted for only three months, when my software programmer dumped the GPS data into the software program it took the program a full day to compile the results. In the Portland Neighborhood Involvement Community Engagement RCT we could not find a computer that could handle the GPS data. The study lasted nine months and had 90 different hot spots sites. It created a large amount of data that crashed every computer we had, and in the end, we could not analyze the GPS data from the officers' squad cars. GPS is the best form of officer locational data as it comes from the cars and most police agencies require officers to put out their proactive stops. Agencies can track officer activity by mapping officers' calls for service by street segment. A street segment is intersection to intersection which will make street segments unequal but makes mapping easier. Mapping can give some insight into where officers are engaging in their activity throughout the day without crashing any computers.

Tracking officer activity is just as important as tracking crime data. Routine activity theory states that crime takes place when a motivated offender encounters a suitable victim in the absence of a capable guardian. Police activity has been shown to reduce crime and calls for service when it is strategic, focused, and tailored. Knowing where the capable guardians are patrolling is important data for police executives to track. Although police patrols are viewed as beneficial, over-policing one community compared to another can increase the amount of social harm felt by a community without increasing any of the crime reduction benefits. Mapping officer activity by street segments would allow police executives to determine if some communities are being over-policed with little improvements in crime outcomes. To evaluate the balance of prevention and harm, indexes have been created to determine the amount of damage a community incurs. As opposed to crime counts as the only outcome measure, harm takes into consideration the difference in harm between one homicide and one shoplift. Social harm takes into consideration the harm from policing and the benefits. It gives us a systematic way of including both benefits and harms into a standardized method for evaluating police interventions.

Harm Indexes

All crimes are not created equal.

Dr. Larry Sherman, Dr. Peter Neyroud, and Eleanor Neyroud

The idea of a crime harm index (CHI) was first suggested in the 2016 article "The Cambridge Crime Harm Index: Measuring Total Harm from Crime" which suggested creating an index based on number of sentencing days a crime received instead of using crime counts. The concept behind the CHI is to create an index based on societal harm that will allow for better comparisons across disparate crimes rather than traditional crime count outputs. To measure the severity of a crime, the authors suggest considering the length of a sentence associated with the crime in the sentencing guidelines. A CHI works in much the same way other indexes as it is a statistical tool designed to measure performance over time. If the objective is to reduce harm to communities rather than simply counting crime, then perhaps our method of benchmarking crime should reflect our goals.

We usually count crime where 1 = 1, for example, one assault with minor injuries equals one assault with major injuries, however the Cambridge CHI article proposed an index where crimes are weighted by severity using sentencing guidelines. Sentencing guidelines reflect the severity of crime, where the offender will receive less of a sentence for an assault that causes minor injuries compared to a sentence for an assault that causes a major injury. The idea behind using sentencing guidelines is to reflect the democratic values of the public. In theory, sentencing guidelines reflect the public's perception of harm associated with each crime. The index accounts for high harm/low occurrence crimes (homicide) and low harm/high occurrence crimes (shoplift) through the sentencing guidelines rather than a simple crime count model. A harm index creates equivalency between these disparate variables and allows agencies to get a better idea of how much harm is occurring in their cities rather than using a unidimensional measure like crime counts.

CHIs have now been created in several different countries: Sweden, Australia, New Zealand, Denmark, Canada, and California in the United States. All the CHIs have been created using sentencing guidelines, however they vary in how the sentencing guidelines are used. The Cambridge CHI (U.K.) uses the minimum number of sentencing days to create the index, so that an offender's previous crimes will not contaminate the index. For example, if a shoplifter is arrested for a shoplift offense, in California it will be tried as a felony if it is their third offense in a year. The Cambridge CHI avoids this overweighting by using the minimum possible sentence for an offender with no previous crimes. Canada uses the Canadian Crime Severity Index (2016) which is based on the actual sentences offenders

DOI: 10.4324/9780367481520-21

receive rather than the proposed sentence to determine the relative seriousness of a crime in comparison to other crimes. Unlike the Cambridge CHI this index does consider an offender's previous crimes. Notably, this type of index can only be created if the prosecutor's office releases offender sentencing data. In the U.S., the state-specific sentencing guidelines make a universal American CHI a little more difficult to create compared to other countries whose sentencing guidelines apply to the whole country. In the U.S. state-specific CHIs would need to be created.

Although the U.S. has federal sentencing guidelines, most police agencies are making arrests based on state statutes rather than federal statutes. For example, crimes like homicide and a battery that occur at a school with an injury did not have a minimum or median sentencing guideline which is why the maximum guidelines were used for the CA-CHI. As I mentioned briefly in Mental Model #9—The Felonious Few, part of my PhD dissertation was the creation of the CA-CHI. I created the CA-CHI from the California Penal Code using maximum sentencing guidelines. I was not able to use a minimum or median sentencing guideline because many of the California statues only list the maximum possible days of imprisonment rather than a minimum or median sentencing guideline. The full table is listed in my dissertation titled, "The Sacramento Hot Spots Policing Experiment: An Extension and Sensitivity Analysis." Table 20.1 displays the first six rows of the table.

Table 20.1 Maximum Penalty by days of Imprisonment for the CA-CHI by Offense Category

Penal Code	Description	Minimum Months	Median Months	Maximum Months	Maximum Days
187	Homicide			180	5400
211	Robbery	36	48	72	2160
212.5	Home Invasion	36	72	108	3240
215	Carjacking	36	60	108	3240
220	Assault with intent to rape	24	48	72	2160
243.2(A)(1)	Battery school injury			12	360

This type of measure can be used in management meetings as well as within the Triple T strategy, where using a CHI as an additional outcome measure when testing an intervention's effect as seen in Mental Model #9—The Felonious Few. In the original Sacramento Hot Spots Policing Experiment, we evaluated the effects of 15-minute high visibility patrols using CFS and Part I crimes as outcome measures. The analysis showed a 7.5 percent reduction in CFS and a 25 percent reduction in Part I crimes, a statistically significant finding when comparing the treatment to the control group assuming the hypothesis was correct. For my dissertation I translated the hot spots outcomes from crime counts to the CA-CHI by following the guidelines listed in the Cambridge CHI article. I created the CA-CHI using the following steps:

1 Counting up the number of crimes of each type in the hot spot;
2 Multiplying the count for each type by the maximum number of prison days recommended for crimes of that type by first time offenders;
3 Calling the product of that multiplication (crime count for a crime type × maximum days in prison) the HST for the crime type (for harm subtotal of days of prison for that offense type);

4   Repeating steps 1, 2, and 3 for every type of crime recorded for the area or person; and
5   Summing up all HSTs to yield the total crime harm (TCH).

When comparing the treatment hot spots to the control hot spots using the CA-CHI for Part I crime, I found the treatment hot spots had a reduction of 23,580 prison days' worth of harm compared to the control area that had an increase of 15,840 prison days. When evaluating the hot spots study using the CA-CHI the overall outcome I observed is that a CHI is useful if you have a lot of variance in the types of crimes that occur in the community or an area. If there is not a lot of variance, say for a small town or city that rarely experiences any type of violent crime, then a CHI might not offer any more information. However, when there is variation in crime data, CHIs offer another lens with which to examine crime data. Examples of this can be found in other countries besides the U.S.

Inspector Dan Jones of the Edmonton Police Service used the Canadian Crime Severity Index (CCSI) to create harm maps for his service. Comparing crime counts versus crime harm maps allowed his officers to see the value of using a CHI. Using seven indicators—assault, break and enter, homicide, robbery, sexual assaults, theft from vehicle, and theft over $500—he mapped out crime by counts. Figure 20.1 shows his kernel density map depicting crime by count. Inspector Jones then mapped the same crimes using the CCSI. Figure 20.2 shows the kernel density map depicting the harm spots.

Figure 20.1 Edmonton Police Service Crime Counts Hot Spots

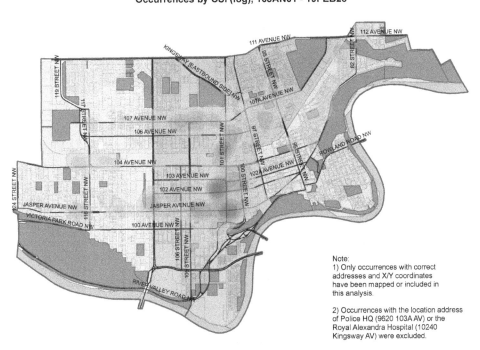

Figure 20.2 Edmonton Police Service Crime Harm Spots

The densest areas of the map shifted from the North area of the district to the central area of the district. Additionally, the density shifted from being more diffuse across the map to being much more concentrated around the areas of 102 and 103 Avenue NW. Observing both maps, executives can make a better decision about where to direct limited resources. Rather than spreading them across the entire area, they can be focused on a very small area. Moreover, the focus can be tailored to the type of harm generated, so rather than a typical saturation patrol strategy, a harm reduction or community engagement strategy could be potentially employed. Saturation patrols or other types of aggressive enforcement policing can lead to frayed relationships with the community.

The Danish Police modeled the Danish Crime Harm Index after the Cambridge CHI. They used their crime management system (POLSAS) to extract crime frequencies. Then with guidance from the 12 Danish police district prosecutors and the guidelines for first time offenders they created a national CHI. Figure 20.3 shows how crime frequencies for the 2016 year were distributed by count.

Theft and related offense accounts for 52 percent of all the crimes in Denmark for 2016 while rape and related offenses only account for 2 percent of the crime. Once the crime frequencies were translated into the Danish CHI you can see how the percentage of crime was redistributed in Figure 20.4.

Theft and related offenses now account for only 16 percent of the total crime and rape and related offenses account for 10 percent of the total crime. Here again you can observe how the translation of a crime count into a crime harm metric takes societal values into consideration and places more weight on crimes that occur to a person than on crime that occurs to property. Using pie charts, graphs, and maps are useful for showing the value of a CHI, for sometimes it isn't until you see the data translated visually that you understand the value of the CHI.

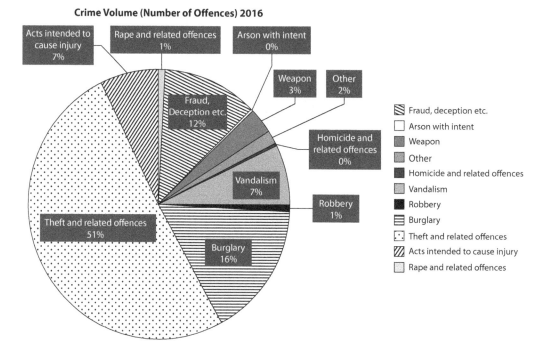

Figure 20.3 Danish Police, Crime Volume (POLSAS)

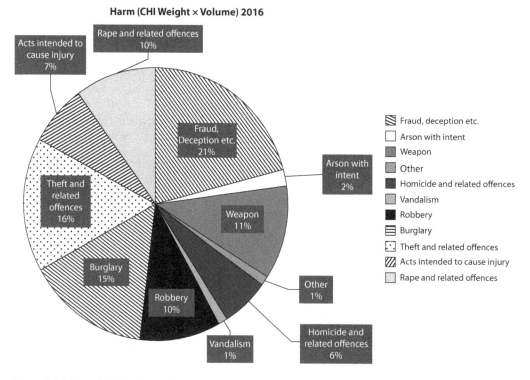

Figure 20.4 Danish Police Crime Harm, Weights Applied to Crime Data 2016 (POLAS)

CHIs are a good first step in contextualizing the harm that is occurring in a community. A similar index that takes this idea a bit more broadly is the harm-focused index. Harm-focused indexes consider the negative outcomes from interventions as well as positive outcomes to provide a more complete picture of the intervention's impact. Harm-focused indexes are relatively new and are only recently being tested. You could view police patrols as akin to chemotherapy, something that is potentially harmful and beneficial at the same time: chemo destroys the cancer cells but at the same time kills off good cells and makes you sick. However, chemotherapy can save your life which is why most cancer sufferers will endure rounds of chemotherapy to save their own lives no matter how ill it makes them. Analogizing chemo to policing, if crime is our cancer, extra patrols can reduce the amount of crime in an area, but at the same time it might take a toll on the law-abiding people of the community and could make residents feel as though they are being over-policed. In the end police want the community to be safe, just like doctors want their patients to be cancer free. The balance with policing, just as with chemotherapy, is to have enough patrol to reduce crime, but not so much that it makes the community unhealthy. Harm focused indexes can help police agencies create a better balance.

In medicine harmful outcomes due to a medical intervention is called "iatrogenesis." Interventions are not a panacea. They do not "cure" everyone 100 percent of the time and they do not harm everyone 100 percent of the time; sometimes there is 90 percent improvement with minor side effects. Medicine is not perfect. Therefore, the medical field makes sure that it understands the effects of their interventions, not just the one or two positive outcomes they are looking for. In policing, many of our interventions can cause harm or at the very least not be effective. One of the ineffective examples that policing continues to employ and can sometimes have harmful outcomes is the DARE program discussed in Mental Model #2—Cognitive Biases. Creating a harm index for the DARE model might assist police agencies with deciding if the benefits outweigh the harms. A 2015 systematic review of drug intervention programs evaluations showed that of the 17 evaluation studies that were completed since the 1980s found 43 different negative outcomes. The researchers stated: "The most common type of negative outcome resulting from prevention programs was behavioral effects consisting primarily of increases in consumption, especially alcohol use." There may be benefits such as a better relationship with the police that accompany the iatrogenic effects, but unless the interventions are tested, policing will remain in the dark about what those effects are. The critical question to ask here is why are police departments continuing to engage in drug and alcohol prevention programs when the most common outcome is increased consumption?

To understand how to reduce crime in any place while creating the least amount of harm, *all data* on *all of variables* that influence crime outcomes will be required. The variable police executives often fail to include in their management meetings is officer proactivity. To understand crime in *your* city you must understand *your* officer proactivity. Without knowing what your officers are doing in the community, where they are doing it, and what laws they are enforcing, an important piece of both the crime and the harm equation is missing. When officers engage in investigatory stops it creates a deterrent effect while reducing the department's legitimacy. Collectively, there are benefits to the community while causing unintended harm to the individual. The community benefits if a person is stopped for speeding, is arrested for drunk driving, or drugs are taken off the street. The individual is harmed if they are stopped and searched, nothing is found (false positive), and a ticket is issued for a broken taillight, nonetheless. To properly evaluate an agency's data, department heads need to examine the numerator (crime) and the denominator (police proactivity) of the crime equation as both influence crime occurring in the city.

Currently, there are very few harm indexes that try to balance the harms *and* benefits of police interventions. Dr. Jerry Ratcliffe at Temple University was one of the first to create a harm index that attempted to balance the positive and negative outcomes of police investigative stops. In his article "Towards an Index for Harm Focused Policing," he acknowledged both the crime reduction benefits of conducting pedestrian and traffic stops and the negative effects of stops in areas with high populations of people of color. His study attempted to use an index that accounted for both the crime reduction effects and the detrimental effects on people's psychological and financial wellbeing of crime and officer proactivity.

Like the other CHIs, Ratcliffe used data from the Philadelphia Police Department and coded all Part I and Part II crimes that occurred from 2004 to 2013 using the Pennsylvania state offense gravity score (OGS). The OGS was adopted in 1997 and was created by the Pennsylvania Commission on Sentencing to assist judges with handing down sentences to offenders. The OGS ranks offenses on a scale of 1-14 with murder and rape of a child under 13 the highest at 14, robbery with the threat of bodily injury scoring mid-rank at 7, and minor misdemeanors scoring the lowest at 1. When the Part I and Part II crimes were ranked by frequency, assaults, vehicle thefts, and thefts were the highest frequency crimes in the previous ten years and accounted for 75 percent of crime in Philadelphia. When depicted in a frequency graph, rape and homicide were barely perceptible.

The number of homicides and rapes that occur within a city or county are, in essence, rare events, yet homicide is often the data point the media uses when discussing the safety of a city. This is because we as a society have deemed this one of the greatest harms one person can do to another, yet homicides when depicted as a crime count on a graph is barely visible. Ratcliffe then takes the Part I and Part II crimes and translates them into a harm index using the OGS. Once they are transmuted, homicide and rape become visible at the bottom of the graph. The graph overall looks more evenly weighted compared to the crime count graph. The graph shifts from assaults, thefts, and vehicle thefts generating 75 percent of the crime count to the OGS harm index graph depicting 75 percent of the harm being generated by assaults, vehicle theft, theft, *burglary, and aggravated assaults*. Thus, using a CHI allows for viewing the data through a different lens. When a CHI is combined with crime counts it can give you a better understanding of what is occurring within any neighborhood, town, or city.

In this same article, Ratcliffe takes the idea of a CHI one step further, by attempting to create a harm index that considers both outcomes of a stop (the harms and benefits), by creating an index reflecting the amount of harm a police pedestrian or traffic stop causes. His approach was one of the first attempts to try and come up with a metric for officer harm, an admirable attempt, but the index weighed a bit heavy on the harm side. Ratcliffe even cautions the reader that his research is "debatable and certainly exploratory."

To do so, he used an arbitrary score for pedestrian and traffic stops, trying to weigh the balance between not overwhelming the harm index model and having a sufficient score to make the harm detectable. He rated officer's proactivity stops at a .25. He mentions in his article that one peer reviewer brought up the issue that a weight of .25 meant 56 stops ($.25 \times 56 = 14$) and equaled one homicide based on the OGS; as such they were not sure that this was the correct weight to give to police proactivity. It would also mean that four stops were equal to a minor misdemeanor. As mentioned before, this is one of the first attempts to quantify the benefits and harms of crime and police activity into one measure and although a brilliant attempt, the weighting measures continue to require further development.

Additionally, Ratcliffe included traffic accidents when he mapped the harm index because accidents also create harm for the individual and the community. As such, his final index included Part I crime, Part II crime, traffic accidents, and officer's proactive stops. Other than one district in Philadelphia, most of the harm generated in the 21 police districts of Philadelphia resulted from Part I crimes. The harm attributed to police proactivity in the districts ranged from 7.4 to 14.2 OGS and police proactivity was highly correlated to areas with high harm from Part I and Part II crimes. This will most likely resonate with officers, as we all know officers tend to make stops in high crime areas. Ratcliffe's attempt to combine crime harm and police-generated harm into one index is commendable as an inspirational starting point for further study and more thorough development. The error here could possibly be found in Ratcliffe's attempt to quantify and combine outcome measures that have separate units of analysis into one index. To clarify, individuals may be the recipient of the harm, however communities are the beneficiary of the crime reduction. The outcome measure is at the microlevel for the individual and at the mesolevel for the community, which means a harm index that combines criminal activity and police activity might not contextually be the best way to think about harm.

Another way to contextualize police-generated harm in a community would include mapping the police proactivity. As previously discussed, mapping out a department's crime and calls for service activity over three years, one year, and 90 days can give a visual depiction of where crime is occurring in the city. I suggest mapping out officer activity over the same time period and then overlaying the maps to determine if officer activity is occurring where the crime and calls for service are occurring (for the most part). The hot spot kernel density map I created in Mental Model #20—Targeting, Testing, and Tracking showed the difference between the high crime/CFS areas and where the officers were patrolling. Recently, Kennedy, Caplan, Piza, and Thomas mapped out NYPD's homicide clearance rates and demonstrated there was a connection between living in socially disadvantaged communities and low homicide clearance rates. They used the Infoshare online website (www.inforshar.org/main/public.aspx) to determine the percentage of families receiving food stamps, percent Black or Hispanic residents, percentage of families below the poverty line, percentage of single-headed female households with children, and median household income to create a disadvantage index as a control variable. An agency could use this disadvantage index and overlap it with the departmental patrol activity to determine if the officers are policing where they should be and policing the way they should be—matching the type of activity to the type of crime occurring in the neighborhood. For example, from those maps, an agency could pull the officer proactivity data and categorize the stops into types. What we would find is that most agencies most likely do not have any manner for collecting data on the *reason* for the stop, meaning the different causes are not documented. Important questions remain unanswered such as: Did the officer stop someone because there is drug or prostitution activity in the area? Was the stop for speeding because there were a lot of accidents in that area? Or was it a regulatory infraction stop because the officer is looking for something else like drugs, a warrant, or a parole violation? Why was the officer patrolling in that area? Collecting and examining the data to determine why officers are making stops in the area is a good first step. Additionally, a police agency could come up with their own determination of harm and create thresholds for the amount of policing activity it conducts in any one area. You could create a legend coding 1-20 stops in an area for a month as green (go), 21-40 stops as yellow (slow down), and once the activity goes over 40, as red (stop). These numbers are absolutely arbitrary. The thresholds could be determined by the amount of crime or harm occurring in the neighborhoods and how much police activity the data revealed it took to keep crime within its upper and lower bounds without exacerbating negative community sentiment. I think this is something every agency would have to evaluate individually, although if enough agencies developed something like this, we might be able to amalgamate the data and analyze if the thresholds were generalizable to other police departments.

Harm is a concept that police agencies should adopt into their operational decision-making models. It is another way of examining data that will assist police agencies with making determinations about resource allocation. While the media drives the national crime narrative with discussions concerning homicide rates, the average citizen is more impacted by thefts from their car and wanting to feel safe walking to the corner store. Furthermore, citizens living in socioeconomically disadvantaged areas want to feel as though they can walk to the corner store without being accosted by a panhandler, drug dealers, or area thugs as much as they do not want to be stopped by the police. Adding a harm metric to a CompStat or management meeting can help police executives balance the needs of their communities by using data and evidence to drive their decision-making processes while reducing the unintended social harm to their communities.

Decision-making Models

When one is dealing with human lives and life opportunities, it is immoral to adopt a mode of decision making which has been demonstrated repeatedly to be either inferior in success rate or, when equal costlier to the client or the taxpayer.

Dr. Paul E. Meehl

The final Mental Model in this book is the decision-making model. Police must make decisions. That is the primary role of being a police officer. When cops are called to a scene, they decide how to handle the situation. Do they make an arrest, give a citation, or leave the person with a warning? Has a law been broken? As officers progress in their career and move up the chain of command, their responsibilities and, therefore, their daily decisions change. They are tasked with setting the strategic priorities of the organization, allocating resources, and dealing with personnel issues. The number of decisions that police make in a week span a variety of topics and the use of a decision-making model is one strategy that can assist an agency with keeping organizational priorities on track. There are many different decision-making models—the rational model, the intuitive model, the recognition primed model, and the creative decision-making model—and by this point in the book it should already be apparent that I am going to suggest the rational model approach to decision-making which takes the following steps:

1 Identification of the problem or opportunity;
2 Gathering and organizing relevant information;
3 Analyzing the situation;
4 Developing a range of options;
5 Evaluating and assigning a value to each of the options;
6 Selecting the options that rank the highest;
7 Acting decisively on that option.

Before I start with Step 1 on the rational decision-making process, I typically have police executives perform two exercises to help them examine their current practices, policies, programs, and strategies to refine their understanding of their organizational and community values.

The first exercise I have police executives conduct is a program and practice evaluation. I have police executives group their programs and practices into four separate categories: Social Programs, Crime Prevention Programs, Juvenile Programs, and Public Relations

DOI: 10.4324/9780367481520-22

(PR) Programs. I have them examine their programs under these separate categories to better understand what they are trying to accomplish in their city and for whom. Many programs may span two categories—if you are doing this exercise then put the program into the category that *primarily* defines the program. Social Programs are the programs that are not specifically targeting a juvenile population and are not crime reduction programs. These programs or practices focus on dealing with a societal issue where the primary problem is not necessarily a crime. The Social Program category are where homeless outreach or mental health programs would fit. Crime Prevention Programs and Juvenile Programs are easy to classify, as the titles are self-explanatory. PR programs are programs that police agencies are engaging in for public relation reasons and are not community engagement. The program is not for any crime reduction purposes or genuine community engagement. PR programs are things like Prescription Drug Take Back Days which are not crime prevention programs nor are they intended to engage the community. The department is not engaging the community directly, but it is a PR campaign. Once the programs have been grouped into categories then you can determine what the goals of the program are and are you meeting them? Police departments are spending taxpayers' monies; thus, executives should be clear about why they are allocating resources to a particular program or practice and what they are trying to achieve. Social programs are the programs that do not specifically target a juvenile population and are not crime reduction programs. These programs (or practices) are focused on dealing with a societal issue where the primary issue is not necessarily crime. This is where homeless outreach programs or a mental health program would fit.

After the programs are organized into the categories, I have police executives evaluate the programs on six topics: cost, goals, metrics, metrics matching the goals, comparison group, and harm. Every program is listed down the left side of the page, and then the evaluation categories are listed across the top. Table 21.1 depicts how the chart should be created.

The first topic—cost—is merely the yearly cost for the officers to participate in and operate the program. This exercise is meant as a quick and dirty evaluation of organizational practices, not a deep analytic dive. Think about how many cops participate in the program, how many days of the week they spend engaged in it, and then multiple that number by 52 to get a rough estimate. Then determine what goals the program is trying to achieve. Is it crime reduction? Is it to improve police perception?

Running police executives through this exercise can be an eye-opening experience. I once ran an executive group through this process and one of the first programs they discussed was a traffic program where everyone in the organization (even the chief) had to do an eight-hour shift of traffic enforcement between Thanksgiving and Spring Break. The hypothesis was a good one; their idea was that there were more people out drinking and driving during the holidays; therefore, an increase in police presence would deter the number of alcohol-related accidents and fatalities. Using the evaluation matrix, they estimated that they spent $700,000 on officers' salaries for participation in the program. The goal of the program was to reduce car accidents, especially fatalities, but at the time they were

Table 21.1 Program Evaluation Matrix

Programs	Yearly Cost	Goals	Metrics	Metrics Match Goals	Comparison Group	Harm
Program A						
Program B						
Program C						

Table 21.2 Program Evaluation Matrix

Programs	Yearly Cost	Goals	Metrics	Metrics Match Goals	Comparison Group	Harm
Program A	$700 K	Reduce traffic fatalities	Citations and warnings	No	No	Increasing the community's negative perception
Program B						
Program C						

measuring citations and warnings. When they compared the program goals to the collected metrics, they realized they had lost focus. The program had run for so long, they forgot about the original intent of the program. At the end of the exercise their evaluation matrix looked like Table 21.2.

Most police executives do not even think about comparison groups or potential harm arising from their interventions. For each program written down, I have executives do a premortem to think through possible harms that could stem from their program. For the Home of the Holidays traffic program, listed potential harms—perceptions of over-policing, reduction of citizen satisfaction with the police, civil unrest, and increased use of force incidents. When a policing program involves stopping citizens involuntarily, thinking through the benefits and the harms should always be a part of the process.

The second exercise is designed to narrow down the organizational values and priorities of a department. During an executive meeting or any meeting have each person anonymously write down:

1 The values they consider important for the organization.
2 The values they consider important for their specific unit.
3 The values they consider important to themselves personally.

To conduct it anonymously, assign the task prior to the meeting. This way people can type their answers and turn them in at the meeting, thus no one's handwriting can be recognized. Once the priorities are collected, a pairwise wiki survey can be created to rank the order of priorities.

A pairwise wiki survey is an online survey where you pit two opposing ideas or values against each other, and you choose which idea is better or which idea you value more. As you start choosing which values or criteria are more important than others, the tool calculates a score ranging from 0 (never preferred) to 100 (always preferred). There is a website called All Our Ideas (www.allourideas.org) that allows people to create their own wiki surveys for free. Their website currently offers the chance to try a survey before you create your own. When I accessed the page, it displayed the following question: "Which do you think is better for creating a green New York City?" the two possible answers were: (1) To create a greener New York City, ban plastic bags, or (2) Replace sodium vapor streetlights with LED or other energy-saving lights. The next time I accessed the site the answers were either: (1) Convert 5 percent of the public park areas into community gardens, or (2) More opportunities for the public to help clean and revitalize public parks. The idea behind wiki surveys is to keep pairing ideas or values against one another to understand where a group ranks the ideas or values against other ideas or values. In the case of policing, depending on what agencies are trying to understand, they could ask questions like: "Which do you think will reduce citizen complaints?" and the two possible answers could be: (1) Introducing implicit bias training, or (2) Training sergeants to supervise patrol activity more closely. The next two answers could be: (1) Introducing implicit bias training, or (2) Incorporating de-escalation tactics into the use of force training. This activity narrows down what types of interventions people think are more useful than others. Another possible question is "How do we improve community perception?": (1) Through outreach programs that citizens enjoy like Coffee with a Cop, reading to elementary school kids, or bike rodeos, or (2) Reducing crime. The next pair of answers could be: (1) Through improving the community's access to resources (education, jobs, medicine, etc.), or (2) Through outreach programs that citizens enjoy like Coffee with a Cop, reading to elementary school kids, or bike rodeos. As you can see, you pair every question or idea until they are all ranked. Even simple questions can be asked: "What is more important to you?": (1) Crime reduction or (2) Community engagement, then (1) Community engagement or (2) Community safety. Creating an internal pairwise wiki survey can help a police department gain a better understanding of their priorities and creating an external wiki survey can help agencies gain a better understanding of their community's priorities.

The pairwise wiki survey (offered by www.alloursources.org) can also be structured to evaluate community priorities. Agencies can advertise a wiki survey via social media to encourage the public to participate. Police departments can have citizens take wiki surveys during Coffee with a Cop, or any community engagement program. By outlining the priorities of an agency and the community, a hierarchy of priorities can be developed. A wiki survey will give the list of criteria and its score between 0 and 100. This ranking process can be developed into a decision-making algorithm for your police department. *Trigger warning*: do not be scared of the algorithm, it is easier than you think.

Algorithms are not as complicated as people think they are. If you have kids, you have had experience with a simple algorithm used as an evaluation tool, the Apgar score. Dr. Virginia Apgar was a Professor of Anesthesiology at Columbia University in 1952 when she created the Apgar score. When babies were born, doctors would use their personal preference about how to determine whether a baby was in distress. Some doctors would rate the baby based on the strength of their cry, others would observe muscle tone or skin color, and some would use a combination of observations to determine whether the baby would be given assistance or left on their own accord to die. It was believed that babies who were born blue and had difficulty breathing would not survive. Therefore, no interventions were offered, and babies were often left to die. Between 1949 and 1952, Dr. Apgar, the director of obstetrics anesthesiology, took an interest in examining the babies directly after birth, looking for birth defects, labor effects, and observing them as to their heart rate, respiratory effort, reflex irritability, muscle tone, and color. She taught her students to do the same. The often repeated legend of the Apgar score started with a simple question during lunch.

As Dr. Apgar was sitting in the cafeteria eating lunch a student approached her and asked: "Dr. Apgar, you always tell us to look at a baby when it is born, but what is it that I am looking for?" Dr. Apgar pulled out a napkin and wrote down five things—color, tone, cry, breathing, and heart rate. Dr. William A. Silverman, who worked with Dr. Apgar, feels that the story was just one of the legends and it was really the work between 1949 and 1952 of trying to resuscitate abandoned babies and documenting the outcomes that led Dr. Apgar to come up with the scoring system. She wrote about her scoring method in a 1953 paper titled "A proposal for a new evaluation of the newborn infant." She evaluated 1,025 neonatal records using her method to score babies one minute after birth on each observable sign as a 0, 1, or 2. She rated the babies 0–2 in poor condition, babies 3-7 in fair condition, and babies rated 8-10 in good condition. Her paper found that mature infants receiving a score between 0-2 had a neonatal death rate of 14 percent, those with a score from 3-7 had a death

Table 21.3 APGAR Score Indicators

Indicators		0 Points	1 Points	2 Points
A	Activity	Absent	Flexed arms and legs	Active
P	Pulse	Absent	Below 100 BPM	Over 100 BPM
G	Grimace	Floppy	Minimal response to stimulation	Prompt response to stimulation
A	Appearance	Blue; Pale	Pink body; blue extremities	Pink
R	Respiration	Absent	Slow and irregular	Vigorous cry

rate of 1.1 percent, and babies with a score of 8-10 had a death rate of .13 percent. Her system was turned into the Apgar scoring system we know today by two doctors, Butterfield and Covey, in 1962, in their article "A practical epigram of the Apgar score." Their article framed the five neonatal scores into Dr. Apgar's name to make it easier for doctors to learn. As the doctors discussed in their article, by 1962, most doctors understood the necessity of evaluating babies a minute after birth and again five minutes later. Still, many doctors had difficulty remembering all the signs to look for. By turning it into an easy-to-recall epigram, the doctors made the practice easier to apply. Table 21.3 shows what we know today as the Apgar scoring system.

The Apgar score is a simple algorithm—a process or a set of rules to be followed in a decision-making process. In the competition between a human's ability to predict and a computer's ability to predict, Dr. Paul E. Meehl's 1954 book *Clinical Versus Statistical Prediction* showed algorithms were better than humans at predicting clinical outcomes in several different areas—clinical psychology, violations of parole, pilot training, and criminal recidivism. With over 200 studies comparing experts and algorithms, algorithms still won— 60 percent of the studies showed that the algorithms were significantly better at prediction.

Using the wiki survey outcomes, police agencies can create an algorithm to rate programs or ideas based on the priorities the organization has created. Wiki surveys can prevent mission creep and help organizations allocate resources to programs, projects, and policies that align with their values. In Table 21.4 I show the fictional results of a wiki survey and how to use an algorithm with a scoring range of 0–2, like the Apgar score. Clearfield and Tilcsik suggest in their book, *Meltdown: What Plane Crashes, Oil Spills, and Dumb Business Decisions Can Teach Us About How to Succeed at Work and at Home*, a range of −1 to 1. For police departments, a range of 0–2 like the Apgar score is a better grading metric and will avoid a zeroed-out score. Rather than ending up with many programs being negatives or zeroes, a 0–2 range should allow for a large enough scale to get an idea of how an agency's policies, practices, and programs rank with their departments and communities' priorities. Table 21.4 depicts a fictional wiki survey score chart.

Table 21.4 Example of Wiki Survey Score Chart

Criteria	Weight	Project A	Project B	Program C	Strategy D
Reduce Social Disorder	89	2	1	2	1
Improve public perception in minority communities	79	2	0	0	0
Reduce Violent Crime	73	1	0	2	1
Improve Morale	67	0	0	2	1
Reduce workload on patrol	62	0	0	2	0
Improve clearance rate	59	1	0	0	1
Total weighted score for project	848	468	89	582	288

As you can see from the total weighted score, if the department only has the resources to run one program and if they want to stay in line with their organizational values then Program C will be the organizational choice rather than Program A and B or Strategy D. This exercise helps police executives with Step 5, assigning values to options, in the rational decision-making process.

1 Identification of the problem or opportunity.
2 Gathering and organizing relevant information.
3 Analyzing the situation.
4 Developing a range of options.
5 **Evaluating and assigning a value to each of the options**.
6 Selecting the options that rank the highest.
7 Acting decisively on that option.

Another suggestion to round out the rational decision-making model would be to add Mental Model #6—Second Order Thinking review after Step 6. Do this by writing down all the possible downstream outcomes that could occur if you implement Program C. Write down the potential positive and negative effects. Think about the secondary or tertiary harm a Program C will create. Sheriff Chris Nocco of Pasco County recently came under fire for using an algorithm to target offenders. His program was based on the idea of intelligence-led policing, targeting high profile repeat offenders to deter them from offending. The Sheriff credits the program with reducing burglaries and theft. Still, the *Tampa Bay Times* accused the Sheriff of harassing people without cause and wrote a several page article about the practice. The *Times* found citizens who reported that the deputies would cite them for minor infractions, contact them in the middle of the night, and would keep coming back several times over the month. Having a discussion about these secondary (people feeling harassed) and tertiary (the newspapers painting the program in a negative light) outcomes will help police executives think through the best way to implement the decisions made in Step 6 to avoid the issues Sheriff Nocco is now facing.

Human thinking is flawed. We automatically use our biases to make decisions, and even when confronted with this information we still don't think we are doing it. We believe we are rational when we are just following gut, intuition, and tradition. Using these two exercises to develop priorities and evaluate departmental programs will help executives make rational, fact-based, data-driven decisions if the steps are followed. My hunch is even if an organization completes both exercises when they arrive at Step 6, "Selecting the option that ranks the highest," someone in the room will tell a powerful anecdotal story about "a guy" as evidence for maintaining a program. Just remember stories are not evidence and a lot of stories still do not equal evidence. Unless the evidence is data and research, it is just opinion. If you want to spend taxpayers' monies effectively and efficiently, then overriding the process is not allowed. As Dr. Laura Huey says in *Implementing Evidence-based Research: A How-to Guide for Police Organizations*, you have to be willing to "kill your darlings" to eliminate programs that are ineffective or inefficient no matter how beloved the program and no matter the rank of the person who created it. If the program, project, or practice is not achieving the priorities and values as ranked by the organization then it should be killed. Imagine how efficient and effective a police agency could be if they ran through this exercise every year at their annual retreat.

Police agencies should take the time to develop a decision-making model to avoid mission creep and ensure that all the current programs align with their organizational values and priorities. Once executives understand the process, they will realize if they want programs or projects to remain in existence, they will have to meet organizational priorities. When the programs are evaluated, they will need to demonstrate (1) The metrics they measure match the goals they are trying to achieve, (2) The program has a comparison group to evaluate against regression to the mean and safeguard their community from unintentional harm.

The Mental Models in Practice VII—Mental Models 19–21

Triple T—Targeting, Testing, and Tracking, Harm Indexes, and Decision-making Models

Mental Models 19–21 are about understanding and testing your assumptions. Policing has many assumptions, ones we created ourselves and others that were passed to us from the academy, field training officers, supervisors, or other officers. Our assumptions come from everywhere. It is our duty to our communities to understand whether the policing practices we engage in are based on credible sources or "best practices." It is also our duty to test our practices to make sure they are the most effective and least harmful to our communities. Here is how to put Mental Models 19–21 into practice:

1 Triple T—Targeting, Testing, and Tracking:

  a Map your city by street segments using crime counts.
  b Target your hot people, hot places, and hot things.
  c Test your interventions.

2 Create a harm index:

  a Map the city by street segment using the harm index.

3 Create a method for making decisions:

  a Rank priorities with a wiki survey.
  b Create an algorithm to measure programs based on priorities.
  c Choose programs based on highest-ranking programs.

4 Test your highest-ranking programs.
5 Choose a control group.
6 Implement the program.

Part VIII

How to Apply It All

Conclusion

How the Twenty-one Mental Models Can Improve Policing and Reduce Cognitive Bias

> Learning to "evaluate evidence and identify inappropriate conclusions," is a critical thinking skill.
>
> Dr. Peter M. Nardi

You might be wondering how these Twenty-one Mental Models can help reduce crime *and* bias, even though the year 2020 made it feel like an either/or proposition. It might feel as though you must stop proactively policing to appear as though your agency is not over-policing (nobody even knows what this means), but it does not have to be this way. Policing can do both and be balanced. To do that, examine your data in the aggregate. This book has laid out an argument to demonstrate it is how you display, interpret, and use data to test police practices that will lead to improving the profession through reducing our cognitive biases and improving our understanding of the effects of police practices on the community. Using data as described in the Twenty-one Mental Models can help police stop "whack-a-mole" reactive policing practices and use their resources in ways that meaningfully reduces crime and disorder while creating the least possible harm to their communities. This section ties all the Mental Models together and explains how to put it into practice.

While trying to finish this book, I listened to a Hidden Brain Podcast called "The Air We Breathe", an NPR podcast hosted by Shankar Vedantam. The podcast was about police shootings and the mindset of the involved officer within the context of the community. Vedantam interviewed some of the top researchers of implicit bias, one of which was Mahzarin Banaji. Dr. Banaji is a Harvard Professor who co-created the Harvard Implicit Association Test (IAT), a timed computer-based test where participants push buttons on a keyboard to sort words into a "white" grouping or a "black" grouping. The IAT is based on the way we group things in our minds, and we group things based on how we associate them. Then the IAT assesses whether you associate black (the color) more negatively or white (the color) more negatively and reveals your implicit bias toward race. In essence, the IAT is attempting to test the Mental Models in our mind related to the things we associate with good/bad and with black/white. The test is controversial within the research community, with research supporting the efficacy of the test *and* research showing the test is not valid or reliable. I only mention the podcast here because what I found interesting was that during the discussion of police shootings and implicit bias, the debate eventually progressed to talking about Implicit Bias Training. Banaji, the creator of the IAT, stated "I don't believe this training is going to do anything." She even made a comment that if she did not try to do something about the explosion of Implicit Bias Training, that when she became an old women she would be disappointed in herself.

DOI: 10.4324/9780367481520-23

The discussion centered around the idea that all humans have bias—bias about race, gender, age, weight, and other types of Mental Models we have created in our minds about other human beings and these Mental Models are based on context. Banaji explained that you cannot try to weed out individual officers with implicit bias, that bias sits within the context of the community. Bias is not an individually created trait. It is a malleable trait that changes over time within the context of where you work and live. Another researcher on the podcast, Eric Hehman, discussed his research that showed geographic areas of the U.S. where citizens had high IAT scores for implicit bias against Blacks and those areas were disproportionately associated with more use of lethal force against Blacks. The research he conducted is correlational rather than causal (MM#13). Hehman demonstrated how a community's implicit bias is linked to police shootings. The IAT test is open for anyone in the world to take and when you take it, you have to enter your zip code. Mapping the zip codes and the IAT results, Hehman compared the IAT measures to police shootings and showed that where implicit bias in the community is higher than average, police shootings of minorities are also higher than average. As Vedantam put it, the individual mind sits within the community, thus the variables that you might not pick up in the individual (due to random fluctuations in small numbers) could be picked up in the aggregate. The data in the aggregate is one of the salient points of this book—if we want to better analyze, understand, interpret, and apply our data to reduce crime while creating the least possible harm to our communities, then we must examine our data in the aggregate. Aggregating data over longer periods of time is the key to better allocating resources, reducing disparate impacts in communities, and focusing our energy on the right problems.

In the medical field it has been discovered that there are disparities in prescribing analgesics for pain when comparing Blacks to Whites, meaning that doctors tend to under-prescribe opioids to Blacks whose complaints of pain are the same as their White counterparts. Because of these ongoing issues, the National Academies of Science Institute of Medicine convened a committee in response to a Congressional request to make suggestions about how to combat "disparities of care" in the health care system. In the report, the Institute of Medicine made several suggestions to combat the systemic bias within the profession, but there were no suggestions of holding doctors individually accountable for bias. There were only suggestions for how to improve the profession through changes in management of the system.

A systematic approach as a profession or a department might be a better way to combat all cognitive bias whether we are talking about bias related to race, numbers, patterns, or availability rather than trying to solve the issues with check-the-box bias training. This is what Banaji also suggested. She argued:

> One of the difficulties we've had in the past is that we have looked at individual people and *blamed individual people*. We've said if we can remove these 10 bad police officers from this force, we'll be fine. And we know as social scientists – and I believe firmly – that that is no way to change anything."

She suggests rather than Implicit Bias Training (which has yet to have an evidence base of efficacy) or eradicating individual officers through the use of the IAT test (as though that is a measure for explicit racism), we should approach the problem using "in-the-moment" reminders. She suggested, for example, in medicine when a doctor types the name of a painkiller into a hospital's prescription system a graph pops up and it says "Please note, in our hospital system, we have noticed that this is the average amount of pain killer we give to White men. This is the average amount we give to Black men for the same reported level of pain." By incorporating in-the-moment reminders, it gives the doctors an opportunity to stop and decide consciously rather than relying on intuition, tradition, or local practice.

The Twenty-one Mental Models have given you a framework in which you can apply the same type of interventions that will help your organization create an overall strategic plan to reduce crime, disorder, and cognitive bias. Cognitive bias manifests itself in our assumptions, heuristics, and beliefs, causing us to make decisions based on gut, tradition, and common practice (MM#1 and MM#2). These cognitive biases cost an organization in efficacy and efficiency, and potentially harm the community, but are difficult to detect and manage individually. Bias does not manifest itself in the individual, but in the aggregate. Individual doctors and officers cannot see their bias when prescribing a medication or writing a ticket. Cognitive biases can only be managed through aggregated data. Police departments can accomplish this by systematically monitoring their aggregated data and if bias is observed, as Banaji suggests, management can figure out ways to give officers "in-the-moment" reminders. This can be accomplished through alerts in a CAD system, reminders in management meetings, or reminders in roll calls. The same way Banaji suggests medical doctors be informed of a hospital's over- or under-prescription of medicines, officers can be given the same reminders for over- or under-policing a particular area of the city.

The Mental Models presented here should give you an understanding that our cognitive biases cause us to react in a way that might be less than optimal for our communities. With this knowledge, step back, slow down, and take the time to make better, more informed decisions about where to allocate police resources. Because now you know that if you look at larger data sets (MM#11), you can observe how phenomenon concentrates based on the Pareto Principle (MM#7)—crime concentrates at place (MM#8), with people (MM#9), and with property. Success and challenges concentrate somewhere in the system, so focus your efforts there. Most of these problems are stable across time, which means changing tactics weekly or monthly is not an effective use of resources. This will be a difficult transition for any organization because it is what you are used to, and you have "always done it that way." Try peer reviewing your organizational perspectives (MM#16) and asking your management team: "How do you know that?" How do you know a weekly management meeting is accomplishing our goals? Do we still examine data as binary percent changes (MM#5)? What measures are we using to determine that it is? Rather than falling back on old habits, think about using a decision-making model to set the priorities of the organization (MM#21) and allocate your resources to figuring out the problem rather than reacting to it. Once you have figured out an appropriate intervention then test it (MM#19) and make sure you have a comparison group (MM#18). This way you will know that the intervention caused (MM#14) the outcome rather than it merely being regression to the mean (MM#12). Think about examining your outcome measures as a harm index (MM#20) rather than a crime count. Does this give you a different perspective as to what is occurring in your community? And finally, use all the principles of thinking, first (MM#3), second (MM#6) and probabilistic (MM#15) to think through all the steps of applying the Mental Models to your organization. The Mental Models are fundamentally scientific (MM#17) theories about how to think about the world. The Twenty-one Mental Models cross disciplines, spanning psychology, sociology, statistics, criminology, and business. I chose these Mental Models to lay out a framework for policing to decrease its psychological footprint on society. Munger first mentioned long ago in a commencement speech that if we want to be successful in our disciplines, then we must hang our experience on a latticework of multiple Mental Models and that is what the *Twenty-one Mental Models That Can Change Policing: A Framework For Using Data and Research For Overcoming Cognitive Bias* offers here.

Mental Model Method—How It All Fits Together, Mental Models 1–21

Combining the Mental Models in Practice Summaries I-VII, here is one method a police organization could take to evaluate and restructure their approach to crime reduction and cognitive bias:

1 Start with your data.
2 Examine your city's crime, calls for service, and officer proactivity data:

   a   Map out your city data by street segment—intersection to intersection no matter the street length.
   b   Map out the data for three years, one year, and 90 days.
   c   See if there is any difference between the data sets—look for stability.
   d   Focus your efforts on the 20 percent of the street segments that generate the highest calls for service and crime.
   e   Evaluate whether your officers' proactivity is occurring on the street segments where 50 percent of your crime is occurring.

3 Examine your city's arrest data:

   a   List out your offenders by number of arrests over the last three years.
   b   Rank offenders from highest frequency to lowest.
   c   Rank offenders from highest harm to lowest harm.
   d   Determine which offenders rank the highest on both lists.
   e   Determine if the offenders who rank high on both lists would qualify as a generalist offender compared to a specialist offender.
   f   Focus diversion efforts on the smallest percent of offenders who are generating the largest percent of harm for the city.
   g   Using a "pulling levers approach" (carrot and the stick) to reducing recidivism will be your best approach for these types of offenders.

4 Examine your departments internal data:

   a   Try to determine if there are any 80/20 ratios in your data for complaints, injuries, use of force, or officer proactivity.
   b   If there are, see if there is an intervention you can use to disrupt or increase behavior depending on what you find.
   c   Determine if there is a particular type of call that generates officer complaints or use of force – can you find ways to intervene on those types of calls?

5 Examine any city data that could have an impact on police calls and see where they overlap:

   a Map your city's fire department and EMS data by street segment and three year, one year, and 90 day data sets to determine if the calls concentrate in any way.
   b Overlap police and fire maps to determine where an intervention might be effective that could reduce calls for both departments.

6 Create Statistical Process Control Charts for crime, calls for service, and harm—figure out the average using at a minimum three years of data:

   a Create an upper control limit and a lower control limit using one standard deviation. One standard deviation will keep you from reacting when crime is 18.26 percent above or below the average. If crime is moving toward the high teens of a standard deviation, it is time to start thinking about an intervention.

7 Create a harm index:

   a Map the city by street segment using the harm index.
   b Map out the data for three year, one year, and 90 days.
   c Overlay the crime harm index map with the crime count map.
   d Overlay the crime harm index map with the officer proactivity map.
   e Are your officers policing in areas that do not have high harm or high crime counts?

      i If they are policing in low crime/low harm areas, what types of stops are they making?
      ii What is the race of citizens they are stopping?

   f Can you create a social harm index for your organization that can takes into consideration both the protective factors of proactivity and the harmful factors of proactivity?

      i Can this social harm index be mapped and overlayed with crime counts?

8 Submit three year, one year, and 90 days of data to the RTI Statistical Traffic Analysis Report www.star.rti.org:

   a Are you finding disparate impacts of traffic stops?
   b Is there a particular type of traffic stop that creates disparity?
   c Is there a particular area of your city that generates the greatest disparity in traffic stops?
   d Is there a team within your agency that creates the greatest disparity in traffic stops in your organization?

9 Examine the last three year of calls for service to determine the frequency of call types:

   a What percent of your calls are non-criminal calls for service?
   b What percent of your calls are related to social services that do not involve criminal activity, such as homelessness, mental illness, or public disorder?
   c What percent of your calls for service could be handled by non-sworn city personnel?

Now that you have your first sets of data and maps, stop examining your data in small data sets and doing binary percent change comparisons. What does the data tell you? What do the maps tell you? How did your STAR analysis come back? Are your officers policing

Table C.1 Program Evaluation Matrix

Programs	Yearly Cost	Goals	Metrics	Metrics match goals	Comparison Group	Harm
Program A						
Program B						
Program C						

where crime is occurring? Are they over-policing? Are they under-policing? Are they over-policing certain areas or certain races? Once you have all this information then you can start examining the programs you have in place to determine if they are helping you with any of the problems the data reveal to you. Using the Program Evaluation Matrix in Mental Model #21—Decision Models, evaluate your current policing programs to determine if they are meeting the goals of your organization. Additionally, use the matrix to determine if your current programs are addressing the issues your data has revealed.

If your programs are not addressing the issues your data is revealing, then "kill your darlings" and get rid of those programs. Once you have identified your problems and jettisoned ineffective programs, now it is time to determine what programs, policies, and practices to implement. First, use the STAR analysis, officer proactivity maps, and arrests as a proxy measure for thinking about how organizational cognitive biases manifest itself in the data.

10   What did the STAR analysis reveal?

    a   Were there disparate traffic stops?

        i   Did they occur in a specific part of the city?
        ii   Were they generated by a particular team?
        iii   Did the disparity occur as a result of the Pareto Principle—were a certain percent of officers creating the largest portion of the disparity?

    b   What percent of your calls are related to social services that do not involve criminal activity such as homelessness, mental illness, or public disorder?
    c   What percent of your calls for service could be handled by non-sworn city personnel?

11   What did the officer proactivity maps reveal?

    a   Were there certain parts of the city that were over-policed?
    b   Were there certain races that were arrested more than others?

        i   Were these discretionary arrests or mandatory?

    c   Were there certain races that were cited more than others?

        i   Were these discretionary arrests or mandatory?

12   What are your organizational assumptions about crime?

    a   Conduct the exercise from Table C.2 in the Putting it into Practice chapter which is available here.
    b   Have your executives anonymously perform the exercise.
    c   Write their assumptions about policing, crime reduction, generators of crime, perpetrators of crime, etc. on the left-had side of a piece of paper.
    d   On the right-hand side of the paper, have them write down where they learned that information from—experience, research, internet, etc.

Table C.2 Assumptions Exercise Table

Assumptions	Source of Information	Empirical Support	MSMS Rank

    e   If the assumption was based on research, then create a column and rank the research design based on the Maryland Scientific Methods Scale.

13 Connect the assumptions in the organization to the officer activity in the field.

    a   How is the community mind affecting the individual mind?

    b   How is the executive management driving individual behavior?

    c   If there is disparity in the data how can the organization create "in-the-moment" reminders for the officers so that disparate contacts in the community are reduced?

    d   If the officers are engaging in proactive behavior that does not reduce crime or improve citizen perceptions, why are they engaging in it?

        i How can the organization create a mechanism in which the officers police in the manner, time, and place in which the management desires? Is this through technology? Pre-loaded directed calls for service. Is this through roll calls? Is this through directed patrols?

14 Create a process to monitor officer proactive behavior to ensure it is reflecting the values and beliefs of the organization and not the values and beliefs of the individual officer.

15 Investigatory stops are still needed to prevent crime thus a balance must be maintained between crime and proactivity.

Now use the Triple T approach.

16 Triple T—Targeting, Testing, and Tracking.

    a   Target your hot people, hot places, and hot things.

        i   Using your maps target the areas with the highest crime harm/count.

        ii   Using offender data, target offenders creating the highest crime harm/count.

        iii Using victim data target victims who are subjected to the highest harm.

        iv Using theft data target high theft items.

    b   Test your interventions.

        i   Use Google Scholar or the U.K.'s College of Policing What Works Crime Reduction Toolkit to find evidence-based interventions.

        ii   Test interventions that have been found to be successful using at the level of a 4 or 5 on the Maryland Scientific Methods Scale.

        iii Use Ratcliffe's ABC spreadsheet to determine if the intervention worked.

    c   Track your data using Statistical Process Control Charts.

        i   Use Statistical Process Control Charts to track the intervention to ensure that its efficacy continues after the testing period.

    d   Track for longer periods of time not just a couple of months.

17 Repeat yearly.

The main idea behind this book is to use empirically based Mental Models to understand and interpret your data. By doing this, you should be able to remove most cognitive biases that exist within policing and provide more effective, more efficient, and less harmful policing to your communities. Implicit bias was one of the main focuses in policing during the 2020 year, yet there are many more cognitive biases besides implicit bias that affect our perceptions of data which alter our approach to policing. If we want to move our profession toward being numerate and understanding how to best approach data in a way that does not bias us toward our vulnerable communities, then the Mental Model Method of Policing is one of the best ways to get you there.

Notes

Prologue: The shoulders of Giants

xv *I wanted to … to understand them.* Goldacre, B. (2010). *Bad science: Quacks, hacks, and big pharma flacks.* McClelland & Stewart.

Introduction: What is a Mental Model and How Does It Help Policing

1 *We should be … associated with hubris.* Vedantam, S. (2020, September). The halo effect: Why its so difficult to understand the past. The Hidden Brain. Retrieved October 5, 2020, from www.npr.org/transcripts/904660038

1 *He explained to … like a nail."* (Munger, 1994) Retrieved May 05, 2020, from https://speakola.com/corp/charli-munger-widom-business-usc-1994

1 *But the concept … world" he declares.* Waldrop, M. M. (1993). *Complexity: The emerging science at the edge of order and chaos.* Simon and Schuster. p. 177.

3 *CompStat weekly data … on these numbers.* Kahneman, D. & Tversky, A. (1972). Subjective probability: A judgment of representativeness. *Cognitive Psychology, 3*(3), 430-454.

3 *In most policing … regress to the mean.* Weisburd, D. & Eck, J. E. (2004). What can police do to reduce crime, disorder, and fear? *The ANNALS of the American Academy of Political and Social Science, 593,* 42-65.

3 *This traditional way … in treading water.* Guilfoyle, S. (2015). Binary comparisons and police performance measurement: Good or bad? *Policing: A Journal of Policy and Practice, 9*(2), 195-209.

5 *If agencies uncover … "kill their darlings".* Huey, L., Mitchell, R. J., Kalyal, H., & Pegram, R. (2021). *Implementing evidence-based research: A how to guide for police organizations.* Policy Press.

5 *It will encourage … their facts upon.* Farnam Street. (2020). A lesson in elementary worldly wisdom as it relates to investment management & business. Retrieved November 7, 2020, from https://fs.blog/great-talks/a-lesson-on-worldly-wisdom/.

Part I: How We Think

Mental Model #1—Systems 1 and 2

9 *The instinctual shortcut … of the rest.* Silver, N. (2012). *The signal and the noise: why so many predictions fail—but some don't.* Penguin. p. 3.

10 *The Invisible Gorilla … of inattentional blindness.* Simons, D. J. & Chabris, C. F. (1999). Gorillas in our midst: Sustained inattentional blindness for dynamic events. *perception, 28*(9), 1059-1074.

11 *This study found … things around them.* Simons, D. J. & Chabris, C. F. (1999). Gorillas in our midst: Sustained inattentional blindness for dynamic events. *Perception, 28*(9), 1059-1074.

11 *They found that … is finished thinking.* Kahneman, D. & Beatty, J. (1966). Pupil diameter and load on memory. *Science, 154* (3756), 1583-1585.

11 *At the end … in the trial.* Kahneman, D., Beatty, J., & Pollack, I. (1967). Perceptual deficit during a mental task. *Science, 157*(3785), 218-219.

12 *System 1 thinking … choice, and concentration.* Kahneman, D. (2011). *Thinking, fast and slow.* Macmillan. p. 20.

13 *This is how … true or false.* Duke, A. (2019). *Thinking in bets: Making smarter decisions when you don't have all the facts.* Portfolio. p. 50.

14 *But because System 1 … difficult to prevent.* Kahneman, D. (2011). *Thinking, fast and slow.* Macmillan. p. 28.

Mental Model #2—Cognitive Bias

15 *Sometimes bad things … evaluating the process.* Vedantam, S. (2020, September). *The halo effect: Why its so difficult to understand the past.* The Hidden Brain. Retrieved October 5, 2020, from www.npr.org/transcripts/904660038

15 *As Kahneman says … purely statistical information.* Kahneman, D. (2011). *Thinking, fast and slow.* Macmillan. p. 36.

16 *Cognitive biases are … by System 1.* Gigerenzer, G. (2006). Bounded and rational. In *Contemporary debates in cognitive science.* Blackwell. pp. 115-133.

16 *Heuristics are our … to act fast.* Gigerenzer, G. (2008). Moral intuition= fast and frugal heuristics?. In *Moral psychology.* MIT Press. pp. 1-26.

16 *In Tversky and Kahneman's … to the world.* Tversky, A. & Kahneman, D. (1974). Judgment under uncertainty: Heuristics and biases. *Science, 185*(4157), 1124-1131.

16 *Insensitivity to sample … of small numbers."* Tversky, A. & Kahneman, D. (1971). Belief in the Law of Small Numbers. *Psychological Bulletin, 76*(2), 105.

17 *Tversky and Kahneman … statistical base rates.* Kahneman, D. & Tversky, A. (1973). On the Psychology of Prediction. *Psychological Review, 80*, 237-51.

17 *This process reminds … should look like.* Lewis, M. (2004). *Moneyball: The art of winning an unfair game.* WW Norton & Company.

17 *From this work … to cluster.* Feller, W. (1968). *An introduction to probability theory and its applications. Vol. 1.* John Wiley & Sons.

17 *Even though one … as equally likely.* Tversky, A. & Kahneman, D. (1974). Judgment under uncertainty: Heuristics and biases. *Science, 185*(4157), 1124-1131.

19 *I have taught … in Southeast Arizona.* Caputi, T. L. & McLellan, A.T. (2017). Truth and D.A.R.E.: Is D.A.R.E.'s new Keepin' it REAL curriculum suitable for American nationwide implementation?. *Drugs: Education, Prevention and Policy, 24*(1), 49-57. DOI: https://doi.org/10.1080/09687637.2016.1208731

19 *They believe that … are merely diluted.* Tversky, A. & Kahneman, D. (1971). Belief in the law of small numbers. *Psychological Bulletin, 76*(2), 105.

20 *The death rate … the midwife side.* Nuland, S. B. (2004). *The doctors' plague: germs, childbed fever, and the strange story of Ignac Semmelweis (great discoveries).* WW Norton & Company.

21 *Simon Sinek, in … of the bullseye.* Sinek, S. (2009). *Start with why: How great leaders inspire everyone to take action.* Penguin.

22 *Thomas Kuhn coined … way of thinking.* Kuhn, T. S. (2012). *The structure of scientific revolutions.* University of Chicago Press.

22 *As Max Planck … familiar with it."* Planck, M. (1949). *Scientific autobiography: And other papers.* Open Road Media.

Mental Model #3—First Principles Thinking

23 *He believed in … the key solution.* Waldrop, M. M. (1993). *Complexity: The emerging science at the edge of order and chaos.* Simon and Schuster. p. 24.

23 *I compiled my … our common beliefs.* Duke, A. (2019). *Thinking in Bets: Making Smarter Decisions when You Don't Have All the Facts.* Portfolio.

23 *Sugar makes kids hyperactive.* Milich, R., Wolraich, M., & Lindgren, S. (1986). Sugar and hyperactivity: A critical review of empirical findings. *Clinical Psychology Review, 6*(6), 493-513.

23 *We have different … visual, and tactile.* An, D. & Carr, M. (2017). Learning styles theory fails to explain learning and achievement: Recommendations for alternative approaches. *Personality and Individual Differences, 116*, 410-416.

24 *First Principles thinking … knowledge from assumption.* Parrish, S. (2019). *The great mental models volume one: General thinking concepts.* Latticework Publishing, Inc.

24 *But because the … international medical establishment.* (Konturek, 2003). Discovery by Jaworski of Helicobacter pylori. *Journal of Physiology and Pharmacology, 54*(S3), 23-41.

24 *Then in 1954 … cause of ulcers.* Weintraub, P. (2010, April, 18) *The doctor who drank infectious broth, gave himself an ulcer, and solved a medical mystery.* Discover. www.discovermagazine.com/health/the-doctor-who-drank-infectious-broth-gave-himself-an-ulcer-and-solved-a-medical-mystery

25 *It was not … to treat it.* Pincock, S. (2005). Nobel Prize Winners Robin Warren and Barry Marshall. *The Lancet, 366*(9495), 1429.

25 *As he explained … been described before?'".* Pincock, S. (2005). Nobel Prize Winners Robin Warren and Barry Marshall. *The Lancet, 366*(9495), 1429.

26 *They were also … for the doctors.* Weintraub, P. (2010, April, 18) *The doctor who drank infectious broth, gave himself an ulcer, and solved a medical mystery.* Discover. www.discovermagazine.com/health/the-doctor-who-drank-infectious-broth-gave-himself-an-ulcer-and-solved-a-medical-mystery

27 *It was purely … the 1970s and 1980s.* Lentz, S. A. & Chaires, R. H. (2007). The invention of Peel's principles: A study of policing 'textbook' history. *Journal of Criminal Justice, 35*(1), 69-79.

27 *CompStat is a … area commanders responsible.* Police Executive Research Forum (PERF) & United States of America. (2013). Compstat: Its Origins, Evolution, and Future in Law Enforcement Agencies.

27 *CompStat was developed … able to consider.* Sparrow, M. K. (2016). *Handcuffed: What holds policing back, and the keys to reform.* Brookings Institution Press.

28 *Studies have shown … the next month.* Johnson, S.D., Bowers, K., & Hirschfield, A. (1997). New insights in the spatial and temporal distribution of repeat victimization. *British Journal of Criminology, 37*(2), 224-224.

28 *Studies have shown … the next month.* Pease, K. (1998). Repeat victimisation: Taking stock, crime detection and prevention series paper 90. London: Home Office.

28 *Studies have shown … the next month.* Townsley, M., Homel, R., & Chaseling, J. (2000). Repeat burglary victimisation: Spatial and temporal patterns. *Australian & New Zealand Journal of Criminology, 33*(1), 37-63.

28 *It has also … period of time.* Sherman, L. W. & Weisburd, D. (1995). General deterrent effects of police patrol in crime "hot spots": A randomized, controlled trial. *Justice quarterly, 12*(4), 625-648.

28 *It has also … period of time.* Weisburd, D., Bushway, S., Lum, C., & Yang, S. M. (2004). Trajectories of crime at places: A longitudinal study of street segments in the City of Seattle★. *Criminology, 42*(2), 283-322.

28 *It has also … period of time.* Weisburd, D. & Eck, J. E. (2004). What can police do to reduce crime, disorder, and fear? *The ANNALS of the American Academy of Political and Social Science, 593*, 42-65.

28 *Displaying crime as … trajectories within data.* Guilfoyle, S. (2015). Binary comparisons and police performance measurement: Good or bad? *Policing: A Journal of Policy and Practice, 9*(2), 195-209.

28 *Shane Parrish in … the reasoning process.* Parrish, S. (2019). *The Great Mental Models Volume One: General Thinking Concepts.* Latticework Publishing, Inc. p. 79.

Part II: How We Think About Math

Mental Model #4—False Linear Thinking

35 *The belief that … their cognitive bias.* Petitti, N. (2020). Personal communication.

36 *In his book … Compared to What?.* Guilfoyle, S. (2013). *Intelligent policing.* Triarchy Press.

36 *When we see … changes are significant.* Guilfoyle, S. (2015). Binary comparisons and police performance measurement: Good or bad? *Policing: A Journal of Policy and Practice, 9*(2), 195-209.

37 *Two emergency room … Dallas, TX from 1993–1999.* Gamble, J. L. & Hess, J. J. (2012). Temperature and violent crime in Dallas, Texas: Relationships and implications of climate change. *Western Journal of Emergency Medicine, 13*(3), 239.

39 *Jordan Ellenberg, in … even in baseball.* Ellenberg, J. (2015). *How not to be wrong: The power of mathematical thinking.* Penguin.

39 *As Ellenberg explains … up 86 Homeruns.* Ellenberg, J. (2015). *How not to be wrong: The power of mathematical thinking.* Penguin.

40 *As Guilfoyle discusses … do precisely that.* Guilfoyle, S. (2013). *Intelligent policing.* Triarchy Press. p. 195.

Mental Model #5—Binary Percent Changes

41 *The only possible … gets really messy.* Guilfoyle, S. (2013). *Intelligent policing.* Triarchy Press. p. 195.

43 *Percent change is … in crime counts.* Wheeler, A. P. (2016). Tables and graphs for monitoring temporal crime trends: Translating theory into practical crime analysis advice. *International Journal of Police Science & Management, 18*(3), 159-172.

44 *To better understand … test this theory.* Guilfoyle, S. (2015). Binary comparisons and police performance measurement: Good or bad?. *Policing: A Journal of Policy and Practice, 9*(2), 195-209.

44 *System 1 thinking … there is none.* Kahneman, D. (2011). *Thinking, fast and slow.* Macmillan. p. 111.

44 *Statistical Process Control … to identify patterns.* Guilfoyle, S. (2013). *Intelligent policing.* Triarchy Press.

46 *The beauty of … the control limits.* Guilfoyle, S. (2013). *Intelligent policing.* Triarchy Press. p. 37.

Mental Model #6—Second Order Thinking

48 *Just as great … start at the end.* Duke, A. (2019). *Thinking in bets: Making smarter decisions when you don't have all the facts.* Portfolio. p. 50.

48 *The farmers flew … the bigger pest.* Israel, B. (2010, June). Cane toads invade, Conquer Australia. www.livescience.com/29560-cane-toad-conquest-invades-australia.html

49 *In reaction to … bullets during protests.* Bowles, N. (2020, August). *Abolish the police? Those who survived Seattle aren't so sure.* www.nytimes.com/2020/08/07/us/defund-police-seattle-protests.html

49 *The area was … a stolen vehicle.* Rufo, C. (2020, July). The end of Chaz. www.city-journal.org/end-of-chaz

50 *It too Lift Master … with the opener.* Affinity Garage Doors (2017, July 31). How LED lights can cause problems with your garage door opener. https://phoenixazgaragedoorrepair.com/1786/how-led-lights-can-cause-problems-with-your-garage-door-opener/garage-door-blog/

50 *The idea of … uncertain future events.* Mitchell, D. J., Edward Russo, J., & Pennington, N. (1989). Back to the future: Temporal perspective in the explanation of events. *Journal of Behavioral Decision Making, 2*(1), 25-38.

50 *When conducting a … the project failed.* Klein, G. (2007, September). Performing a project premortem. *Harvard Business Review.* Retrieved October 1, 2020, from https://hbr.org/2007/09/performing-a-project-premortem

51 *X-rays, a powerful … Würzburg in Germany.* Glasser, O. (1993). *Wilhelm Conrad Röntgen and the early history of the Roentgen rays (No. 1).* Norman Publishing.

51 *Dr. Stewart fought … X-raying pregnant women.* Greene, G. (2017). *The woman who knew too much, Revised Ed.: Alice Stewart and the secrets of radiation.* University of Michigan Press.

51 *CompStat has been … the 20th century.* Kelling, G. L. & Sousa, W. H. (2001). *Do police matter? An analysis of the impact of New York City's police reforms.* CCI Center for Civic Innovation at the Manhattan Institute.

51 *Yet, it also … than they were.* Eterno, J. A. & Silverman, E. B. (2012). *The crime numbers game: Management by manipulation.* CRC Press.

51 *Guilfoyle argued in … sector performance management."* Guilfoyle, S. (2013). *Intelligent policing.* Triarchy Press. p. 195.

52 *The fishbone diagram … a specific event.* Kenett, R. S. (2008). Cause-and-effect diagrams. *Encyclopedia of statistics in quality and reliability, 1.*

Part III: How Things Concentrate

Mental Model #7—Pareto Principle

59 *The 80/20 rule … power law distribution.* Pareto, V. Cours d'économie politique (Droz, Geneva) 1896. *Manual of political economy.*

59 *There are many … a web page.* Newman, M. E. (2005). Power laws, Pareto distributions and Zipf's law. *Contemporary Physics, 46*(5), 323-351.

60 *U.S. cities are … total land area.* U.S. Census Bureau (2015) U.S. cities are home to 62.7 percent of the population but comprise 3.5 percent of land area. Retrieved December 13, 2020, from www.census.gov/newsroom/press-releases/2015/cb15-33.html.

60 *Typically, the most … the whole manuscript.* Powers, D. M. (1998). Applications and explanations of Zipf's law. In *New methods in language processing and computational natural language learning.* ACL. pp. 151-160.

60 *He wanted businesses … most quality issues.* Juran, J. M. (1951). *Quality control handbook,* McGraw-Hill Book Company Inc.

60 *Take the case … made it susceptible.* Vedantam, S. (2020, September). *The halo effect: Why it's so difficult to understand the past.* The Hidden Brain. Retrieved October 5, 2020, from www.npr.org/transcripts/904660038

61 *This means that … that has gets.."* Waldrop, M. M. (1993). *Complexity: The emerging science at the edge of order and chaos.* Simon and Schuster. p. 17.

61 *Aaron Clausett from … the 2000 census.* Clauset, A. (2011). Inferences, models, and simulations for complex systems. PDF retrieved August 13, 2020, from http://tuvalu.santafe.edu/~aaronc/courses/7000/csci7000-001_2011_L2.pdf

61 *Heather Prince from … administrative Statistics (LEMAS) survey..* (Inter-university Consortium for Political and Social Research Michigan State, 2020). Statistics 2016 Law Enforcement. Retrieved August 30, 2020, from www.icpsr.umich.edu/web/NACJD/studies/37323.

62 *This concentration of … coding defects arise.* Brooks, A (2019, October 1). The vital few and the useful many. Retrieved June 13, 2020, from https://shadowdragon.io/blog/the-vital-few-and-the-useful-many/

Mental Model #8—The Law of Crime Concentration

64 *Perhaps stability in … as a whole.* Weisburd, D. (2015). The law of crime concentration and the criminology of place. *Criminology, 53*(2), 133-157, 149.

64 *He began pushing … trained police officers.* Oliver, W. M. (2017). *August Vollmer: The father of American policing.* Carolina Academic Press.

64 *He established the … research in policing.* American Society of Criminology (2020). History of the American Society of Criminology. Retrieved September 24, 2020, from https://asc41.com/History.html

65 *Thus, routine preventive … reassure the public.* Kelling, G. L., Pate, T., Dieckman, D., & Brown, C. E. (1974). *The Kansas City preventive patrol experiment.* Police Foundation.

65 *The Standard Model of Policing … are patrol related activities* Weisburd, D. & Eck, J. E. (2004). What can police do to reduce crime, disorder, and fear? *The ANNALS of the American Academy of Political and Social Science, 593,* 42-65.

65 *That report laid … of controlling crime.* President's Commission on Law Enforcement and the Administration of Justice, 1967. *The Challenges of Crime in a Free Society* (Washington, DC: U.S. Government Printing Office).

66 *The Police Foundation … police-related mobile patrol.* National Police Foundation (n.d.). The Kansas City Preventative Patrol Experiment. Retrieved November 18, 2020, from www.policefoundation.org/projects-old/the-kansas-city-preventive-patrol-experiment/

66 *Unfortunately, the belief … This is a myth.* Bayley, D. H. (1994). *Police for the future.* Studies in Crime and Public Policy.

67 *The RECAP experiment … the same locations.* Sherman, L., Buerger, M.E. & Gartin, P. (1989). *Repeat call address policing: The Minneapolis RECAP experiment.* Crime Control Institute.

67 *The Pareto Principle … and individual buildings.* Sherman, L. W., Gartin, P. R., & Buerger, M. E. (1989). Hot spots of predatory crime: Routine activities and the criminology of place. *Criminology, 27*(1), 27-56.

67 *I conducted the … calls for service.* Mitchell, R. J. (2017). Frequency versus duration of police patrol visits for reducing crime in hot spots: non-experimental findings from the Sacramento hot spots experiment. *Cambridge Journal of Evidence-Based Policing, 1*(1), 22-37.

67 *Additionally, Pierce, Spaar, & Briggs … and auto thefts.* Pierce, G. L., Spaar, S. & Briggs, L. R. (1988). *The character of police work: Strategic and tactical implications.* Center for Applied Social Research, Northeastern University.

67 *Additionally, Pierce, Spaar, & Briggs … and auto thefts.* Eck, J. E., Gersh, J., & Taylor, C. (2000). *Finding crime hot spots through repeat address mapping. In Analyzing Crime Patterns: Frontiers of Practice,* eds. V. Goldsmith, P. McGuire, J. Mollenkopf, and T. Ross. Sage.

68 *Sherman called these … them small worlds.* Weisburd, D. (2015). Small worlds of crime and criminal justice interventions: Discovering crime hot spots. In *Envisioning criminology.* Springer. pp. 261-267.

68 *Sherman and Weisburd … or control groups.* Reiss, A. J., Jr. (1985). *Policing a city's central district: The Oakland story.* National Institute of Justice.

68 *Since Sherman and Weisburd's … 65 studies and 78 tests.* Braga, A. A., Turchan, B. S., Papachristos, A. V., & Hureau, D. M. (2019). Hot spots policing and crime reduction: an update of an ongoing systematic review and meta-analysis. *Journal of Experimental Criminology, 15*(3), 289-311.

69 *He asserted "This … cumulative proportion of crime.* Weisburd, D. (2015). The law of crime concentration and the criminology of place. *Criminology, 53*(2), 133-157.

69 *The formulation of … of universal validity".* Weisburd, D. (2015). The law of crime concentration and the criminology of place. *Criminology, 53*(2), 133-157, 151.

69 *The police managers … the street robberies.* Braga, A. A., Hureau, D. M. & Papachristos, A. V. 2010. The concentration and stability of gun violence at micro places in Boston, 1980–2008. *Journal of Quantitative Criminology 26,* 33–53.

70 *They also knew … segments in Seattle.* Weisburd, D., Morris, N. A., & Groff, E. R. (2009). Hot spots of juvenile crime: A longitudinal study of arrest incidents at street segments in Seattle, Washington. *Journal of Quantitative Criminology, 25*(4), 443.

70 *Finally, they knew … is now available".* National Research Council. 2004. Effectiveness of police activity in reducing crime, disorder and fear. Wesley G. Skogan and Kathleen Frydl (eds.), *Fairness and Effectiveness in Policing: The Evidence. Committee to Review Research on Police Policy and Practices. Committee on Law and Justice, Division of Behavioral and Social Sciences and Education.* The National Academies Press.

70 *Moreover, in that … of the crime.* Weisburd, D., Bushway, S., Lum, C., & Yang, S. M. (2004). Trajectories of crime at places: a longitudinal study of street segments in the City of Seattle★. *Criminology, 42*(2), 283-322.

70 *Over the course … increase in crime.* Weisburd, D., Bushway, S., Lum, C., & Yang, S. M. (2004). Trajectories of crime at places: a longitudinal study of street segments in the City of Seattle★. *Criminology, 42*(2), 283-322.

Mental Model #9—The Felonious Few

73 *The folklore of … damage they inflict.* Flynn, E. (2020). Personal communication.

73 *This Pareto Principle … of the misogyny.* Lorenz, M. O. (1905). Methods of measuring the concentration of wealth. *Publications of the American statistical association, 9*(70), 209-219.

73 *This Pareto Principle … of the misogyny.* Spelman, W. & Eck, J. E. (1989). *Sitting ducks, ravenous wolves and helping hands: New approaches to urban policing.* Lyndon B. Johnson School of Public Affairs, University of Texas at Austin.

73 *This Pareto Principle … of the misogyny.* Rhoades, S. A. (1993). The Herfindahl-Hirschman index. *Fed. Res. Bull., 79*, 188.

73 *This Pareto Principle … of the misogyny.* Fauset, S., Johnson, M. O., Gloor, M., Baker, T. R., Monteagudo, A., Brienen, R. J. … & Pitman, N. C. (2015). Hyperdominance in Amazonian forest carbon cycling. *Nature communications, 6*(1), 1-9.

73 *This Pareto Principle … of the misogyny.* Bartlett, J., Norrie, R., Patel, S., Rumpel, R., & Wibberley, S. (2014). Misogyny on twitter.

73 *In an article … offenders, and places.* Spelman, W. & Eck, J. E. (1989). *Sitting ducks, ravenous wolves and helping hands: New approaches to urban policing.* Lyndon B. Johnson School of Public Affairs, University of Texas at Austin.

73 *They stated, "These … crime is concentrated."* Spelman, W. & Eck, J. E. (1989). *Sitting ducks, ravenous wolves and helping hands: New approaches to urban policing.* Lyndon B. Johnson School of Public Affairs, University of Texas at Austin.

74 *Sherman named this … The Miscreant Many.* Sherman, L. W., Bland, M., House, P., & Strang, H. (2016). *The felonious few vs. the miscreant many.* Cambridge: Cambridge Centre for Evidence Based Policing.

74 *These are the … crime from occurring.* Cohen, L. E. & Felson, M. (1979). Social change and crime rate trends: A routine activity approach. *American Sociological Review*, 588-608.

74 *Eck expanded on … of Offending Concentration."* Martinez, N. N., Lee, Y., Eck, J. E., & SooHyun, O. (2017). Ravenous wolves revisited: A systematic review of offending concentration. *Crime Science, 6*(1), 10.

75 *Thus, they stipulate … of all crime."* Martinez, N. N., Lee, Y., Eck, J. E., & SooHyun, O. (2017). Ravenous wolves revisited: A systematic review of offending concentration. *Crime Science, 6*(1), 10.

75 *Liggins, Ratcliffe, & Bland … arrested in Northamptonshire, U.K.* Liggins, A., Ratcliffe, J. H., & Bland, M. (2019). Targeting the most harmful offenders for an English police agency: Continuity and change of membership in the "felonious few". *Cambridge Journal of Evidence-Based Policing, 3*(3-4), 80-96.

75 *The Cambridge CHI … raw crime count.* Sherman, L., Neyroud, P. W., & Neyroud, E. (2016). The Cambridge crime harm index: Measuring total harm from crime based on sentencing guidelines. *Policing: A Journal of Policy and Practice, 10*(3), 171-183.

75 *The Cambridge CHI … a maximum one.* Mitchell, R. J. (2016). The Sacramento hot spots policing experiment: An extension and sensitivity analysis. Unpublished dissertation, University of Cambridge.

75 *This outcome shows … to the community.* Liggins, A., Ratcliffe, J. H., & Bland, M. (2019). Targeting the most harmful offenders for an English police agency: Continuity and change of membership in the "felonious few". *Cambridge Journal of Evidence-based Policing, 3*(3-4), 80-96.

75 *Individuals were identified … victim or offender.* Hiltz, N., Bland, M., & Barnes, G. C. (2020). Victim-offender overlap in violent crime: Targeting crime harm in a Canadian suburb. *Cambridge Journal of Evidence-based Policing*, 1-11.

Part IV: How Things Vary

Mental Model #10—Distributions

81 *The statistician knows ... the real world.* Box, G. (1976). Science and statistics. *Journal of the American Statistical Association* 71(356), 791-799.

81 *The Merriam-Webster dictionary ... through scientific method.* (MM#17)." science. (2020). In Merriam-Webster. com Retrieved October 5, 2020, from www.merriam-webster.com/dictionary/science

81 *On a lighthearted ... to pull it off."* Science. In Urban Dictionary. Retrieved November 28, 2020 from www. urbandictionary.com/define.php?term=science

82 *Howard Wainer in ... in the world.* Wainer, H. (2009). *Picturing the uncertain world: How to understand, communicate, and control uncertainty through graphical display.* Princeton University Press.

82 *De Moivre's book, The ... for probability theory.* de Moivre, A. (1718). *The doctrine of chances: or, a method of calculating the probability of events in play.* W. Pearson.

83 *However Wainer calls it ... ignorance has caused.* Wainer, H. (2009). *Picturing the uncertain world: How to understand, communicate, and control uncertainty through graphical display.* Princeton University Press.

85 *His finding led ... samples over 30.* Brosamler, G. A. (1988, November). An almost everywhere central limit theorem. In *Mathematical Proceedings of the Cambridge Philosophical Society*, 104(3). Cambridge University Press. pp. 561-574.

85 *Today scientists understand ... understanding the world.* Renn, J., Damerow, P., Rieger, S., & Giulini, D. (2001). Hunting the white elephant: When and how did Galileo discover the law of fall?. *Science in Context*, 14(s1), 29.

85 *The power law ... right (positive skew).* Guerriero, V. (2012). Power law distribution: Method of multi-scale inferential statistics. *Journal of Modern Mathematics Frontier*, 1(1), 21-22.

86 *In the end ... ignorance can be."* Wainer, H. (2009). *Picturing the uncertain world: How to understand, communicate, and control uncertainty through graphical display.* Princeton University Press.

Mental Model #11—Law of Large Numbers

88 *I groan when ... the Sistine Chapel.* (2020). Ratcliffe, J. Personal Communication.

88 *It was as ... 2002 to 2006.* Bratton, W. (June, 2020). *Like it or not, broken windows works. New York Daily News.* Retrieved July 10, 2020, from www.nydailynews.com/opinion/ny-oped-like-it-or-not-broken-windows-works-20190602-jmit2osnyvbyhhzllcvxqc4z2q-story.html

88 *However, there was ... New York was unparalleled.* Baumer, E. P. & Wolff, K. T. (2014). Evaluating contemporary crime drop (s) in America, New York City, and many other places. *Justice Quarterly*, 31(1), 5-38.

88 *However, there was ... New York was unparalleled.* Fagan, J., Zimring, F. E. & Kim, J. (1997). Declining homicide in New York City: A tale of two trends. *J. Crim. L. & Criminology*, 88, 1277.

88 *However, there was ... New York was unparalleled.* Levitt, S. D. (2004). Understanding why crime fell in the 1990s: Four factors that explain the decline and six that do not. *Journal of Economic Perspectives*, 18(1), 163-190.

88 *However, there was ... New York was unparalleled.* Weisburd, D., Telep, C. W., & Lawton, B. A. (2014). Could innovations in policing have contributed to the New York City crime drop even in a period of declining police strength?: The case of stop, question and frisk as a hot spots policing strategy. *Justice Quarterly*, 31(1), 129-153.

88 *However, there was ... New York was unparalleled.* Zimring, W. D. S. F. E. (2006). *The great American crime decline.* Oxford University Press.

90 *In thinking, fast ... in large samples."* Kahneman, D. (2011). *Thinking, fast and slow.* Macmillan. p. 111.

90 *Bill Gates funded ... the best grades.* (Tabarrok, September 2010). The Small Schools Myth. Retrieved on November 26, 2020, from https://marginalrevolution.com/marginalrevolution/2010/09/the-small-schools-myth.html

90 *If Bill Gates ... equally compelling results.* Wainer, H. (2009). *Picturing the uncertain world: How to understand, communicate, and control uncertainty through graphical display.* Princeton University Press.

90 *By examining crime ... method of research.* Kahneman, D. (2011). *Thinking, fast and slow.* Macmillan. p. 111.

90 *Tim Mashford an ... spots policing scheme.* Mashford, T. & Davidson, S. (2020). Optimising parameter selection for predicting volume crime using hotspot mapping. *Journal of Police Science*, 4(2), 46-48.

91 *Dr. Jerry Ratcliffe ... stop doing them.* Ratcliffe, J. (2017, July 13). Year to date comparisons and why we should stop doing them [Blog]. Retrieved October 1, 2020, from www.jratcliffe.net/post/year-to-date-comparisons-and-why-we-should-stop-doing-them

92 *Kahneman's book Thinking ... connection is spurious.* Kahneman, D. (2011). *Thinking, fast and slow.* Macmillan. p. 110.

Mental Model #12—Regression to the Mean

93 *Excellence doesn't persist … mediocrity asserts itself.* Ellenberg, J. (2015). *How not to be wrong: The power of mathematical thinking.* Penguin. p. 301.

93 In the *Lady* … and their sons. Salsburg, D. (2001). *The lady tasting tea: How statistics revolutionized science in the twentieth century.* Macmillan.

93 *In How Not … safely be forgotten."* Ellenberg, J. (2015). *How not to be wrong: The power of mathematical thinking.* Penguin. p. 74.

94 *Tversky, Gilovich and … a hot hand.* Tversky, A. & Gilovich, T. (1989). The cold facts about the "hot hand" in basketball. *Chance, 2*(1), 16-21.

94 *During the 1980s … receiving the prize.* Dickson, P. (2009). *The Dickson baseball dictionary.* WW Norton & Company.

94 *Toronto Blue Jays … the poor performance.* Howarth, J. (1986). *Baseball lite.* Protocol Books.

94 *When Sports Illustrated … the following year.* The cover no one would pose for: Is the SI jinx real? Sports Illustrated. Retrieved October 10, 2020, from https://vault.si.com/vault/2002/01/21/that-old-black-magic-millions-of-superstitious-readersand-many-athletesbelieve-that-an-appearance-on-sports-illustrateds-cover-is-the-kiss-of-death-but-is-there-really-such-a-thing-as-the-si-jinx

94 *Sports Illustrated even … SI jinx real?"* Sports Illustrated Cover Jinx. (n.d.) In *Wikipedia.* Retrieved October 10, 2020, from https://en.wikipedia.org/wiki/Sports_Illustrated_cover_jinx#cite_note-2

94 *In most policing … to the mean.* Goldstein, H. (1990). *Problem-oriented policing.* Philadelphia: Temple University Press.

95 *This traditional way … in treading water.* Guilfoyle, S. (2015). Binary comparisons and police performance measurement: Good or bad?. *Policing: A Journal of Policy and Practice, 9*(2), 195-209.

95 *In a review … on reducing crime.* Braga, A. A., Welsh, B. C., & Schnell, C. (2015). Can policing disorder reduce crime? A systematic review and meta-analysis. *Journal of Research in Crime and Delinquency, 52*(4), 567-588.

95 *As they suggested in … and improving legitimacy.* Braga, A. A., Brunson, R. K., & Drakulich, K. M. (2019). Race, place, and effective policing. *Annual review of sociology, 45*, 535-555.

Part V: How to Determine Causality

Mental Model #13—Correlation is Not Causation

101 *Facts are the … a certain phenomenon.* Naskar, A. *All for acceptance.* Neuro Cookies. p. 20.

102 *Correlation is a … least two variables.* Nardi, P. (2017). *Critical thinking: Tools for evaluating research.* University of California Press.

103 *The strength of … and large effects.* Cohen, J. (1988). *Statistical power analysis for the behavioral sciences* (2nd ed.). Lawrence Erlbaum.

103 *This finding comes … produce large outcomes.* Braga, A. A., Turchan, B. S., Papachristos, A. V., & Hureau, D. M. (2019). Hot spots policing and crime reduction: An update of an ongoing systematic review and meta-analysis. *Journal of Experimental Criminology, 15*(3), 289-311.

104 *Additionally, I found … p < .05 level.* Mitchell, R. J. (2016). The Sacramento hot spots policing experiment: An extension and sensitivity analysis. Unpublished dissertation, University of Cambridge.

104 *If we have lto … to make decisions.* Kahneman, D. (2011). *Thinking, fast and slow.* Macmillan.

106 *Weisburd and Petrosino … inappropriate policy recommendations.* Weisburd, D. & Piquero, A. R. (2008). How well do criminologists explain crime? Statistical modeling in published studies. *Crime and Justice, 37*(1), 453-502.

Mental Model #14—Causal Inference

107 *Testing of police … is most cost-effective.* Sherman, L. W. (2015). *Evidence-based Policing in 100 milestones: A video course in 26 chapters.* The Cambridge Centre for Evidence-Based Policing.

108 *One very simple … the www.reducingcrime.com website.* Ratcliffe, Jerry H. (2019) *ABC spreadsheet calculator* (version 1.4) [Computer Software], reducingcrime.com

109 *Weisburd and Petrosino … variable of interest.* Weisburd, D. & Piquero, A. R. (2008). How well do criminologists explain crime? Statistical modeling in published studies. *Crime and Justice, 37*(1), 453-502.

109 *Created in the … crisis intervention process.* Everly Jr, G. S., & Mitchell, J. T. (1995). *Prevention of work-related posttraumatic stress: The critical incident stress debriefing process.* In L. R. Murphy, J. J. Hurrell, Jr., S. L. Sauter,

& G. P. Keita (Eds.), *Job stress interventions* (p. 173–183). American Psychological Association. https://doi.org/10.1037/10183-012

109 *In 2000 Mayou … victim's PTSD symptoms.* Mayou, R. Ehleers, A., & Hobbs, M. (2000). Psychological briefing for road traffic victims: Three-year follow-up of a randomized controlled trial. *British Journal of Psychiatry 176*, 589-593.

110 *The intervention included. … the traumatic experience.* Mayou, R. Ehleers, A., & Hobbs, M. (2000). Psychological briefing for road traffic victims: Three-year follow-up of a randomized controlled trial. *British Journal of Psychiatry 176*, 589-593, 590.

111 *here is the … the stars apart.* cummings, e. e. & Firmage, G. J. (1991). *Complete poems, 1904–1962.* Liveright Publishing Corporation.

112 *Mental Model #14 … to establish causality.* Pearl, J. & Mackenzie, D. (2018). *The book of why: The new science of cause and effect.* Basic Books.

112 *We know, for … places, and property.* Weisburd, D., Bushway, S., Lum, C., & Yang, S. M. (2004). Trajectories of crime at places: a longitudinal study of street segments in the City of Seattle★. *Criminology, 42*(2), 283-322.

113 *We know there … of taxpayers' monies.* Walsh, W. F. (2001). CompStat: An analysis of an emerging police managerial paradigm. *Policing: An International Journal of Police Strategies & Management, 24*(3), 347-362.

Mental Model #15—Bayesian (Probabilistic) Reasoning

114 *Bayes is all … and universal truths.* Pease, K. (2017, May) *Bayes Theorem and policing.* East Midlands Police Academic Collaboration. Retrieved October 25, 2020, from www.empac.org.uk/bayes-theorem-policing/

114 *The work was … Doctrine of Chances.* Salsburg, D. (2001). *The lady tasting tea: How statistics revolutionized science in the twentieth century.* Macmillan.

115 *Clark was a … within two years.* Shaikh, T. (2007, March). *Sally Clark, mother wrongly convicted of killing her sons, found dead at home.* The Guardian. Retrieved October 25, 2020, from www.theguardian.com/society/2007/mar/17/childrensservices.uknews

116 *In a later … the first death.* Hill, R. (2005). Reflections on the cot death cases. *Significance, 2*(1), 13-16.

117 *In this blog … crime in Scotland.* Ashby, M. (2020, May 13). Why you can't identify changes in crime by comparing this month to last month [Blog post]. *Social Research Association.* Retrieved July 10, 2020, from https://the-sra.org.uk/SRA/Blog/whyyoucantidentifychangesincrimebycomparingthismonthtolastmonth.aspx

119 *Policing knows this … "real world" use.* Pease, K. (2017, May) *Bayes Theorem and Policing.* East Midlands Police Academic Collaboration. Retrieved October 25, 2020, from www.empac.org.uk/bayes-theorem-policing/

120 *Pease related Bayesian … evaluators have left).* Pease, K. (2017, May) *Bayes Theorem and Policing.* East Midlands Police Academic Collaboration. Retrieved October 25, 2020, from www.empac.org.uk/bayes-theorem-policing/

120 *Klein studied how … really recognized experience.* Klein, G. A. (2017). *Sources of power: How people make decisions.* MIT Press.

120 *They decided to … have an intuition?* Kahneman, D. (2011). *Thinking, fast and slow.* Macmillan. p. 235.

121 *As Kahneman himself … best, sometimes worse.* Kahneman, D. (2011). *Thinking, fast and slow.* Macmillan. p. 241.

121 *Even when they … of the time.* Kahneman, D. (2011). *Thinking, fast and slow.* Macmillan. p. 224.

Part VI: How to Think Scientifically

Mental Model #16—Peer Review Your Perspectives

125 *Some years ago … likely to last.* Descartes, R. (2013). *Meditations on first philosophy.* Broadview Press.

126 *Before I understood … practices for recruiting.* Police Officer Standards and Training (POST) (2006). Recruitment & Retention: Best Practices Update. Retrieved October 29, 2020, from http://annex.ipacweb.org/library/conf/08/ca_post.pdf

126 *POST included both … magazine, Police Chief.* Johnson, K. (2005, June). The Community Recruiter. *The Police Chief.*

127 *Two people separated … to span decades.* Weisburd, D. & Petrosino, A. (2004). Experiments, criminology. In K. Kempf-Leonard (Ed.), *Encyclopedia of social measurement.* Academic Press. pp. 877–884.

127 *The Massachusetts Reformatory … the intended effect.* Cabot, R.C. (1930). Foreword. In S. Glueck & E.T. Glueck (Eds.), 500 criminal careers. Knopf. pp. vii-xiii.

129 *The intervention he … in existence today.* Jolliffe, D. & Farrington, D. P. (2008). The influence of mentoring on reoffending. National Council for Crime Prevention.

129 *It was believed … their delinquent tendencies.* deQ, P. S. (1940). A long-term study of children: The Cambridge-Somerville Youth Study. *Child Development, 1,* 143-151.

129 *In hindsight, this … later in life.* Powers, E. & Witmer, H. L. (1951). *An experiment in the prevention of delinquency: The Cambridge-Somerville Youth Study.* Columbia University Press.

129 *This sample aptly … the hardest cases.* Powers, E. & Witmer, H. L. (1951). *An experiment in the prevention of delinquency: The Cambridge-Somerville Youth Study.* Columbia University Press.

129 *When the data … of offenses committed.* Powers, E. & Witmer, H. L. (1951). *An experiment in the prevention of delinquency: The Cambridge-Somerville Youth Study.* Columbia University Press.

129 *When the data … of offenses committed.* McCord, J. & McCord, W. (1959a). A follow-up report on the Cambridge-Somerville Youth Study. *The Annals of the American Academy of Political and Social Science, 322,* 89–96.

129 *When the data … of offenses committed.* McCord, W. & McCord, J. (1959b). *Origins of crime: A new evaluation of the Cambridge-Somerville Youth Study.* Columbia University Press.

129 *In fact, the … the control group.* McCord, J. (2003). Cures that harm: Unanticipated outcomes of crime prevention programs. *The Annals of the American Academy of Political and Social Science, 587,* 16–30.

129 *In hindsight, this … later in life.* Powers, E. & Witmer, H. L. (1951). *An experiment in the prevention of delinquency: The Cambridge-Somerville Youth Study.* Columbia University Press.

129 *Once again she … were left alone.* McCord, J. & McCord, W. (1959a). A follow-up report on the Cambridge-Somerville Youth Study. *The Annals of the American Academy of Political and Social Science, 322,* 89–96.

129 *Once again she … were left alone.* McCord, W. & McCord, J. (1959b). *Origins of crime: A new evaluation of the Cambridge-Somerville Youth Study.* Columbia University Press.

130 *As she stated … towards their children.* Dubner, S. (2017). When helping hurts. *Freakonomics.* Retrieved October 31, 2020, from https://freakonomics.com/podcast/when-helping-hurts/.

130 *As her son … a death certificate?"* Dubner, S. (2017). When helping hurts. *Freakonomics.* Retrieved October 31, 2020, from https://freakonomics.com/podcast/when-helping-hurts/.

130 *Research has shown … out of crime.* Farrington, D. P. (1986). Age and crime. *Crime and Justice, 7,* 189-250.

130 *The men in … the control group.* McCord, J. (1978). A thirty-year follow-up of treatment effects. *The American Psychologist, 33,* 284–289.

131 *The men in … the control group."* McCord, J. (1981). Consideration of some effects of a counseling program. In S. E. Martin, L. B. Sechrest, & R. Redner (Eds.), *New directions in the rehabilitation of criminal offenders.* National Academy Press. pp. 394–405.

131 *She had several … disillusioned with life.* McCord, J. (1981). Consideration of some effects of a counseling program. In S. E. Martin, L. B. Sechrest, & R. Redner (Eds.), *New directions in the rehabilitation of criminal offenders.* National Academy Press. pp. 394–405.

131 *Her work culminated … in backfire effects.* McCord, J. (2003). Cures that harm: Unanticipated outcomes of crime prevention programs. *The Annals of the American Academy of Political and Social Science, 587,* 16–30.

131 *Program advocates and … involvement with crime.* Petrosino, A., Turpin-Petrosino, C., Hollis-Peel, M. E., & Lavenberg, J. G. (2013). "Scared Straight" and other juvenile awareness programs for preventing juvenile delinquency. *Cochrane Database of Systematic Reviews, (4),* 3.

132 *It took 20 years … of the program.* Finckenauer, J. O. (1982). *Scared straight and the panacea phenomenon.* Prentice-Hall.

132 *When the outcomes … the control group.* Finckenauer, J. O. (1982). *Scared Straight and the Panacea Phenomenon.* Prentice-Hall.

Mental Model #17—The Scientific Method

133 *I apologize for … sense of data.* Ioannidis, J. P. (2016). Evidence-based medicine has been hijacked: a report to David Sackett. *Journal of Clinical Epidemiology, 73,* 82-86.

133 *Police departments can … could be negative.* Mitchell, R. J. & Lewis, S. (2017). Intention is not method, belief is not evidence, rank is not proof. *International Journal of Emergency Services, 6(3).*

133 *This is how … increased recidivism instead.* Petrosino, A., Turpin-Petrosino, C., & Finckenauer, J. O. (2000). Well-meaning programs can have harmful effects! Lessons from experiments of programs such as Scared Straight. *Crime & Delinquency, 46(3),* 354-379.

134 *Today the scientific … hypotheses or predictions.* The Scientific Method. Retrieved November 26, 2020, from https://www.khanacademy.org/science/high-school-biology/hs-biology-foundations/hs-biology-and-the-scientific-method/a/the-science-of-biology

135 *The Maryland Scientific … Based Crime Prevention.* Farrington, D. P., Gottfredson, D. C., Sherman, L. W., & Welsh, B. C. (2002). The Maryland scientific methods scale. *Evidence-based Crime Prevention*, 13-21.

135 *The Maryland Scientific … Based Crime Prevention.* Sherman, L., Gottfredson, D., MacKenzie, D. L., Eck, J., Reuter, P., & Bushway, S. (1998). Crime prevention: What works, what doesn't, what's promising. Report to the U.S. Congress.

135 *The scale translates … Evidence-Based Practices.* Cook, T. D., Campbell, D. T., & Day, A. (1979). *Quasi-experimentation: Design & analysis issues for field settings* (Vol. 351). Houghton Mifflin.

136 *In order to … outcome is observed.* Sherman, L., Gottfredson, D., MacKenzie, D. L., Eck, J., Reuter, P., & Bushway, S. (1998). Crime prevention: What works, what doesn't, what's promising. Report to the U.S. Congress. p. 12.

138 *They were able … the control areas.* Henning, K. Stewart, G., Kahn, K., Peterson, C., Renauer, B., Mitchell, R., Labissiere, Y., & Sothern, S. (2017). Portland's Neighborhood Involvement Locations Project (final report). Criminal Justice Policy & Research Institute, Portland State University.

Mental Model #18—Evidence-based Practice

140 *It all comes … feels rather pointless.* Briner, R. (2021). Personal communication.

140 *Dr. David Sackett, one … of individual patients."* Thoma, A. & Eaves III, F. F. (2015). A brief history of evidence-based medicine (EBM) and the contributions of Dr David Sackett. *Aesthetic Surgery Journal*, *35*(8), NP261-NP263.

141 *Before evidence-based medicine … Evidence-Based Medicine.* Guyatt, G. H. & Busse, J. W. (2006). The philosophy of evidence-based medicine. In *Evidence-based Endocrinology*. Humana Press. pp. 25-33.

142 *"The terms 'small' … as behavioral science."* Cohen, J. (1988). *Statistical power analysis for the behavioral sciences* (2nd ed.). Lawrence Erlbaum. p. 25.

142 *Anthony Braga and … overall effect size."* Braga, A. A., Turchan, B. S., Papachristos, A. V., & Hureau, D. M. (2019). Hot spots policing and crime reduction: an update of an ongoing systematic review and meta-analysis. *Journal of Experimental Criminology*, *15*(3), 289-311.

144 *Jan Baptista van Helmont … that were never proven.* Donaldson (2016). van Helmont's proposal for a randomised comparison of treating fevers with or without bloodletting and purging. *JLL Bulletin: Commentaries on the history of treatment evaluation.* Retrieved August 23, 2020, from www.jameslindlibrary.org/articles/joan-baptista-van-helmonts-proposal-around-1643-for-a-randomised-comparison-of-using-or-withholding-bloodletting-and-purging-when-treating-fevers/

144 *In addition to … into your doctrine."* van Helmont, J. B. (1966). *Ortus Medicinae, id est initia physicae inaudita.* Sumptibus Ioannis Baptistæ Deuenet.

144 *In 1967, when … ever did before.* Gawande, A. (2014). *Being mortal: Medicine and what matters in the end.* Metropolitan Books.

144 *Before the 1950s … in the United States.* Gawande, A. *The Checklist Manifesto–How to Get Things Right*, 2009. Henry Holt and Company, New York, 13.

145 *The truth he … and clinical expertise.* Guyatt, G. (2016). Dave Sackett and the ethos of the EBM community. *Journal of Clinical Epidemiology*, *73*, 75.

145 *A decade later … Practice of Medicine."* Guyatt G, Cairns, J., & Churchill, D. (1992) Evidence-Based Medicine: A new approach to teaching the practice of medicine. *Journal of the American Medical Association*, *268*(17), 2420-2425.

145 *This article was … evidence-based medicine.* Eddy, D. M. (1990). Practice policies—guidelines for methods. *JAMA*, *263*(13), 1839-1841.

145 *This series had … and applicability steps.* Montori, V., Ioannidis, J., & Guyatt, G. (2008). Reporting bias. *Users' guides to the medical literature: A manual for evidence-based clinical practice.* McGraw-Hill.

145 *"In Evidence-Based… and clinical practice."* Sackett, D. L., Rosenberg, W. M., Gray, J. M., Haynes, R. B., & Richardson, W. S. (1996). Evidence based medicine: What it is and what it isn't. *BMJ: British Medical Journal*, *313*(7050), 170.

145 *Assessing the landscape … needs to change.* Millenson, M.L. (1997). *Demanding medical excellence.* Chicago University Press.

146   *One of the … a peaceful resolution.* Sherman, L. W. (2020). Personal communication.

146   *The difference in … side of justice.* Sherman, L. W. (2020). Personal communication.

147   *The relationship led … Domestic Violence Experiment.* Sherman, L. W. & Berk, R. A. (1984). The specific deterrent effects of arrest for domestic assault. *American Sociological Review*, 49(2), 261-272.

147   *At the end … of reducing recidivism.* Sherman, L. W. & Berk, R. A. (1984). The specific deterrent effects of arrest for domestic assault. *American Sociological Review*, *49*(2), 261-272.

147   *That seminal article … intersections and places.* Sherman, L. W., Gartin, P. R., & Buerger, M. E. (1989). Hot spots of predatory crime: Routine activities and the criminology of place. *Criminology*, *27*(1), 27-56.

148   *When Sherman started … service—"hot spots."* Sherman, L., Buerger, M., & Gartin, P. (1989). *Repeat call address policing: The Minneapolis RECAP experiment*. Crime Control Institute.

148   *In Police for … defense against crime.* Bayley, D. H. (1994). *Police for the future*. Studies in Crime and Public Policy. Oxford University Press on Demand.

148   *This study showed … all hot spots.* Weisburd, D. & Green, L. (1995). Policing drug hot spots: The Jersey City drug market analysis experiment. *Justice Quarterly*, *12*(4), 711-735.

149   *The article was … American Policing" series.* Sherman, L. W. (1998). *Evidence-based policing*. Police Foundation.

149   *He described evidence-based … units, and officers.* Sherman, L. W. (1998). *Evidence-based policing*. National Police Foundation.

149   *Evidence-based policing … research in practice.* Sherman, L. W. (1998). *Evidence-based policing*. National Police Foundation.

Part VII: How to Make Decisions

Mental Model #19—Targeting, Testing, and Tracking

155   *Knowledge is very … same as action.* Millenson, M. L. (1997). *Demanding medical excellence*. Chicago University Press.

155   *He called it … tracking the outcome.* Sherman, L. W. (2013). The rise of evidence-based policing: Targeting, testing, and tracking. *Crime and Justice*, *42*(1), 377-451.

155   *The science author … into a science.* Clegg, B. (2013). *Roger Bacon: The first scientist*. Hachette UK.

155   *Clegg went on … a conclusion certain."* Clegg, B. (2013). *Roger Bacon: The first scientist*. Hachette UK.

156   *Sherman describes the … perceptions of police legitimacy.* Sherman, L. W. (2013). The rise of evidence-based policing: Targeting, testing, and tracking. *Crime and Justice*, *42*(1), 377-451.

157   *She found that … were never victims.* Hiltz, N., Bland, M., & Barnes, G. C. (2020). Victim-offender overlap in violent crime: Targeting crime harm in a Canadian suburb. *Cambridge Journal of Evidence-Based Policing*, *4*, 1-11.

157   *One good example… theft from autos.* BetaGov. (2020). Police vehicle lights. Retrieved November 29, 2020, from www.betagov.org/completed-trials/Police-Vehicle-Lights.pdf

158   *Ellie Macbeth, a … both on maps.* Macbeth, E. & Ariel, B. (2019). Place-based statistical versus clinical predictions of crime hot spots and harm locations in Northern Ireland. *Justice Quarterly*, *36*(1), 93-126.

158   *This study was … at predicting hot spots.* Oatley, G., Barnes, G. C., Clare, J., & Chapman, B. (2019). Crime concentration in Perth CBD: A comparison of officer predicted hot spots, data derived hot spots and officer GPS patrol data. *Australian Journal of Forensic Sciences*, *51*(sup1), S136-S140.

158   *This finding was … Talking to Strangers.* Gladwell, M. (2019). *Talking to strangers: What we should know about the people we don't know*. Penguin UK.

160   *Binary outcomes, pre/post … predicting the future.* Guilfoyle, S. (2013). *Intelligent policing: How systems thinking methods eclipse conventional management practice*. Triarchy Press.

160   *As Donald Wheeler … out the noise.* Wheeler, Donald J. (1998). *Avoiding man-made chaos: And other essays*. SPC Press.

160   *In another study…number of visits.* Ariel, B., Farrar, W. A., & Sutherland, A. (2015). The effect of police body-worn cameras on use of force and citizens' complaints against the police: A randomized controlled trial. *Journal of Quantitative Criminology*, *31*(3), 509-535.

160   *I have policing … number of visits.* Williams, S., & Coupe, T. (2017). Frequency vs. length of hot spots patrols: A randomised controlled trial. *Cambridge Journal of Evidence-based Policing*, *1*(1), 5-21.

160   *It created a … officers squad cars.* Henning, K. Stewart, G., Kahn, K., Peterson, C., Renauer, B., Mitchell, R., Labissiere, Y., & Sothern, S. (2017). Portland's neighborhood involvement locations project (final report). Criminal Justice Policy & Research Institute, Portland State University.

Mental Model #20—Harm Indexes

162   *All crimes are not created equal.* Sherman, L., Neyroud, P. W., & Neyroud, E. (2016). The Cambridge crime harm index: Measuring total harm from crime based on sentencing guidelines. *Policing: A Journal of Policy and Practice, 10*(3), 171-183.

162   *The idea of … using crime counts.* Sherman, L., Neyroud, P. W., & Neyroud, E. (2016). The Cambridge crime harm index: Measuring total harm from crime based on sentencing guidelines. *Policing: A Journal of Policy and Practice, 10*(3), 171-183.

162   *The idea behind … of the public.* Sherman, L., Neyroud, P. W., & Neyroud, E. (2016). The Cambridge crime harm index: Measuring total harm from crime based on sentencing guidelines. *Policing: A Journal of Policy and Practice, 10*(3), 171-183.

162   *Crime Harm Indexes (CHI) … the United States.* Andersen, H. A., & Mueller-Johnson, K. (2018). The Danish Crime Harm Index: How it works and why it matters. *Cambridge Journal of Evidence-Based Policing, 2*(1-2), 52-69.

162   *Crime Harm Indexes (CHI) … the United States.* Curtis-Ham, S., & Walton, D. (2018). The New Zealand crime harm index: Quantifying harm using sentencing data. *Policing: A Journal of Policy and Practice, 12*(4), 455-467.

162   *Crime Harm Indexes (CHI) … the United States.* House, P. D., & Neyroud, P. W. (2018). Developing a crime harm index for Western Australia: The WACHI. *Cambridge Journal of Evidence-Based Policing, 2*(1-2), 70-94.

162   *Crime Harm Indexes (CHI) … the United States.* Kärrholm, F., Neyroud, P., & Smaaland, J. (2020). Designing the Swedish crime harm index: An evidence-based strategy. *Cambridge Journal of Evidence-Based Policing,* 1-19.

162   *Crime Harm Indexes (CHI) … the United States.* Mitchell, R. J. (2019). The usefulness of a crime harm index: Analyzing the Sacramento Hot Spot Experiment using the California Crime Harm Index (CA-CHI). *Journal of Experimental Criminology, 15*(1), 103-113.

162   *Crime Harm Indexes (CHI) … the United States.* Ransley, J., Murphy, K., Karstedt, S., Bartlett, D., Forrester, L., & Carless, M. (2018). Developing and applying a Queensland crime harm index—implications for policing serious and organised crime. *Research Report,* (10), 105-116.

162   *Canada uses the … to other crimes.* Wallace, M. (2009). *Measuring crime in Canada: Introducing the crime severity index and improvements to the Uniform Crime Reporting Survey.* ProQuest.

163   *The full table … and Sensitivity Analysis.* (2017). Mitchell, R. J. (2016). The Sacramento hot spots policing experiment: An extension and sensitivity analysis. Unpublished dissertation, University of Cambridge.

163   *The analysis showed … hypothesis was correct.* Telep, C. W., Mitchell, R. J., & Weisburd, D. (2014). How much time should the police spend at crime hot spots? Answers from a police agency directed randomized field trial in Sacramento, California. *Justice Quarterly, 31*(5), 905-933.

163   *If there is … any more information.* Mitchell, R. J. (2019). The usefulness of a crime harm index: analyzing the Sacramento Hot Spot Experiment using the California Crime Harm Index (CA-CHI). *Journal of Experimental Criminology, 15*(1), 103-113.

163   *The researchers stated … especially alcohol use.* Werch, C. E. & Owen, D. M. (2002). Iatrogenic effects of alcohol and drug prevention programs. *Journal of Studies on Alcohol, 63*(5), 581-590.

167   *When officers engage … the department's legitimacy.* Engel, R. S. (2005). Citizens' perceptions of distributive and procedural injustice during traffic stops with police. *Journal of Research in Crime and Delinquency, 42*(4), 445-481.

168   *In his article … people of color.* Ratcliffe, J. H. (2015). Towards an index for harm-focused policing. *Policing: A Journal of Policy and Practice, 9*(2), 164-182.

168   *Ratcliffe even cautions … review his approach.* Ratcliffe, J. H. (2015). Towards an index for harm-focused policing. *Policing: A Journal of Policy and Practice, 9*(2), 164-182.

169   *Recently, Kennedy, Caplan … homicide clearance rates.* Kennedy, L. W., Caplan, J. M., Piza, E. L., & Thomas, A. L. (2020). Environmental factors influencing urban homicide clearance rates: a spatial analysis of New York City. *Homicide Studies.* https://doi.org/10.1177/1088767920976183

Mental Model #21—Decision-making Models

171   *When one is … or the taxpayer.* Meehl, P. E. (1954). *Clinical versus statistical prediction: A theoretical analysis and a review of the evidence.* Echo Point Books & Media. p. viii.

173   *As you start … 100 (always preferred).* Clearfield, C., & Tilcsik, A. (2018). *Meltdown: What Plane Crashes, Oil Spills, and Dumb Business Decisions Can Teach Us About How to Succeed at Work and at Home.* Penguin.

174 *Dr. William A. Silverman ... the scoring system.* Finster, M. & Wood, M. (2005). The Apgar score has survived the test of time. *Anesthesiology: The Journal of the American Society of Anesthesiologists, 102*(4), 855-857.

175 *Her paper found ... rate of .13 percent.* Apgar, V. (1953). A proposal for a new method of evaluation of the newborn infant. *Current Researches in Anesthesia & Analgesia,* Jul-Aug, *32*(4), 260–267.

175 *Her system was ... the Apgar score".* Butterfield, J. & Covey, M. J. (1962). Practical epigram of the Apgar score. *Jama, 181*(4), 353-353.

175 *In the competition ... and criminal recidivism.* Meehl, P. E. (1954). *Clinical versus statistical prediction: A theoretical analysis and a review of the evidence.* Echo Point Books and Media.

175 *Now with over ... are significantly better.* Kahneman, D. (2011). *Thinking, fast and slow.* Macmillan. p. 223.

175 *Clearfield and Tilcsik ... of -1 to 1.* Clearfield, C. & Tilcsik, A. (2018). *Meltdown: What plane crashes, oil spills, and dumb business decisions can teach us about how to succeed at work and at home.* Penguin.

176 *Having a discussion ... is now facing."* McGory, K. & Bedi, N. (2020, September). Targeted. *Tampa Bay Times* https://projects.tampabay.com/projects/2020/investigations/police-pasco-sheriff-targeted/intelligence-led-policing/

176 *As Dr. Laura Huey ... who created it.* Huey, L., Mitchell, R. J., Kalyal, H. & Pegram, R. (2021). *Implementing evidence-based research: A how to guide for police organizations.* Policy Press.

Conclusion: How the Twenty-one Mental Models can improve policing and reduce cognitive bias

181 *Learning to evaluate ... critical thinking skill.* Nardi, P. (2017). *Critical Thinking: Tools for evaluating research.* Univ. of California Press.

181 *The test is ... valid or reliable* Fiedler, K., Messner, C., & Bluemke, M. (2006). Unresolved problems with the "I", the "A", and the "T": A logical and psychometric critique of the Implicit Association Test (IAT). *European Review of Social Psychology, 17*(1), 74-147.

181 *The test is ... valid or reliable.* Greenwald, A. G., McGhee, D. E., & Schwartz, J. L. K. (1998) Measuring individual differences in implicit cognition: The Implicit Association Test. *Journal of Personality and Social Psychology, 74*(6): 1464-1480.

181 *The test is ... valid or reliable.* Karpinski, A. & Hilton, J. L. (2001). Attitudes and the implicit association test. *Journal of Personality and Social Psychology, 81*(5), 774.

181 *Banaji the creator ... to do anything.* Vedantam, S. (2017, June). The air we breathe: The hidden brain. Retrieved November 8, 2020, from www.npr.org/transcripts/531587708

182 *Another researcher on ... force against Blacks.* Hehman, E., Flake, J. K., & Calanchini, J. (2018). Disproportionate use of lethal force in policing is associated with regional racial biases of residents. *Social Psychological and Personality Science, 9*(4), 393-401.

182 *In the medical ... their white counterparts.* Meghani, S. H., Byun, E., & Gallagher, R. M. (2012). Time to take stock: A meta-analysis and systematic review of analgesic treatment disparities for pain in the United States. *Pain Medicine, 13*(2), 150-174.

182 *Because of these ... health care system.* Smedley, B. D., Stith, A. Y., & Nelson, A. R. (2003). Institute of Medicine, Committee on Understanding and Eliminating Racial and Ethnic Disparities in Health Care. Unequal treatment: confronting racial and ethnic disparities in healthcare.

182 *We've said if ... to change anything.* Vedantam, S (2017, June). The air we breathe: The hidden brain. Retrieved November 8, 2020, from www.npr.org/transcripts/531587708

182 *This is the ... level of pain.* Vedantam, S. (2017, June). The air we breathe: The hidden brain. Retrieved November 8, 2020, from www.npr.org/transcripts/531587708

About the Author

Renée J. Mitchell served in the Sacramento Police Department for twenty-two years and is currently a Senior Police Researcher with RTI International. She holds a B.S. in Psychology, a M.A. in Counseling Psychology, a M.B.A., a J.D., and a Ph.D. in Criminology from the University of Cambridge. She has taught and lectured internationally on evidence-based policing and is best known for being the first policing pracademic to run a randomized controlled trial. She was a Fulbright Police Research Fellow and is the co-founder and executive committee member of the American Society of Evidence-Based Policing. She has two TEDx talks, "Research Not Protests" and "Policing Needs to Change: Trust me I'm a Cop", where she advocates for evidence-based policing. She has published her research in the *Journal of Experimental Criminology, Justice Quarterly,* and the *Cambridge Journal of Evidence-Based Policing.* Her books include *Evidence Based Policing: An introduction* and *Implementing Evidence-Based Research: A How to Guide for Police Organizations*

She is also a full-time mom and wife and without the love and support of her family and friends none of the preceding would have been possible.

Index